The Black Press

The Black Press

New Literary and Historical Essays

edited by
TODD VOGEL

RUTGERS UNIVERSITY PRESS
New Brunswick, New Jersey, and London

Library of Congress Cataloging-in-Publication Data

The black press : new literary and historical essays / edited by Todd Vogel
    p. cm
    Includes bibliographical references and index.
    ISBN 0-8135-3004-0 (cloth : alk. paper) — ISBN 0-8135-3005-9
    (pbk. : alk. paper)
    1. African American press—History.   I. Vogel, Todd, 1959–

PN4882.5 B59 2001
813.009'12—dc21   2001019292

Manufactured in the United States of America

For Karen

Contents

Acknowledgments

I CAN'T COUNT THE number of academics who told me that they had organized an anthology once, but they'd never do it again. I naively thought, what's it take? Gather a bunch of people with a common interest. Create a group of compelling essays, and bind it all up. The project appeared to be like holding a scholarly party with great conversation. Well, I learned. Parties that flow smoothly take the most work. Many people helped this particular soiree go well.

First, I'd like to thank the contributors to this volume who have been a blast to work with. They took material in unexpected directions and taught me about wonderful parts of the black press. Among those contributors, several stand out in the support they gave to this project. Shelley Fisher Fishkin first turned me on to the black press as a subject of study. Her energy, enthusiasm, and support make her a dream mentor. Robert Levine and Robert Fanuzzi lent important moral support through the process.

Others stepped in to offer support and important comments. Elizabeth McHenry has provided encouragement, critique, and friendship. Maureen Reed lent her valuable editing eye to a piece in the collection. Margo Perkins, Barbara Sicherman, and Corrie Martin read early drafts of my introduction. Cheryl Greenberg, William Forbath, Robert Abzug, Robin Kilson, Kevin Kenny, and Jan Cohn helped with my

chapter on black labor. Kevin Gaines and Eric Sundquist offered inci-
sive comments on the volume as a whole and individual chapters. Maren
Stange helped root out cover art. My colleagues at the University of
Texas at Austin and at Trinity College have made scholarship excit-
ing. Leslie Mitchner believed in this book and saw it through. Finally,
I want to thank Karen Hust, my first and best reader.

The Black Press

Introduction

TODD VOGEL

THE ESSAYS IN THIS VOLUME rewrite our understanding of the black press. They dispense with narrow readings that claim the press focused only on slavery or elite African Americans' concerns, for, in fact, articles in the black press addressed a surprising array of issues such as antebellum trade unions, the Spanish Civil War, and cold war consumer culture. Beneath this array of topics, moreover, the press sought to do something more: it filled its pages with critiques and worked to change American culture. The essays here demonstrate that the black press redefined class, restaged race and nationhood, and reset the terms of public conversation. Moving past a narrow definition of the press also opens a trove of materials and challenges traditional scholarly methods. And we gain a fuller understanding of not just African-American culture but also the varied cultural battles fought throughout our country's history.

This collection begins with the first publications of the 1820s and ends in the twenty-first century. Analysis covering this period of time allows the essays to reveal how the press's content and its very form changed with evolving historical and cultural conditions in America. The earliest papers fought for abolitionism as well as rights for free blacks in the North. When racist *New York Enquirer* editor Mordecai M. Noah questioned free blacks' right to live as citizens in a republic, John Russwurm and Samuel Cornish founded *Freedom's Journal* in 1827, publishing news about the free black community. Later Frederick Douglass sought a voice independent of Garrisonian abolitionists, and he started *The North Star*. After Emancipation, free blacks in the South created scores of black newspapers to stitch freedmen into the community and protect their rights. The early twentieth-century black press sought to define itself and its community amid American modernism. Midcentury writers analyzed the impact of international events, like the growth of fascism, on America's black community. Writers in the 1960s took on the task of defining revolution in that decade's ferment.[1]

Each of the thirteen essays in this volume examines an important phase of African-American and mainstream American culture. Each also illuminates the press's cultural work, and each does this by moving beyond a simple analysis of texts. If we seek to understand not just the words on the page but the way the page peeled off a letterpress, traveled to far-flung towns, landed in the hands of literate people, and then accelerated to the speed of sound through the voice of a reader who broadcast to friends and community, we mine the publications for their complex meanings. The essays here interpret the press as both a performance and as a commodity within the culture at large. And the press's meaning at any one of these points in the cycle, from letterpress production to a reading society's reception, depends in part on other points of alignment in the cycle.

For example, relatively economical newsprint and frequency of publication of the press itself broadened black writers' freedoms. Blacks who struggled to get into print because of proscriptions by white-dominated publishers could turn to the ephemeral weekly or monthly. And the ephemeral nature of press led to another benefit: it made the writers nimble. They could plunge into the public conversation and get their views out nearly immediately. Writers in the *Negro Digest* during the turbulent 1960s, for example, did not publish their views in books that emerged in fossilized hard-cover volumes long after the fact. The *Digest* writers could print their ideas in response to events, and, as the world changed, rewrite them, with each article floating the idea into the moment. A complex understanding of production, distribution, regulation, and reception allows us to grasp a more textured public discourse, one that exchanges ideas within not just the black community but the nation at large.[2]

A periodical analyzed as a cultural production creates an ideal stage for examining society. Periodical editors must find fresh ways to address discrimination, government economic policy, and other big questions that receive gallons of ink elsewhere. And they sometimes must find an up-to-the-minute pretext to write these articles weekly or even daily. Their stories, then, become staged pieces, often connecting local anecdote or recent event to broader, more sweeping issues. In Douglass's *North Star*, for example, the disappearance of a local man becomes the basis for ranging far afield. People feared that the local man had been murdered, and several citizens heard "mysterious rappings" in houses around the city. Soon, these "rappings" turned into directions from a "spirit" to dig beneath a specific tree's roots to find bones. Hundreds of townspeople showed up for three days of digging, and they found nothing. But the writer turned the tale of this wild chase into a meditation on superstition, the power of the mind and natural law—and how these abstract issues fit into the broader political and cultural role of blacks in America. Each local event gives writers the chance to tackle a broader topic anew.[3]

In this way, the press gives us the chance to see writers forming and reforming ideologies, creating and recreating a public sphere, and staging and restaging race itself. Societal ideals about the creation of races change enormously in our history as westward expansion and a market economy reconstruct the roles of blacks and race. Writers who addressed the spirit and the status of blacks in America of the 1820s might have been ostracized from the community, but they had not yet been stripped of their citizenship by the Dred Scott case thirty years later. Their stories necessarily reflected that difference. And, of course, this process has continued as economic rights and societal ideas about race have changed up to the present moment. David Walker's writings in his *Appeal*, for example, created a discourse that crossed borders by opposing the racial, political, and geographical segregation prompted by the Missouri Compromise of 1820. Other antebellum editors recrafted the meaning of the republic and of citizenship by using success narratives to stage repeated performances of what it meant to be a citizen. And the photographs of Gordon Parks and others at *Ebony* sought to create a new public definition of blackness.

Of course, redrafted meanings of nation and race did not spring fully formed from the minds of the writers. They worked out these ideas over time, revised them to account for new ideas or new circumstances, and positioned themselves for the battle they fought with the white majority in the nation. The articles of the press amount to verbal exchanges between community members over crucial questions, such as the Missouri Compromise, but also over less plangent but important questions such as economic oppression of blacks in the 1970s. Writing, here, becomes a social act. Thus, this volume aims not only to analyze the press but also to encourage scholars to grapple with this crucial primary resource by setting it in its complex historical and cultural moment.

Because these exchanges also move beyond the African-American community, the writings in the black press help us understand not just that community but the nation as a whole. Writers who wanted to successfully address their position in society had to craft a story that made sense of a country torn by an economic and social system based on racial injustice. In the black press, for example, readers find excerpts from the *New York Herald* commenting on the early black conventions. James Gordon Bennett argued that if Frederick Douglass and other conventioneers had their way, whites would have to black their own boots and shave their own beards. The paper took pleasure in situating the racist Bennett's screed among articles calling for a very different world and printed the New York editor's argument without immediate comment. In the black press's stories, poems, and narratives, we find jeremiads, creative negotiations, and proposals for alternative paths for the nation.[4]

The difficulty black writers faced in getting published made them work creatively to broadcast their ideas in a variety of mediums. This raises important genre questions for scholars. Black authors wrote for newspapers and magazines, self-published in pamphlets, and turned to large houses to put out their novels. For instance, David Walker wrote for *Freedom's Journal* and served as an agent for the distribution of the paper. Robert Levine finds that Walker's experience as a distribution agent helped Walker disseminate the *Appeal*; and his aggressive distrubution likely gave his words a more powerful force. The question of distribution becomes key to analyzing this writing. Is there an important difference between a newspaper or magazine and something called a "pamphlet," revised and distributed throughout the land? Shelley Fisher Fishkin and Carla Peterson push this analysis one step further when they demonstrate the importance of Frederick Douglass's journalism to his novel *The Heroic Slave*. So we must ask these questions: In a society in which black writers struggled to get anything into print, how might the particular forms in which they wrote affect our understanding of the publication and its cultural work? Do we need to think more broadly about what we consider African-American literary production?

Similarly, the very distribution of the press and its use by black Americans raises the important question of how many people actually read or heard the press articles. For example, Mary Ann Shadd Cary hoped that Toronto's population of fifty thousand blacks would buy five thousand copies of her *Provincial Freeman* each week.[5] Even had Cary gained five thousand subscribers (and she did not), we have no way of knowing how many people heard the paper's contents in parlors or reading societies throughout the city. Peter Hinks notes that David Walker intended for his *Appeal* to be read aloud to others. And Elizabeth McHenry discusses the role of the press in clubs and reading societies. Just as advertisers today count "readers" rather than "subscribers" to understand their ad's impact, more people than simple subscribers likely read or heard material from the black press.[6]

One major challenge to studying the press is getting our hands on the papers themselves. Newspapers and magazines arrive to readers unbound and printed on relatively cheap paper, making them much more difficult to preserve than a book. The social belief that newspapers and magazines are ephemeral—no matter the quality of their content—also keeps people from saving them. Furthermore, many libraries did not believe that the black press was worthy of preservation, and they relegated copies to the dust bin. James P. Danky reports that institutions have been one of the biggest impediments to studying the black press. In 1937, only nine institutions reported copies of the antebellum *Freedom's Journal*. Thousands of titles reported published cannot be located today. Mississippi, for example, was the home of many black newspapers in the nineteenth and twentieth centuries, but the first title in its state archives starts in 1937.[7]

Until recently, even extant issues of a paper resisted analysis by the researcher. Often, copies of the black newspapers came only on microfilm. Eager scholars received the rolls through interlibrary loan and found themselves staring endlessly into the microfilm reader, hunting

for articles in papers without indices.[8] Eyestrain from staring at microfilm copies with small text and scarred film drove away all but the most
hardy; any research budget on the black press needed to include money
for a new eyeglass prescription. And professors could forget about as-
signing the articles to a class of uninitiated undergraduates.

However, interest in recovering "lost" texts and the help of technology is making the press more accessible than ever. Antebellum newspapers now appear in both book form and as web documents. Several
publishers have released David Walker's *Appeal*, and James Danky at
the University of Wisconsin is posting images of all 103 issues of
Freedom's Journal on the web. Accessible Archives of Malvern, Pennsylvania, digitized *The Journal*, *The Rights of All*, *The Provincial Freeman*,
The North Star, and the *Christian Recorder*, and subscribers can search
forty-five thousand items on the web. The Library of Congress offers
the late nineteenth-century *Baptist Magazine* at its web site. For the Modern Library, Sondra Kathryn Wilson has collected a trove of twentieth-
century material with stories, poetry, and essays from black magazines,
including *Opportunity*, *The Messenger* and *The Crisis*.[9] The migration to
the Internet has changed not only the black press, as Anna Everett details, but also how scholars and students study the history of the black
press.

Everett's work and other essays in this volume show how the press's
meaning changes depending on the audience it creates. One important
common thread connecting these essays is their exploration of how the
black press shaped the public sphere. Many essays use Jürgen Habermas
as a starting point and demonstrate that we must modify Habermas if
we are to understand the full impact of the black press. Habermas argues that as a bourgeois class grew in early modern Europe, a public
sphere of lively and free discussion coalesced to battle an absolutist government that was trying to enforce its will on the people. In this sphere,
individuals rose up to discuss the common good and thus challenged
and monitored the state's authority. Participants in this sphere, he says,
welcome all into the conversation, use rational arguments to hammer
out their case, and set aside any inequalities to deliberate as peers.[10]

Houston Baker says in his 1994 essay, "Critical Memory and the
Black Public Sphere," that the public sphere could not be composed of
Habermas's free actors who make rational arguments. He offers one

simple reason: black American slaves did not have the same rights as Habermas's property-holding men. Baker argues that as marginalized people, blacks created a world that allowed them to form a counter-language to the dominant discourse, which stripped them of their rights. Thus, to understand the full force of African-American dissent, critics must carefully consider the position of blacks as critics.[11]

Nancy Fraser agrees that Habermas too narrowly defines the public sphere, and in "Rethinking the Public Sphere" she tries to tease out the implications of crafting a broader definition. Her work generates crucial questions about black writers, the press, and their roles in society. Habermas wrongly assumes, says Fraser, that an open forum exists and that rational individuals participate in discussion on equal footing. Even as the discourse lauds a sphere that is accessible, rational, and equally open to all, the very discourse itself creates distinctions. The result ironically keeps political domination in place. Because the public sphere has never had open access or one "common good" to discuss, American society lacks even one public sphere.

The remedy, says Fraser, is to broaden our notion of the public sphere. First, we must recognize that social and economic inequality has created multiple public spheres. These multiple spheres, which Fraser calls "subaltern counterpublics," embody some concerns that overlap one another and some concerns that remain distinct. One challenge for society is to reduce inequality so that the overlapping concerns grow even as we respect the discrete concerns. To this end, asking questions—such as, how the black press sought to change political and economic inequality, how the press defined a public question, and how it sought to intervene in the public dialogue—leads us to a better understanding of this complex of discourse. We can also ask how identity and counterpublics became intertwined in trying to bring change to society. Black newspapers' messages assume their full meaning only as we revise the public sphere and the ways it works with marginalized peoples.[12]

But we must make one more modification of Habermas, Baker, and Fraser to account for the special conditions of the black press. As Baker and Fraser note, Habermas developed his theory to account for the rise of the public sphere in the *bourgeois* world. These public spheres remain tethered to *print*. Michael Warner points out in *Letters of the Republic* that print does not do its work alone. Each use of print—by individuals in a particular time and place—creates a different outcome.[13] The black newspapers alone help us recover an approximate trail of dissent, but they do not show us how African Americans used these newspapers to debate in reading societies, conventions, and barber shops. Through convention proceedings, reading society minutes, and letters to the editor we catch snatches of the interpretation and performance of newspaper articles. But, in the end, they deliver only glimpses. Again, we must use the popular culture of the period and changing societal definitions of race to put together the mosaic of the press and its effects. Historical and cultural context become key to understanding the press.[14]

Although the essays in this volume stand on their own, they appear arranged in four chronological sections. The first section, dealing with the antebellum black press, illustrates the linkages between political rights, racial language, print culture, and public discourse. In the first essay of this volume, "Circulating the Nation: David Walker, the Missouri Compromise, and the Rise of the Black Press," Robert Levine shows how David Walker sought to change the nation's spacial and racial borders. He argues that in *Appeal*, David Walker fashioned a riposte to the racial, political, and geographical segregation prompted by the Missouri Compromise of 1820. Walker found ingenious ways to distribute his papers in the slave South. He used his *Appeal* to unify blacks around a system of literacy and political rights, and his paper in effect created a national black population.

In my essay, "The New Face of Black Labor," I illustrate how the press reworked class and racial boundaries around whiteness by using popular discourses of the period. The antebellum black editors created a discourse of elevation that linked a democratic vision with self-improvement, natural rights, and republican virtue, allowing them to stake out an alternative path in the republic. I argue that the black press articles about elevation amounted to a performance that rewrote the code of race, class, and labor in early America. Their path, had the nation followed the lead of the black press, might have delivered us from the bloody struggles produced by racial ideology.

Robert Fanuzzi's "Frederick Douglass's 'Colored Newspaper': Identity Politics in Black and White" examines the newspaper war between Frederick Douglass and William Lloyd Garrison. By studying print culture and identity politics, Fanuzzi shows that when Douglass split from

Garrison's *Liberator*, he sought to create a newspaper that proved blacks' ability to fulfill their civic duty and highlight the injustice of enslaving someone capable of full citizenship. But Douglass's *North Star* and Garrison's *Liberator* struggled for largely the same readers. The fight became acrimonious, and both editors used racialized language—claiming to pilot the authentic "colored" paper—to gain an edge. In the end, both "colored" newspapers created a conflicted public sphere, mixing white and black worlds. Yet Douglass also strived to place this discourse in the community and thus used his paper's racial identity to rework the public sphere.

The next contribution reprints an important work by Shelley Fisher Fishkin and Carla L. Peterson in which they flesh out the role of oratory and literacy in Frederick Douglass's writing. In " 'We Hold These Truths to Be Self-Evident': The Rhetoric of Frederick Douglass's Journalism," Fishkin and Peterson argue that Douglass learned about the rights of man by reading a bootleg copy of a rhetoric text, *The Columbian Orator.* He then turned those rhetorical techniques into a counter-discourse in his writings that sought to change blacks' status. His writing transformed the individual "I" into a collective "I," one that stood for the black body politic. Later, Douglass used these journalistic techniques in his novel, *The Heroic Slave.* Douglass's work illustrates an important example of how journalism and the black press play a key role in shaping the dominant discourse and how the margins work to reverse that discourse.

The two essays in Part Two about the press in postbellum America examine how one writer responded to being shut out by the white publishing world and how black newspapers changed their rhetoric about Native Americans to create what Fraser might call a "counterpublic." Wendy Wagner's "Black Separatism in the Periodical Writings of Mrs. A. E. (Amelia) Johnson" overturns our understanding of the late nineteenth-century writer Amelia Johnson, converting her from an assimilationist with domestic interests to someone who assumed a confrontational tone for social protest. Johnson called for separate publishing houses for African-American writers and even sought to put the black separatist movement in a long tradition of revolution. Her views about the black press presaged the rise of major black periodicals like the *Crisis* and *Opportunity.*

Hannah Gourgey's "Poetics of Memory and Marginality: Images of the Native American in African-American Newspapers 1870–1900 and 1970–1990" bridges the nineteenth and twentieth centuries as she illustrates how the black press changed its language about Native Americans. In the nineteenth century, the press bought into the Romantic idea of the noble-but-doomed savage in its descriptions of Native Americans as "children of nature" and the "exotic other." But in the 1970s, African Americans and Native Americans sought to rewrite their history to ally the groups. This rhetorical process shows the fluidity of the margins and the mainstream and of a public and a counterpublic.

The black press of the early twentieth century, the focus of Part Three, struggled to define African Americans within the United States and in relation to struggles in other countries. Adam McKible inspects the Harlem-based *Messenger* and a series of articles about each of the United States to understand how the paper sought to influence views about citizenship. He finds in "Our(?) Country: Mapping 'These "Colored" United States' in *The Messenger*" that the writers of this series showed a remarkable "example of commitment, a spirit of experimentation, and a refutation of despair." The black newspaper here served as a space where the community could state its ideals and discuss the reality that the black community faced. In promoting this vision, the black press created a space where a new community could be made.

In "'Bombed Out in Spain': Langston Hughes, the Black Press, and the Spanish Civil War," Michael Thurston unites poetry, the black press and international politics to argue that Langston Hughes wrote about the conflict in Spain in a way that brought the war home to black Americans. Thurston shows us that the newspapers can be read as a text with more than one layer. The deeper he goes, with close readings, contextualization, analysis, and theoretical framework, the more the papers reveal that Hughes's analysis of the Spaniards' vision of a more egalitarian society with racial equality said something about black life in America. Further, Hughes provided a model for other black writers such as Edwin Rolfe and Richard Wright.

C. K. Doreski's "Kin in Some Way": The *Chicago Defender* Reads Japanese Interment, 1942–1945" illustrates the *Chicago Defender*'s evolving understanding of race and citizenship as it moved from a binary black-and-white understanding of race to something more subtle. The columns of the *Defender* in effect "regraphed race, nation, and ethnicity on a cross-cultural grid of citizenship and identity," Doreski writes. Langston Hughes used his column in the paper to question a country that would place citizens in internment camps and examines parallels between Chicago blacks locked in the ghetto and California Japanese locked in the camps. S. I. Hayakawa also called for a cross-racial unity that would more sharply define the political rights of all American citizens. But Hayakawa, who condemned the internment in only the blandest language, failed to address the politics of race and nation during war. The black press, then, tracks the changing sense of self, community, and country amid the enormous tumult of World War II.

The articles in Part Four, addressing the last half of the twentieth-century, show writers grappling with consumer culture, the iconography of African Americans, and changing technology. In "On Sale at Your Favorite Newsstand: *Negro Digest/Black World* and the 1960s," James Hall turns to post–World War II America and the *Negro Digest* to ask first how magazines affect race and culture and second what happens when black cultural activism becomes fused with "black capitalism." Previous accounts, Hall maintains, steer clear of the socioeconomic concerns of writer and audience. Hall shifts our vision to the interaction between the *Digest*'s irrepressible owner, James Johnson, and America's consumer culture to find that Johnson's magazine "performed" its answers to social and economic questions every day with the stories and photographs it chose to run and the editorial stands it took. During two decades, the magazine maintained its "experimental" sensibility through transforming cultural performances, exploration of democracy, ideas about cultural nationalism, and inquiries into the links between the arts and corporate funding.

Maren Stange argues in "'Photographs Taken in Everyday Life': *Ebony*'s Photojournalistic Discourse" that, although *Ebony Magazine* modeled itself on *Life*, it used photography much differently in an effort to remodel the icons of black life. *Life* attempted to stretch the medium to explore photography as art; *Ebony* chose instead to treat its images transparently—as a "true-to-life" depiction of what's going on in the black world. Like the editors of the antebellum black press, the photographers in *Ebony* wanted to break the linkages between black skin and degradation. Stange finds that the magazine drew on the talent of photographers Gordon Parks and Wayne Miller; yet it remained more interested in entering the public discourse about the iconography of African Americans than in photography as art. It sought to naturalize a new iconic blackness.

Rodger Streitmatter embarks on a reconstruction project in "*Black Panther* Newspaper: A Militant Voice, A Salient Vision" by investigating a paper ignored by journalism historians. The paper, which carried circulation that could have run as high as two hundred thousand, articulated a call for societal change and organized the black community. Although the paper could not attract advertising—the mainstay of most newspapers' revenues—Streitmatter's fact-finding article shows that its subscriptions made so much money that the paper supported other party activities. The *Black Panther* focused most of its energy on economic oppression, but under withering harassment by the FBI, the paper lost its way as editors cycled through the paper's top leadership position. Streitmatter concludes that the paper not only served the traditional role of the black press by covering issues that the mainstream press refused to discuss, but it also created a voice and a set of demands that activists still use.

Some scholars worry that the Internet, like other technological changes, will push the traditional black press aside. But Anna Everett's essay, "The Black Press in the Age of Digital Reproduction: Two Exemplars," argues that the Internet holds out the promise of an alternative public sphere working in ways called for by Houston Baker and Nancy Fraser. A web page's hypertext, which prompts readers to explore a diverse network of meaning, allows producers and consumers of text to build multiple layers of analysis, information, and opinion. At the same time, the Internet and web pages allow people to bypass the expensive process of printing and distributing a newspaper. This open access, along with a form that masks the particulars of identity, helps to open the borders of discourse. Everett examines the 120–year-old *Charlotte Post* and the on-line *Afro-Americ@* to show how the black press on the Internet changes the traditional gate-keeping practices of the newspapers. The Internet, Everett argues, becomes a postmodern public sphere. Everett's conclusions underscore that historians and literary scholars of the press in every time period must tackle the confluence of technology, public discourse, definitions of race, and political rhetoric if they are to make full use of black press. And the topics in this volume—ranging from reactions to the Missouri Compromise to blacks' strategic portrayal of Native Americans to the black press's adaptation to the Internet—show that the black press has many more functions than scholars have been willing to use. Understanding the press alone, while important, is not an end in itself. Rather, the perspective on cultural analysis that newspapers require—combining culture, history, and theory—is the very challenge that will push the study of American culture to the next level. Our work is only beginning.

Notes

1. See Armistead S. Pride and Clint C. Wilson II, *A History of the Black Press* (Washington, D.C.: Howard University Press, 1997), 18. For more on the antebellum black press, see Frankie Hutton, *The Early Black Press in America, 1827 to 1860* (Westport, Conn.: Greenwood Press, 1993). "Our Paper and Its Prospects," *The North Star,* 3 December 1847. See also William S. McFeely, *Frederick Douglass* (New York: W. W. Norton & Co., 1991), 147–50. I. Garland Penn writes short biographies of these writers and editors in *The Afro-American Press and Its Editors* (1891; reprint, New York: Arno Press, 1969). Roland E. Wolseley, *The Black Press U.S.A.* (Ames: Iowa State University Press, 1971). Abby Arthur Johnson and Ronald Maberry Johnson, *Propaganda and Aesthetics: The Literary Politics of Afro-American Magazines in the Twentieth Century* (1979; reprint, Amherst: University of Massachusetts Press, 1991).

2. Stuart Hall, "Notes on Deconstructing the Popular," *People's History and Socialist Theory,* ed. Raphael Samuel (London: Routledge and Kegan Paul, 1981), 227–40; Fredric Jameson, "Reification and Utopia in Mass Culture," *Social Text* 1 (1979): 130–48; and Michael Denning, "The End of Mass Culture," *International Labor and Working-Class History* 37 (Spring 1990), 4–18. See also Chandra Mukerji and Michael Schudson, "Introduction: Rethinking Popular Culture," in *Rethinking Popular Culture: Contemporary Perspectives in Cultural Studies,* ed. Mukerji and Schudson (Berkeley: University of California Press, 1991), 1–61. My approach here also draws on the work of Lila Abu-Lughod and Robin D. G. Kelley. Abu-Lughod in "Romance of Resistance: Tracing Transformations of Power Through Bedouin Women," *American Ethnologist* 17, 1 (1990): 41–55, encourages us to examine resistance by marginalized groups but to avoid romanticizing it. Rather, we should investigate how this resistance clarifies the way power works. Instead of defining politics by "how" people participate, we should investigate "why." See Kelley, "'We Are Not What We Seem': Rethinking Black Working-Class Opposition in the Jim Crow South," *Journal of American History* 80 (June 1993); 75–112.

3. "Where Are We?" *The North Star,* 22 September 1848.

4. See "From Bennett's N.Y. Herald," *The North Star,* 10 November 1848.

5. "Our Next Number," *Provincial Freeman,* April 1856. On Cary and the *Freeman,* see Jane Rhodes's biography, *Mary Ann Shadd Cary: The Black Press and Protest in the Nineteenth Century* (Bloomington: Indiana University Press, 1998).

6. Hinks, "Introduction," in *David Walker's Appeal to the Coloured Citizens of the World* (University Park: Pennsylvania State University Press, 2000), xxxviii.

See Elizabeth McHenry, *Forgotten Readers: African-American Literary Societies, 1830–1940* (Durham, N.C.: Duke University Press, forthcoming). See also McHenry's "Forgotten Readers: African-American Literary Societies and the American Scene," in *Print Culture in a Diverse America*, ed. James P. Danky and Wayne A. Wiegand (Urbana: University of Illinois Press, 1998), 149–72.

7. James P. Danky, "Introduction: The Black Press and White Institutions," *African-American Newspapers and Periodicals: A National Bibliography*, ed. James P. Danky and Maureen E. Hady, (Cambridge: Harvard University Press, 1998), xxxi–xxxiii.

8. Several indices exist. See, for example, work by Philip Foner, especially his edited *The Life And Writings of Frederick Douglass* (New York: International Publishers, 1950). Also see *Antebellum Black Newspapers: Indices To New York Freedom's Journal (1827–1829), The Rights Of All (1829), The Weekly Advocate (1837), And The Colored American (1837–1841)*, Donald M. Jacobs, Heath Paley, Susan Parker, and Dana Silverman, eds. (Westport, Conn.: Greenwood Press, 1976.) But even these works, as helpful as they are, leave much to be desired.

9. For a thorough bibliography of the black press with more than six thousand entries, see *African-American Newspapers And Periodicals: A National Bibliography*, ed. James P. Danky and Maureen E. Hady (Cambridge, Mass.: Harvard University Press, 1998). See, for example, David Walker, *David Walker's Appeal: To the Coloured Citizens of the World*, ed. Peter P. Hinks (University Park: Pennsylvania State University Press, 2000). Danky's digitized issues of *Freedom's Journal* can be found at http://www.shsw.wisc.edu/library/aanp/freedom/index.html. And Accessible Archives' documents are available at http://www.accessible.com/. *The Baptist Magazine*, Library of Congress, Rare Book and Special Collections Division, Daniel A.P. Murray Pamphlets Collection, available on-line at: http://memory.loc.gov/ammem/aap/aaphome.html. *The Opportunity Reader: Stories, Poetry, and Essays from the Urban League's Opportunity Magazine*, ed. Sondra Kathryn Wilson (New York: Modern Library, 1999), *The Messenger Reader: Stories, Poetry, and Essays from the Messenger Magazine*, ed. Sondra Kathryn Wilson (New York: Modern Library, 2000) and *The Crisis Reader: Stories, Poetry, and Essays from the Urban League's Opportunity Magazine*, ed. Sondra Kathryn Wilson (New York: Modern Library, 1999).

10. Jürgen Habermas, *The Structural Transformation of the Public Sphere: An Inquiry into a Category of Bourgeois Society*, trans. Thomas Burger (1962; Cambridge, Mass.: MIT Press, 1991).

11. Houston A. Baker, Jr., "Critical Memory and the Black Public Sphere," *Public Culture* 7, 1 (1994): 3–33.

12. Nancy Fraser, "Rethinking the Public Sphere," *Social Text* 25/26 (1990): 56–80.

13. Michael Warner, *Letters of the Republic: Publication and the Public Sphere in Eighteenth-Century America* (Cambridge: Harvard University Press, 1990).

14. I greatly benefited from discussions with Corrie Martin for the material in this paragraph.

The Antebellum Years

Part I

Chapter 1	Circulating the Nation

ROBERT S. LEVINE

David Walker, the Missouri Compromise and the Rise of the Black Press

Dᴀᴠɪᴅ Wᴀʟᴋᴇʀ's *Appeal*, published in three editions between September 1829 and June 1830, is generally regarded as one of the most influential and explosive black nationalist documents authored by an African American. Urging the slaves to "kill or be killed,"[1] Walker has gained a reputation for militancy, even though much of the *Appeal* is concerned with countering white racial prejudice and developing strategies for black empowerment in the United States. Whether viewed through the lens of black militancy or black uplift, it is fair to say that Walker has emerged, in Sterling Stuckey's words, as the "father of black nationalist theory."[2] But what exactly is that theory, and how is it presented? We can begin to answer these interrelated questions by considering a passage in Article I of the *Appeal*. Walker remarks: "I saw a paragraph, a few years since, in a South Carolina Paper, which, speaking of the barbarity of the Turks, it said: 'The Turks are the most barbarous people in the world—they treat the Greeks more like *brutes* than human beings.' And in the same paper was an advertisement, which said: 'Eight well built Virginia and Maryland *Negro fellows* and four *wenches* will positively be *sold* this day, *to the highest bidder!*" (12–13). More is going on in this passage than Walker's obvious attack on the hypocrisy and blindness of southern enslavers. In discussing his newspaper reading, Walker positions the *Appeal* in relation to what could be termed the newspaper print culture of the 1820s. It is worth noting that the newspaper is southern, a portion of which Walker in effect now circulates in the North and then recirculates nationally in this appropriated and ironic form. Throughout the *Appeal* there are numerous references to northern and southern newspapers, and I argue in this essay that central to Walker's black nationalist strategies in the *Appeal* is an effort to achieve a circulation of his text rivaling that of the nation's increasingly sectionalized newspapers. For Walker, black nationalism was a matter of circulation, and in *Appeal* he sought to achieve a national circulation with a national (and even international) black voice—a voice, it must be emphasized, that exists in print.

In his invaluable *To Awaken My Afflicted Brethren: David Walker and the Problem of Antebellum Slave Resistance*, Peter P. Hinks argues that the "*Appeal* issued from a well-established tradition of black antislavery and religious oratory."[3] Although I would not want to deny the important influence of those traditions on the *Appeal*, this essay focuses on the close relationship between the rise of the black press and the publication of Walker's *Appeal*. Walker and other black activists regarded print, rather than oratory, as promising to link together the disparate and scattered black communities of the early republic. Significantly, Walker served as an authorized subscription agent of John Russwurm and Samuel Cornish's *Freedom's Journal*, the first African-American newspaper, and he continued to demonstrate his commitment to the African-American press by working as an agent for *The Rights of All*, a short-lived newspaper edited by Cornish between May and October 1829. The *Appeal* appeared shortly after the demise of *Rights*, as if Walker were attempting to carry on the mission of that journal by circulating his own call for black uplift and resistance. Circulation as a desideratum, material practice, and ideology were also central to the debates of 1819–1821 on Missouri. The Missouri Compromise led to a refashioning of not only American nationalism in relation to issues of section and race but also the American press. The early black press, and Walker's *Appeal*, creatively responded to these developments.

Briefly, the Missouri controversy of 1819–1821 revealed that beneath the surface of the celebratory national rhetoric generated by the War of 1812 and its aftermath lay sectional and racial tensions that threatened to fracture the Union. For when the New York congressman James Tallmadge, Jr., proposed amendments to the Missouri statehood bill that would have banned entry of additional slaves into Missouri and the remaining territories of the Louisiana Purchase, a furor erupted in Congress. The subsequent debates of 1819–1820, highly polarized by sections, forced congressional leaders to address issues of territorial expansionism, sectional identity, and the ideological foundations of the government. Was the Constitution an antislavery document, or did the three-fifths clause commit the nation to slavery in perpetuity? In March 1820 with the help of Henry Clay a compromise was achieved: Maine was admitted as a free state and Missouri as an unrestricted state, and slavery was banned in the territory of the Louisiana Purchase north of 36° 30'. But sectional tensions remained, and controversy flared again in November 1820 when Missouri proposed a constitution that would have excluded free blacks and mulattoes from entering the state. In 1821, the Congress, again with Clay's help, approved a rather vague compromise in which it was agreed that Missouri's constitution would not impinge on the rights of U.S. citizens.

Although the immediate controversy on Missouri came to an end, the debates of 1819–1821 intensified the conflict between proslavery and antislavery forces, raised new questions about the problematics of borders on both the state and national level, and engaged Americans in the ideological challenge of rethinking the meaning of the American Revolution and reconsidering broad issues of citizenship.[4] The debates also generated a tremendous amount of print. As the press historian Carol Sue Humphrey notes, "Missouri's application for statehood in 1818 sparked a major debate over the status of slavery in the United States, and the press provided a major mechanism for communicating the various arguments." That process of communication and dissemination contributed to two significant developments: the founding of several hundred newspapers and the increasing sectionalization of those newspapers. Among the newly created newspapers were Philadelphia's antislavery paper, the *National Gazette and Literary Register*, and Charleston's proslavery paper, the *Southern Patriot and Commercial Advertiser*. Whereas earlier newspapers were closely tied to particular parties, which sometimes crossed sectional lines, newspapers around the time of the Missouri crisis came to reflect, as David Paul Nord notes, "the disaggregation and decentralization of the country."[5]

As the increasing sectionalization of newspapers makes clear, lurking beneath the glories of Clay's nationalistic "American System" were unresolved questions of territory, nation, race, and citizenship, particularly in relation to Missouri's proposed constitution prohibiting free blacks and mulattoes from entering the state. Henry Clay's compromise on Missouri's constitution, which asserted that no law shall be passed that excludes citizens "from the enjoyment of any of the privileges and immunities to which such citizen is entitled under the Constitution of the United States," allowed Congress to avoid having to address the issue of blacks' citizenship and the implications of the Constitution's three-fifths clause.[6] Were free blacks citizens of the United States? Did they have the right to circulate from state to state? Did they have any rights at all? These are some of the large questions addressed in the post–Missouri Compromise writings of David Walker and other free blacks of the period.

Born in the late eighteenth century in Wilmington, North Carolina, David Walker was a free black who, sometime between 1815 and 1820, made his way to South Carolina, where he may have participated in Denmark Vesey's 1822 slave conspiracy. That conspiracy was inspired, in part, by the debates on Missouri. In the main trial record, "An Official Report of the Trials of Sundry Negroes, Charged with an Attempt to Raise an Insurrection in the State of South Carolina" (1822), Charleston's legal authorities emphasized the role of print in fomenting the insurrrectionism of Vesey and his accomplices. For example, the Report's prefatory "A Narrative of the Conspiracy and Intended Insurrection" declares that the "number of inflammatory pamphlets on slavery brought into Charleston from some of our sister states, within the last four years . . . furnished him [Denmark Vesey] with ample means for inflaming the minds of the colored population of this state; and by distorting certain parts of those speeches, or selecting from particular passages, he persuaded but too many that Congress had actually declared them free, and that they were held in bondage contrary to the laws of the land." As one of the recruited (and eventually executed) blacks affirmed to the court, Vesey's coconspirator Monday Gell recruited blacks by reading newspaper accounts of antislavery speeches by northern congressmen: "THE PRISONER stated that Monday read daily the newspapers, and told him that Congress was going to set them free (alluding to the Missouri question); he said, to hear about that carried him to Monday's." If, in fact, Walker was in South Carolina during the time of this ultimately aborted conspiracy, he would have learned of the importance of print not only in radicalizing but also in linking blacks as part of a shared community.[7]

But even if Walker had not been in South Carolina, the evidence suggests that he quickly came to understand the importance of print to the creation of a black nationalist consciousness. Walker moved to Boston in 1824 or 1825, and in 1826 he was initiated into the Boston order of the Prince Hall Masons. He also came to have a key role in the Massachusetts General Colored Association (MGCA). Crucial to the evolving goals of these organizations was an effort to counter the increasing prestige of the American Colonization Society (ACS), which sought to make the United States into an all-white nation by shipping the free blacks to their "native" Africa. For Henry Clay and other members of the ACS, the Missouri debates only further revealed that blacks did not belong in the United States. In an effort to circulate these views nationally, in 1825 the ACS founded its own monthly newspaper, or journal, *The African Repository and Colonial Journal*. Walker noted in *Appeal* that he read *African Repository and Colonial Journal* "from its commencement to the present day" (69). Ironically, this particular journal demonstrated to Walker and other free blacks how print could help to develop black pride and black nationalism, for the ACS made its case for colonization by celebrating the historical greatness of Africa. As the writer "T. R." remarked in "Observations on the Early History of the Negro Race," those who "were called *Ethiopians*" helped to transform Egypt from "a state of barbarism" to "the mother of science" and ultimately "gave to Africa, and through her to Europe and America, all the wisdom of the Egyptians." Boston's blacks were influenced not only by the journal's regular accounts of the important influence of Ethiopia and Egypt on the development of Western civilization, which they took to legitimate African Americans' place in the United States, but also by the journal's efforts to achieve a national reach. In the lead editorial of the August 1825 issue, for example, the editors declared:

"It appears to be an obvious truth, that an Institution which proposes to effect any very desirable purpose, in reference to our coloured population, must act upon some principle and plan, which both the Southern and Northern States will unite to maintain."[8] Similar desires for a national reach were among the large goals of the *Freedom's Journal*, the first African-American newspaper, which began publishing in New York City in March 1827.

Edited by the Jamaican-born John Russwurm, a graduate of Bowdoin College, and the New York Presbyterian minister Samuel Cornish, *Freedom's Journal* challenged the *African Repository and Colonial Journal's* colonizationist agenda by presenting strategies for black uplift in the United States. In the inaugural 16 March 1827 issue of *Freedom's Journal*, the editors underscored just how important it was for blacks to have their own newspaper to plead their "own cause," particularly as such a newspaper would help to develop transsectional connections among its readers: "It is our earnest wish to make our Journal a medium of intercourse between our brethren in the different states of this great confederacy." Aspiring, as one historian puts it, "to produce a nationally circulated newspaper which would develop a sense of . . . a black consciousness, as it were, among the freemen and ex-slaves living in scattered communities," the material fact of the newspaper itself, circulating from county to county and state to state, can be regarded as a synecdoche for the black national body, which the editors imagined as a single body with "a single voice." That "voice" is very different from the oratorical voice, which simply cannot perform the same circulatory work as a newspaper. As part of their mission to create a black national body, Russwurm and Cornish attempted to develop black pride as *The African Repository and Colonial Journal* did, by printing articles that celebrated the African origins of western culture.[9] But what I want to emphasize here is not so much the content of the various editorials and articles that appeared in the newspaper during its approximately two-year run, but rather a figure of circulation: the "Authorized Agent."

According to Hinks, four months before the appearance of *Freedom's Journal's* first issue, there was a meeting at David Walker's house of "the People of Colour of the City of Boston" to discuss the newspaper's prospects. At that meeting the participants produced a resolution pledging "to use our utmost exertion to increase its patronage." The final page of the inaugural issue, in the lower bottom corner, lists fourteen "Authorized Agents," including David Walker, entrusted to achieve the goal of building the paper's circulation.[10] Implicit in the boxed presentation of those agents, who are based in northern states and the District of Columbia, is a suggestion of their representative relationship to the relatively small subscribing body. One dramatic development of the paper through its succeeding issues is the regular, steady increase of the list of authorized agents, for the small box at the bottom of the page eventually grows to one full column; such growth was meant to imply a simultaneous growth of black readership and community.

As the editors made clear by regularly printing the list of authorized agents, the agents were gradually extending their reach into the southern states, thereby challenging the anticirculatory border politics of the Missouri Compromise. The list of authorized agents in the issue of 23 March 1827 included a new agent in Hayti; twenty-two agents were listed in the issue of 3 August 1827, including an agent in Virginia. In the issue of 14 September 1827, Russwurm informed his readers that Cornish was leaving the coeditorship to devote himself to his ministry but would continue to serve as "General Agent" overseeing the now twenty-three authorized agents. Cornish's departure may have been motivated by his dissent from Russwurm's increasing attraction to colonizationism, but he stayed on as general agent until the final issue. Perhaps as a result of his work, the list of agents continued to grow, with the most significant increases coming in the southern states: the issue of 16 November 1827 noted the addition of two agents each in Virginia and Maryland, and the issue of 11 January 1828 noted the addition of three new agents in North Carolina and one in England.[11]

For Russwurm, the work of the authorized agents was absolutely central to the financial survival of the paper. But equally important was the authorized agents' role in extending a sense of black community beyond the borders of the northern states. Russwurm's "Prospectus" in the issue of 25 April 1828 underscored the importance of gaining new "subscribers in different parts of the country." Over the next year or so new agents continued to be added to the list, including one in Upper Canada and even one in New Orleans. By the time Russwurm makes his support for African colonization explicit, which he confirms by declaring in his farewell editorial of 28 March 1829 that he has accepted "the expediency of emigration to Liberia," he has a total of thirty-eight authorized agents from four countries, including a number from the southern states.[12] Though Walker rejected Russwurm's colonizationism, he remained committed to the mission of disseminating a national black newspaper. In addition to continuing his work as an authorized agent, in late 1828 he began to advertise his clothing store in the paper. That advertisement also appeared in every issue of the six-month run of *The Rights of All*.

Cornish began publishing *Rights* approximately two months after the demise of *Freedom's Journal*. In an editorial in the inaugural issue of 29 May 1829, similar to his editorial in the inaugural issue of *Freedom's Journal*, Cornish emphasizes the importance of challenging African colonization and representing "the rights, & interests of the coloured population." Again, literal circulation of the paper is crucial to this agenda, and he makes a special plea to potential black readers not to "withhold [their] patronage from this publication, it being devoted to all the interests of the coloured population." Central to extending the paper's circulation throughout that populace are the authorized agents: "The first number will mostly be sent to the care of the several agents, who will please to obtain the names and residences of the subscribers, and hand them their papers." On the final page of the first issue Cornish lists thirty-two authorized agents, including David Walker. Among the thirty-one other agents are people based in Hayti, England, Canada, North Carolina, Virginia, Louisiana, the District of Columbia, and Maryland.[13]

Because of the precarious financial standing of Cornish's paper, over the next several months he paid particular attention to the role of the authorized agents in keeping the paper afloat, stating rather urgently in the issue of 12 June 1829: "The Agents throughout the country, are requested to extend the circulation of this paper." Central to his goals is a vision of blacks themselves circulating "throughout the country"; the very process of disseminating *Rights* poses a challenge to the post–Missouri conviction among white compromisers that the place for free blacks is the North (or, as the ACS would have it, Africa). In his most sustained reflection on the connection between the authorized agents and black community, Cornish remarks in the issue of 18 September 1829:

let the executive committees employ one general agent, whose
duty it shall be to continue travelling from one extremity of our
country to the other, forming associations, communicating with
our people and the public generally, on all subjects of interest,
collecting monies and delivering stated lectures on industry,
frugality, enterprise &c., thereby linking together, by one solid
chain, the whole free population, so as to make them think and
feel, and act, as one solid body, devoted to education and
improvement.[14]

As was true for *Freedom's Journal*, the very circulatory nature of that
publicized, textualized voice is imagined as having the power to link
(and create) "brethren."

A similar vision of black community linked (and created) by print
informs Walker's one extant speech, "Address, Delivered before the
General Colored Association of Boston," which appeared in the 19 December 1828 issue of *Freedom's Journal*. In the speech, Walker laments
the "yet unorganized condition" of blacks in the United States and asserts that the primary goal of the Massachusetts General Colored Association should be "to unite the colored population, so far, through
the United States of America, as may be practicable and expedient;
forming societies, opening, extending, and keeping up correspondences."
Of note here is the emphasis on written communication, the ways in
which the circulation of "correspondences" would help to achieve black
nationalist goals of united community. For Walker, literacy remained a
key to such goals. As reported in the 25 April 1828 issue of *Freedom's
Journal*, when Walker spoke to Boston's blacks on a different occasion,
he "stated largely the disadvantages the people of Colour labor under,
by the neglect of literature." In his MGCA address he argues similarly
that literacy and printed communications can contribute to black uplift and community. The support for such a claim, he states, is best evident in southern whites' efforts to keep the slaves illiterate. He thus
reports of how "a slaveholder upon finding one of his young slaves with
a small spelling book in his hand (not opened) . . . beat him almost to
death." Interestingly, by the end of his speech he moves from what could
be termed a U.S. black nationalism to a Pan-Africanism, enjoining "the
dejected, degraded, and now enslaved children of Africa . . . to take their
stand among the nations of the earth."[15]

Border-crossing, circulation, and a tension between nationalism and transnationalism are crucial to David Walker's *Appeal*. It is therefore appropriate, as I suggested at the start, to think of the *Appeal* as taking up the mission that Cornish's *The Rights of All* was forced to leave off. Like Cornish, Walker attempts to "speak to our brethren at a distance." Such an effort to "speak" in print to distant blacks, and in this way "link[ ] together, by one solid chain, the whole free population," can be taken as one of the principal goals of the *Appeal*. As suggested by the evocative title of his tract, *David Walker's Appeal, in Four Articles, Together with a Preamble, to the Coloured Citizens of the World, but in Particular, Very Expressly, to Those of the United States of America*, Walker simultaneously sought to legitimate blacks' claims to the national narrative of the United States while at the same time developing a transnational perspective on the place of blacks in the Americas and throughout the world. But more often than not, as suggested by his opening reference to his black readers as "My *dearly beloved Brethren and Fellow Citizens*" (1), Walker's concerns are focused on the United States and are conceived in relation to the issues of territory and citizenship brought to the fore by the Missouri crisis and its aftermath.

The *Appeal* is best known for its aggressive response to Jefferson's racism in *Notes on the State of Virginia* (1785), its effort to develop black pride by linking blacks to ancient Egyptians and contemporary Haitians, its hortatory calls for black uplift, and its militancy. My focus here, however, is on figures of circulation. Walker begins the *Appeal* in this way: "Having traveled over a considerable portion of these United States, and having, in the course of my travels, taken the most accurate observations of things as they exist—the result of my observations has warranted the full and unshaken conviction, that we, (coloured people of these United States,) are the most degraded, wretched, and abject set of beings that ever lived since the world began" (1). The opening presents Walker's literal circulation as a way of gaining access to knowledge and power, and as an act of transgression. For unlike the Jews enslaved in ancient Egypt, who were allowed to intermarry and circulate—"And Joseph went out over all the land of Egypt" (8)—African Americans are bound either to the plantation or to particular states or regions. Thus Walker presents blacks' lack of free mobility as one of the central aspects of their degradation: "If any of you wish to know how FREE you are, let one of you start and go through the southern and western States of this country, and unless you travel as a slave to a white man . . . or have your free papers, (which if you are not careful they will get from you) if they do not take you up and put you in jail, and if you cannot give good evidence of your freedom, sell you into eternal slavery, I am not a living man" (28).

Walker's emphasis on "free papers," or print, as a sign of freedom helps to make it clear that his subsequent attack on Jefferson less decries the man (who is dead) than the text, *Notes*, that continues to circulate and influence white Americans on blacks' supposed inferiority. Reading is presented as central to an ability to contest white racism. Responding to Jefferson's remarks on why (white) Roman slaves were able to become writers while American (black) slaves have supposedly failed to distinguish themselves in this way, Walker asserts, "Every body who has read history, knows, that as soon as a slave among the Romans obtained his freedom, he could rise to the greatest eminence in the State" (16). And he remarks, in effect, that everybody who has read U.S. laws forbidding slave literacy knows that blacks do not have similar opportunities: "Read the laws of Virginia, North Carolina, &c." (16).

That it is incumbent upon blacks to gain the skills that would allow them to interact with print is emphasized in Article II of *Appeal*, "OUR WRETCHEDNESS IN CONSEQUENCE OF IGNORANCE" (19), for what Walker argues, echoing and revising the *African Repository and Colonial Journal*, is that blacks need to recover the learnedness of "the sons of Africa" (19) who had such a large impact on ancient Greece and Rome. In so doing, blacks would simultaneously renew and build their sense of community in the United States. So that blacks might better learn history *and* participate in the Jacksonian marketplace, he calls for "the dissemination of education" (30). He also reprints an anecdote from a newspaper, "the Columbian Centinel of this city, for September 9, 1829," about blacks' participation in quelling a black uprising against a white master, an article which he alleges shows "the degraded ignorance and deceit among us" (23). Desirous that blacks become more aggressive toward the masters, he urges them to "read the history particularly of Hayti" (20), while at the same time condemning

whites' efforts to prevent blacks from learning how to read. In attacking whites for such practices, Walker ironically states, "No doubt some
will say I write with a bad spirit" (20).

Walker's choice of the word *write* over *speak* in referring to his "bad
spirit" is appropriate, for virtually throughout the *Appeal* he emphasizes
the textuality of his analyticial performance. Even the hyperbolic type-
face—the repeated multiple exclamations, pointing fingers, and so on—
are primarily intended for the reading eye. But there is an important
oral dimension to the *Appeal* as well, and Hinks's argument that
"Walker's *Appeal* has its roots in an oral, not a print, culture" is best
supported by the relatively short Article III, "OUR WRETCHEDNESS
IN CONSEQUENCE OF THE PREACHERS OF THE RELIGION OF
JESUS CHRIST" (35). Aggressively attacking the hypocrisy of nomi-
nally Christian preachers, Walker himself assumes the persona of a
preacher lashing out against what he terms the "mockery of religion . . .
conducted by the Americans" (43). After describing a sermon by a
South Carolina preacher who insists on the slaves' Biblical duty to obey
their masters, Walker, in the manner of a Jeremiah, concludes with an
apocalyptic prediction of divine vengeance against the United States
should white Americans not abolish slavery and renounce their racist
ways: "I call God—I call angels—I call men, to witness, that your DE-
STRUCTION *is at hand*, and will be speedily consummated unless you
REPENT" (43). There is something wonderfully audacious about
Walker's willingness here to appropriate the preacherly role and stand
in judgment of white religious and cultural authorities.[16] Although the
admonitions exist in print and have a compelling presence on the page,
it is difficult not to "hear" Walker's prophetic words. Even so, Walker
makes it clear that he is responding not just to a sermon that he claims
to have heard at a camp meeting in South Carolina but also to his own
reading of southern newspapers: "They have newspapers and monthly
periodicals, . . . on the pages of which, you will scarcely ever find a paragraph respecting slavery" (39).

The failure of the South and, more generally, the nation to discuss
slavery in a print context replete with dissenting minority voices can
be regarded as the implicit subject of the *Appeal's* longest section, the
concluding Article IV, "OUR WRETCHEDNESS IN CONSE-
QUENCE OF THE COLONIZING PLAN" (45). For this section con-

sists almost entirely of Walker's remarks on various newspaper articles, which he puts into conversation with one another. In doing so, he makes one of his boldest interventions into U.S. public culture, as he attempts to insert a black nationalist voice, particularly as it was developing in the black press, into discussions about section, race, and nation.

My reading of Article IV is guided by recent debates on Jürgen Habermas's notion of the public sphere. In his influential *The Structural Transformation of the Public Sphere*, Habermas idealizes a moment in eighteenth-century British culture when (he claims) various public institutions—coffee houses, literary societies, novels, and newspapers—contributed to the emergence of a rational, participatory public culture. In Habermas's formulation, newspapers were of particular importance in helping to develop this culture, for "the press institutionalized regular contacts and regular communication." A number of recent critics have challenged Habermas for what they allege is his elitist or hegemonic conception of the public sphere. Houston A. Baker, Jr., contends, for example, that Habermas's notion of a participatory public sphere is inapplicable to antebellum black Americans, most of whom were either socially disenfranchised or regarded as property: "Insofar as the emergence and energy of Habermas's public sphere were generated by property ownership and literacy, how can black Americans, who like many others have traditionally been excluded from these domains of modernity, endorse Habermas's beautiful idea?" And yet what Walker proposes, I want to suggest, is that we regard the black public, particularly as developed and publicized by its recent newspapers, as a constitutive part of a public sphere that is anything but monolithic. Rather, one gets the sense from reading the *Appeal* that the public sphere consists of a variety of competing publics, what Nancy Fraser has termed "*subaltern counterpublics*."[17] As represented in *Appeal*, the conversational or dialogical nature of early national print culture has everything to do with the publicity and circulation of print. Such circulation can be taken as a model of the circulatory freedom that Walker desired for black Americans. Within Walker's dialogical model, then, which is not all that different from Habermas's imaginings of a productive and rational public sphere, black newspapers, and the *Appeal* itself, participate in a national conversation.

The *Appeal's* final section focuses precisely on the national conversation about the American Colonization Society's (ACS) project of colonizing the free blacks to Africa. Those plans, announced at the December 1816 founding of the ACS, were reported in the Washington, D.C., newspaper the *National Intelligencer*, one of the preeminent newspapers of the day. According to Frank Luther Mott, during this time "all papers based their news of the government on the reports of the *National Intelligencer*." In his journalistic Article IV, Walker proves no exception to this practice, for he quotes several times from the 24 December 1816 report on the ACS in the *National Intelligencer*.[18] Walker's conception of his own (black) nationalism may well have emerged as a response to this now republicized newspaper discussion. Walker asserts that Clay and others formulated "a plan to get those of the coloured people, who are said to be free, away from among those of our brethren whom they unjustly hold in bondage, so that they may be enabled to keep them the more secure in ignorance and wretchedness, to support them and their children, and consequently they would have the more obedient slaves" (47). As Walker develops his analysis of the newspaper account of the meeting, it becomes clear that the colonizationists' plan is of a piece with that of the Missouri legislators: to curtail the circulation of ideas among free and enslaved African Americans and thereby undercut the possibility of cross-sectional, national unity among blacks. Throughout his discussion, he underscores the textual dimension of his response to the ACS: "I shall now pass in review the speech of Mr. Elias B. Caldwell, Esq. of the District of Columbia, extracted from the same page on which Mr. Clay's will be found" (51). Like Clay, Caldwell talks of the importance of denying blacks knowledge, of keeping them in "the condition of brutes" (52), and Walker goes on to describe the *National Intelligencer's* report of John Randolph making a similar plea to separate the educated free blacks from the uneducated slaves.

Immediately following the discussion of the article from the *National Intelligencer*, Walker prints excerpts from a letter by Philadelphia's Richard Allen, the noted founder of the African Methodist Episcopal Church, which excoriates the racist work of the ACS in denying blacks' claims to U.S. citizenship. Significantly, Walker cites as his source for Allen's letter the 2 November 1827 issue of *Freedom's Journal* (56); and after reprinting selections from the letter, he once again reminds his readers of its source: "I have given you, my brethren, an extract verbatim, from the letter of that godly man, as you may find it on the aforementioned page of Freedom's Journal" (58). To some extent, the battle of words between Allen and the ACS is presented as part of a newspaper war, or public debate, which actually had not received much attention until (re)publicized by Walker in *Appeal's* Article IV. In his *Freedom's Journal* letter, Allen asserts African Americans' rights to U.S. citizenship in no uncertain terms—"This land which we have watered with our *tears* and *our blood*, is now our *mother country*, and we are well satisfied to stay where wisdom abounds and the gospel is free" (58). Walker echoes Allen's criticisms, presenting blacks as even more legitimately of the land than whites: "America is more our country, than it is the whites—we have enriched it with our *blood and tears*" (65). Walker then invokes "the language of the Rev. Mr. S. E. Cornish, of New York, editor of the Rights of All," in asserting that any black who (like Russwurm) supports the agenda of the ACS "should be considered as a traitor to his brethren" (67), and he offers his resounding support for *Rights*. Without acknowledging the recent failure of that newspaper, he makes an "appeal" for "circulation": "Let me make an appeal brethren, to your hearts, for your cordial co-operation in the circulation of 'The Rights of All,' among us. The utility of such a vehicle conducted, cannot be estimated. I hope that the well informed among us, may see the absolute necessity of their co-operation in its universal spread among us" (67). The circulation of the paper, and by extension of an imagined black community, would serve the national ends of the thrice-stated "among us" of this proclamation, thereby countering the separatist program of the ACS and the anticirculatory politics of the Missouri Compromise.

After attacking the *African Repository and Colonial Journal* for belittling blacks' claims to U.S. citizenry, Walker makes his final reference to a newspaper near the end of the *Appeal*, when he urges his readers to "see my Address, delivered before the General Coloured Association of Massachusetts, which may be found in Freedom's Journal, for Dec. 20, 1828" (71). The very idea of "seeing" a speech once again underscores the crucial place of print in an age of oratory, for without print that speech would not have circulated beyond the confines of the

Colored Association. The reference to what for many would have been a rather obscure speech also points to the role of black newspapers (and Walker's tract) in publicizing black perspectives and making those perspectives integral to the public sphere. As Nancy Fraser remarks in her revisionary critique of Habermas, "the concept of a counterpublic militates in the long run against separatism because it assumes a *publicist* orientation. . . . After all, to interact discursively as a member of a public, subaltern or otherwise, is to aspire to disseminate one's discourse to ever widening arenas."[19] The very processes of dissemination can be taken as central to the *Appeal*'s project of widening the arena of participatory democracy and thus central as well to the text's emancipatory potential.

Circulation, dissemination, and publicity were not only textual thematics but also material strategies of the *Appeal*. As W. Jeffrey Bolstor and others have documented, Walker developed a number of tactics for circulating the text outside of Massachusetts. One of his most effective was to deploy free black seamen as his "Authorized Agents" in the South. Bolster explains, "From the used-clothing store that he operated on Brattle Street, near the Boston wharves, Walker buttonholed sailors and asked them to spread his message. It was no coincidence that the *Appeal* circulated first in seaports." In the wake of the Missouri debates and the Vesey conspiracy, some southern states incarcerated black sailors during their visits, though many of these sailors continued to have exchanges with the free and enslaved blacks of port cities. By the time of the third edition of the *Appeal*, southern efforts to ban Walker's tract had intensified. In North Carolina, authorities were particularly cognizant of circulation as an issue; in attempting to halt the text's distribution by approving "An Act to prevent the circulation of seditious publications," they adopted anticirculatory regulations reminiscent of the Missouri Constitution. As part of its revised "Free Negro Code," the legislature voted to quarantine black sailors, to forbid the entrance of other free blacks into the state, and to make it illegal for North Carolina's free blacks to return to the state should they choose even temporarily to cross its borders.[20]

In a footnote to the final edition of *Appeal*, Walker rhetorically queries southern policing efforts: "Why do they search vessels, &c. when entering the harbours of tyrannical States, to see if any of my Books can be found, for fear that my brethren will get them to read. Why, I thought the Americans proclaimed to the world that they are a happy, enlightened, humane, and Christian people" (72). He supplies his own answer: "But perhaps the Americans do their very best to keep my Brethren from receiving and reading my 'Appeal' for fear that they will find in it an extract which I made from their Declaration of Independence, which says, 'we hold these truths to be self-evident, that all men are created equal,' &c. &c. &c" (72). That fear of a revolutionary rearticulation of the Declaration speaks to lingering fears raised by the debates on Missouri, in which northern congressmen, as Glover Moore observes, "invoked the concept of natural law and the most famous American document which expounded it—the Declaration of Independence—to sustain their . . . positions." The assertions by some northern congressmen, as reported in northern newspapers, that the Declaration was a document mandating freedom for all helped to inspire Denmark Vesey to conceive of his conspiracy in American Revolutionary terms; those speeches also further inspired northern free blacks to mobilize their antislavery and antiracist efforts. Precisely such invocations of the Declaration during and immediately following the debates on Missouri led Thomas Jefferson, who himself had originally publicized the Declaration in various colonial newspapers, to assert that there was nothing in the Declaration that challenged the states' powers to determine their own sovereign actions.[21] Walker's debate with Jefferson in *Appeal* can thus be read as yet another aspect of that tract's waging of a newspaper war.

Walker's decision to conclude *Appeal* by quoting Jefferson's foundational Declaration brings us back to the question of the relationship between Walker's politics of print and his politics of black nationalism. Anticipating Benedict Anderson's notion of the connection of newspapers to the formation of the nation, Walker's politics of (black) nationalism champions the circulation of black texts and views that circulation as central to linked efforts to develop black citizenship and community. An inevitable result of what Stuckey terms "Walker's disregard for geographical barriers," however, is that circulation can be viewed simultaneously as both a tenet of and a challenge to the nation, particularly at those moments when the *Appeal* suggests Walker's larger hemispheric concerns about the "coloured persons" (63) of the

West Indies and South America. With his final remarks on the failure
of the United States to live up to its founding ideals, Walker brings
the focus back to the situation of African Americans.

Nevertheless, there remains an animating tension in Walker's rhetorically canny *Appeal* and his equally canny efforts at circulating it, a
tension between nationalistic notions of "our country" (65) and
transnational or black nationalist notions of "[our] *enslaved brethren all
over the world*" (29). This tension informs much African-American literature of the nineteenth century. A reconceived literary history that
puts Walker's post–Missouri writings more at the center of a tradition
of African-American writing will pay greater attention to such writers
as Martin Delany and Mary Ann Shadd Cary, who similarly addressed
connections between nationalism and transnationalism and racial and
geographical borders and were similarly involved in efforts to develop
a black press and community.[22] Walker's (and other early national African Americans') linkage of circulation to black nationalism helped
to insure the continuing importance of the African-American press to
blacks' struggles for freedom in the United States.

Notes

1. *David Walker's Appeal, in Four Articles; Together with a Preamble; to the Coloured
   Citizens of the World, but in Particular, and Very Expressly, to Those of the United
   States of America*, ed. Sean Wilentz (New York: Hill and Wang, 1995), 25. This
   text reprints the third and final edition of June 1830. All future page references to the *Appeal* are supplied parenthetically in the main body of the text.
2. Sterling Stuckey, *Slave Culture: Nationalist Theory and the Foundations of Black
   America* (New York: Oxford University Press, 1987), 120.
3. Peter P. Hinks, *To Awaken My Afflicted Brethren: David Walker and the Problem
   of Antebellum Slave Resistance* (University Park: Pennsylvania State University
   Press, 1997), 173. Though I depart from his reading of the *Appeal*, I am indebted to Hinks's excellent study for much of my knowledge of Walker and
   his times.
4. The best study of the Missouri Compromise remains Glover Moore, *The Missouri Controversy, 1819–1821* (Lexington: University of Kentucky Press, 1953).
   On connections between the Missouri debates and American literary nationalism, see Robert S. Levine, "Section and Nation: The Missouri Compromise
   and the Rise of 'American' Literature," *REAL: Yearbook of Research in English
   and American Literature* 14 (1998): 223–40.
5. Carol Sue Humphrey, *The Press of the Young Republic, 1783–1833* (Westport,
   Conn.: Greenwood Press, 1994), 102; David Paul Nord, "Newspapers and
   American Nationhood, 1776–1826," in *Three Hundred Years of the American
   Newspaper*, ed. John B. Hency (Worcester, Mass.: American Antiquarian Society, 1991), 404. Nord estimates that approximately four hundred newspapers
   were founded between 1810 and 1825.

6. Clay's compromise on the Missouri constitution may be found in Moore, *Missouri Controversy*, 155.

7. "An Official Report of the Trials of Sundry Negroes, Charged with an Attempt to Raise an Insurrection in the State of South Carolina," in *The Trial Record of Denmark Vesey*, ed. John Oliver Killens (Boston: Beacon Press, 1970), 11–12, 128. On Walker's possible involvement in the Denmark Vesey slave conspiracy, see Hinks, *To Awaken My Afflicated Brethren*, 30–37.

8. T. R., "Observations on the Early History of the Negro Race," *The African Repository and Colonial Journal* 1 (1825): 7, 8; "Colonization Society," *The African Repository and Colonial Journal* 1 (1825): 161.

9. "To Our Patrons," *Freedom's Journal*, 16 March 1827, 1; Kenneth D. Nordin, "In Search of Black Unity: An Interpretation of the Content and Function of *Freedom's Journal*," *Journalism History* 4 (1977–1978): 123; "Proposals for Publishing the Freedom's Journal: Prospectus," *Freedom's Journal*, 16 March 1827, 4. On Egypt, see for example the three-part series "Mutability of Human Affairs," which appears in issues of 6 April, 13 April, and 20 April of the 1827 *Freedom's Journal*. For useful discussions of *Freedom's Journal*, see also Bella Gross, "*Freedom's Journal* and the Rights of All," *The Journal of Negro History* 17 (1932): 241–86; and Lionel C. Barrow, Jr., "'Our Own Cause': *Freedom's Journal* and the Beginnings of the Black Press," *Journalism History* 4 (1977–1978): 118–22. Good general accounts include Frankie Hutton, *The Early Black Press in America, 1827 to 1860* (Westport, Conn.: Greenwood Press, 1993), and Armisted S. Pride and Clint C. Wilson II, *A History of the Black Press* (Washington, D.C.: Howard University Press, 1997).

10. Hinks, *To Awaken My Afflicated Brethren*, 75; *Freedom's Journal*, 16 March 1827, 4.

11. On Cornish's departure, see "To the Patrons and Friends of 'Freedom's Journal,'" *Freedom's Journal*, 14 September 1827, 107.

12. *Freedom's Journal*, 25 April 1828, 37, and 28 March 1829, 410. The issue of 25 April 1828 also included a report on a meeting of Boston's blacks, including David Walker, which produced as one of its resolutions: "That we view the Freedom's Journal . . . well worthy of our unremitted exertions for its support" (*Freedom's Journal*, 38).

13. See *The Rights of All*, 29 May 1829, 2, 8.

14. *The Rights of All*, 12 June 1829, 15; 18 September 1829, 34.

15. "Address, Delivered before the General Colored Association of Boston, by David Walker," *Freedom's Journal*, 19 December 1828, 296; "Freedom's Journal," *Freedom's Journal*, 25 April 1828, 38; "Address," *Freedom's Journal*, 19 December 1828.

16. On Walker and the American Jeremiad, see Carla L. Peterson, *"Doers of the Word": African-American Women Speakers and Writers in the North (1830–1880)* (New York: Oxford University Press, 1995), 64–66.

17. Jürgen Habermas, *The Structural Transformation of the Public Sphere: An Inquiry into a Category of Bourgeois Society* (Cambridge: MIT Press, 1992), 16; Houston A. Baker, Jr., "Critical Memory and the Black Public Sphere," in *The Black Public Sphere: A Public Culture Book*, ed. The Black Public Sphere Collective (Chicago: University of Chicago Press, 1995), 13; Nancy Fraser, "Rethinking the Public Sphere: A Contribution to the Critique of Actually Existing Democracy," in *Habermas and the Public Sphere*, ed. Craig Calhoun (Cambridge: MIT Press, 1992), 123.

18. Frank Luther Mott, *American Journalism, A History: 1690–1960* (New York: Macmillan Company, 1962), 177.

19. See Fraser, "Rethinking the Public Sphere," 124.
20. W. Jeffrey Bolster, *Black Jacks: African American Seamen in the Age of Sail* (Cambridge: Harvard University Press, 1997), 197. On North Carolina and Walker, see John Hope Franklin, *The Free Negro in North Carolina, 1790–1860* (1943; reprint, Chapel Hill: University of North Carolina Press, 1995), 64–70. For discussions of other southern states' efforts to block circulation of the *Appeal*, see Clement Eaton, "A Dangerous Pamphlet in the Old South," *Journal of Southern History* 2 (1936): 323–34; William H. Pease and Jane H. Pease, "Walker's *Appeal* Comes to Charleston: A Note and Documents," *Journal of Negro History* 59 (1974): 287–92; and Hinks, *To Awaken My Afflicted Brethren*, chap. 5.
21. Moore, *Missouri Controversy*, 307. On the newspaper context of the Declaration of Independence and Jefferson's pro–Missouri views, see Pauline Maier, *American Scripture: Making the Declaration of Independence* (New York: Alfred A. Knopf, 1997), esp. chap. 4.
22. Stuckey, *Slave Culture*, 135. For his influential discussion of nationalism and print culture, see Benedict Anderson, *Imagined Communities: Reflections on the Origin and Spread of Nationalism* (New York: Verso, 1991), esp. chaps. 2 and 3. On Martin Delany and Mary Ann Shadd Cary, see Robert S. Levine, *Martin Delany, Frederick Douglass, and the Politics of Representative Identity* (Chapel Hill: University of North Carolina Press, 1997), esp. chaps. 1 and 5; and Jane Rhodes, *Mary Ann Shadd Cary: The Black Press and Protest in the Nineteenth Century* (Bloomington: Indiana University Press, 1998).

Chapter 2

The New Face of Black Labor

TODD VOGEL

ANTEBELLUM BLACK NEWSPAPERS strikingly illustrate how the editors borrowed, revised, and asserted new rules for black life in America. The editors joined many free blacks to use the mainstream's pervasive discourse of republicanism in an attempt to redefine their role in the nation. The editors brandished this discourse to punch through the web of discrimination that whites had crafted to keep them "in their place." Their aims become especially apparent when the editors write about labor. They crafted stories to recast images of blacks as mere workers or servants in a society run by whites and to thereby redefine their role in the nation. In these free black newspapers, authors used narratives of elevation—stories about getting ahead in society through work—to create an alternative social understanding about jobs and citizenship that overturned the antebellum system of privilege given to those considered "white." They broadcast their stories to a wide audience and critiqued a market economy that exploited racial division. Their lessons of elevation and tales of the elevated—at once inspiration and proof—refuted any public perception that blacks were a passive people suited only to serve, established that their minds proved as effective a tool as their muscles, and further asserted that, as people capable of considering the rights of everyone, they could participate in a republican government as full citizens. Thus, reformers of the 1830s and 1840s reworked the mainstream version of elevation to break the links between black skin, menial jobs, and inferior political rights.

The black editors' discourse of elevation went beyond a sophisticated critique of racism in antebellum America. It offered a check on the growing ideology of whiteness. When the editors linked a democratic vision with self-improvement, natural rights, and republican virtue, they staked out an alternative path in the republic. In this vision, black skin erected no roadblocks on their route. Jobs and political honors went to those who mastered the classical practice of putting the good of the whole above one's narrow interests. This discourse recalled some of the nation's earliest founding principles while it healed some of its fatal contradictions. Indeed, the black editors' vision destabilized whiteness itself in the new republic. Had history run differently, their path might have delivered the nation from the bloody struggles that the ideology produced.

Newspapers prove an especially useful tool for teasing out these ideas. Between 1827 and 1855, as many as one hundred African-American newspapers, written for audiences of both whites and blacks, may have found their way into print.[1] In examining the antebellum period, when a growing market economy squeezed the labor force, we can use free blacks' newspapers to follow Stuart Hall's advice to look for oppositions on the margins of capitalism. The free black writers possessed all the tools to compete successfully in the market economy, while racist laws, racist employers, and racist economic and social mores excluded them. Thus, their attitudes about labor and "elevation" in their newspapers offer an ideal test case of how race and class fit together in the growing market economy in early America.[2]

Further, we can treat the newspapers as a stage, where free blacks acted out their views about citizenship and race. Here they write and rewrite their personal stories and profiles and present them to fit their current struggles. Stories about the formation of a reading society, the rise of a Cincinnati carpenter, or the inspiring success of a St. Louis businessman become opportunities for crafted tales that remake the iconography of citizenship. They articulate an alternative vision for race, labor, and political participation. And this reworking overturns scholars' preconceptions of elevation and black life. Nearly fifty years ago Arthur Schlesinger, Jr., set the tone for modern scholars when he called purveyors of elevation, "men of good will" who "indulge[d] an honest compassion for the working classes without facing the economic implications of the problem." Well-meaning rich people, in other words, did not understand the working class's real needs.[3]

We know, looking backward, that twelve steps toward individual empowerment would never cure divisions wrought by slavery, prejudice, or a market economy. The editors themselves seemed to believe that their strategy of elevation brought change only slowly, at God's speed. But antebellum reformers, unlike Schlesinger's New Dealers, enjoyed no precedent for government intervention. The laissez-faire economy in the North and a slave economy in the South left a free black population with a crisis over the relationship between labor and citizenship. A population defining itself and American political rights as "white" threatened to permanently lock out free blacks, and they had no place to turn but to themselves. We must examine their look inward to understand their agenda for broader change and their efforts to combat a white ideology. First, offer blacks education and other forms of elevation, demanded a writer of *Freedom's Journal*, and, if they cannot succeed, "then shall we be convinced that really we are of a different species . . . and that the Creator has, in his providence, designed for us 'hewers of wood' and 'drawers of water,' and 'beasts of burden,' for our fairer brethren."[4] Elevation offered free blacks a chance; it promised—as an alternative path to the ideology of whiteness that a market economy reproduced and reinforced—to transform their role in society.

Clergy members like Samuel E. Cornish and, later, successful business people like James McCune Smith edited the papers and wrote with a fever for change. They acutely felt their outsider status in a country that excluded them all from any reasonable definition of citizenship. Cornish grew up in Delaware with a free black family, and as a young man moved to Philadelphia, where he trained as a Presbyterian minister. He ministered to slaves on the Eastern Shore of Maryland and later to blacks in Manhattan. As he labored to help individuals, he fought broader struggles. In the late 1820s, free blacks in New York state came under intense attack. Major M. Noah at the *New York Enquirer* argued that free blacks could not be strong citizens. States and cities introduced laws restricting free blacks' freedoms, and the rise of the American Colonization Society threatened to send all African Americans out of the country. Cornish left social work and teamed up with John Russwurm, a recent graduate of Bowdoin College. Together they formed *Freedom's Journal* in 1827.[5]

The paper fiercely opposed popular colonization schemes and published writers like David Walker to attack its foes. It folded in 1829 after Cornish and Russwurm split over whether blacks should join colonizationists and expatriate themselves.[6] Eight years later, Cornish founded *The Colored American* and hired James McCune Smith, a medical doctor turned journalist. Smith was born the son of a slave and a self-emancipated bond woman and attended the African Free School No. 2 in New York. Although he won prizes as a student, medical schools at Columbia College and at Geneva, New York, denied Smith entry. He moved overseas for his education and earned degrees at the University of Glasgow. On his return to the United States in 1837, he became the first university-trained black physician in America. Alexander Crummell called him the most learned Negro of his day.[7] Frederick Douglass said that Smith was his "foremost" influence and supporter among his black peers and "a keen and polished writer."[8]

Smith and Cornish marshaled their considerable rhetorical skills to lance those who shut out blacks. They encouraged skilled laborers in the free black community to fight those who assumed that blacks were inferior and should not enjoy full citizenship. Smith accused the American Colonization Society, for example, of "disseminat[ing] the idea of the natural inferiority of the colored people, by creating and keeping alive a feeling of prejudice or pity in regard to us." He argued that "men do not pity their equals. . . . What object links together these men of title? . . . They are the aristocracy of the republic."[9]

Articles that pillory colonizationists as aristocrats sound like Tom Paine railing against George III. Yet Smith here chose a different reading of republicanism than most whites at the time. Many early republicans followed Jefferson's lead to embrace "benevolence" and "affection" and "virtue." These traits bound the country together in the absence of old-world hierarchy, and only "virtuous" citizens—those who put the interests of all above their own—should lead. But Jefferson and others in the early nineteenth century also stated that these traits did not cross racial lines. Jefferson's thinking convinced James Madison, a president of the American Colonization Society, and many others that African

Americans represented a destructive, "heterogeneous" force.[10] In 1832, the Massachusetts Colonization Society trod in well-worn tracks when it warned that African Americans' difference always would shut them out of the republic. "Emancipation can never make the African, while he remains in this country, a real free man," claimed the Society. "Degradation must and will press him to the earth."[11] Like Jefferson, the Society in 1832 argued that "difference" kept citizens from forming the necessary bonds in a republic. Race—and the conditions that blacks endured in the United States—enforced a distance from which neither they nor the country would recover. The result: the United States would never really become the country republicanism destined it to be unless it maintained its "whiteness" and followed a colonization scheme to expatriate blacks. Cornish and Smith saw the result's damning assumption: African Americans could never become leaders who bridged the difference. Consequently, they could never become full-fledged participants in the republic.[12]

So Smith invoked a more fully inclusive notion of republicanism, one in line with the nation's ideal of equality as stated in the Declaration of Independence. Important as this shift was from the way the Founding Fathers had used the term, it was in many ways further still from the usage of republicanism in Smith's own day. Circumstances brought him to the question of labor. By 1820, the term "virtue" in the republic had shifted to designate those with commercial power. Workers interpreted rising up in society to mean that they could become their own boss. At the same time, free blacks felt economic pressure in the workplace, for the industrializing economy demanded fewer skilled craft laborers and more drudge manual laborers. Despite the Jacksonian rhetoric of broader voting powers and individual rights, the republican promise of becoming one's own master—of rising from apprentice to master— began to fade.[13]

This collision of economic power and dwindling opportunity threatened the tenuous success free blacks had won. Those who developed a journeyman's refined skills or used their brains for work enjoyed more respect than those who toiled in a factory or performed "drudge" labor like digging ditches. As Jonathan Glickstein has shown, even the self-help of the day, which tried to uphold the American myth of rising through the ranks, reinforced this lowly status of manual workers. William

Ellery Channing and his cohort of self-help writers believed that manual work held honor only if laborers used their brains. This mental work prepared the laborer to rise up to other, less muscle-intensive, jobs where they could become wealthy. This scheme applied one of Jefferson's key recipes for attaining virtue—education—to the labor market and encouraged the accumulation of money as a worthy end. But power and money in this new formulation became the end. If workers continued as manual laborers, then their hope for a better life shrank.[14]

White workers feared that wage slavery would make them appear as chattel slaves, and they created the term "white slave" to define a whiteness and a republic that secured their rights on the backs of blacks. This whiteness forged a link between skin color—race—and political status that locked the northern free blacks out of the political process.[15] States codified these restraints with a raft of restrictive laws. New York, Connecticut, and Ohio, among others, began to further limit blacks' right to vote. Property requirements of black voters in New York meant that in an African-American population of exceeding twelve thousand in 1825, only sixteen could vote. Cincinnati, Ohio, required blacks who wanted to live in the city to post a $500 bond. A special Ohio Senate committee even admitted in 1838 that the state had passed what it called "the most odious and oppressive laws, to degrade and depress" free blacks.[16]

Black newspapers and books complained bitterly that society blocked free blacks from its higher jobs and thus closed off their rights as citizens in the antebellum North. Philip Bell, *The Colored American's* proprietor, complained to whites about the lack of opportunities for his sons. Give them business training, and "you will not employ them as clerks," said Bell. "If they are taught navigation, you will not employ them as captains. If we make them mechanics, you will not encourage them, nor will white mechanics work in the same shop with them."[17] White Baltimore shipbuilders on a job with Frederick Douglass threatened to quit unless the foreman fired black employees; the workers beat Douglass and almost knocked his eye from the socket.[18] And William J. Brown said that the local carpenter and shoemaker refused him work. When one man promised a clerk's job, his boss refused to hire a black. "No colored men except barbers had trades," grumbled Brown. "If I possess the knowledge of a Demosthenes or Cicero, it would not bring to me flattering prospects for the future," he said. "To drive a carriage, carry a market basket after the boss, brush his boots, or saw wood and run errands was as high as a colored man could rise."[19] A colored man would never rise to be his own master. Indeed, job statistics confirm Brown's frustration. Even in 1855, 87 percent of New York's employed blacks languished in menial or unskilled jobs, the lowest rung on the ladder in the antebellum North.[20]

Restrictive laws and lowly jobs, with all of their associated meanings of dim-wittedness and unsuitability for citizenship, meant that whiteness not only preserved rights for white workers but also forged a link between black skin and free black workers' inferior status as persons. "Foul prejudice," said one *Colored American* article, "consigns [the free black] to the most menial and unprofitable occupations. . . . It places him, however virtuous and intelligent, politically and socially, below the mere vagabond." This prejudice, the article continued, "denies the colored man his inalienable rights—Life, liberty, and the pursuit of happiness." Prejudice, manifested in low jobs and low status, drives free blacks out of the republic.[21]

Yet signs of elevation that might break blacks out of drudge work and assumptions of low intellect only drew derision from whites, even those who claimed to be blacks' friends. In 1830, John F. Watson used his *Annals of Philadelphia* to explain concerns about "rising" free blacks:

> Their aspirings and little vanities have been rapidly growing. . . .
> Once they submitted to the appellation of servants, Blacks, or
> negros, but now they require to be called coloured people, and
> among themselves, their common call for salutation is—
> gentlemen and ladies. Thirty to forty years ago, they were much
> humbler, more esteemed in their place, and more useful to
> themselves and others. . . . With the kindest feelings for their
> race, judicious men wish them wiser conduct, and a better use
> of the benevolent feelings which induced their emancipation
> among us.

Watson here regrets that African Americans no longer responded to the call of "servant, Blacks or negros"—as if the three terms were interchangeable; instead, blacks had the gall to ask, as did James McCune Smith a few years later, for respect and their rights. Later in his piece Watson argues that Philadelphia's free blacks were happier as slaves.[22]

Free blacks then had their tasks cut out for them. They had to re-define the social rules of whiteness that kept African Americans out of skilled jobs. They had to drive a wedge between skin color and job to show that blacks could do mental work. *The Colored American* editors exhorted readers to write themselves into the Jacksonian Republic that included all "producers." "Until we have the means, and adopt the mea-sures which will make us the producers, the mechanics, the manufac-turers, and the business men of the country," argued the writer, who then borrowed a phrase that white Jacksonian America used to elide class and maintain racist barriers: "we cannot be of *its bone and sinew*, nor numbered and held as its parts and pillars."[23] Thus did the editors link the equality in the labor market to the equality inherent in the rights of man.

Blacks filled their antebellum writing with these efforts to prove themselves mental workers and citizens. We find evidence in the black community's emphasis on education. Jefferson and other republicans believed that education created members of the necessary virtuous class because it taught them to lead by putting the good of the whole above their own narrow interests. Education also created a common set of val-ues and a communal language of freedom.[24]

But the schools in antebellum America regularly excluded black children or offered them separate and inferior facilities. Belleville, New Jersey, officials in 1839 refused to allow the children of Samuel Cor-nish, editor of *The Colored American*, into the public school. Even if a church-supported school took a black student, "they have turned him into the field," complained *The Colored American*. An oasis to develop the mind became a field for drudge manual labor. So the act of estab-lishing an educational system for blacks in itself was to deny the pre-vailing order and to begin the process of stitching blacks into the republic. The paper touted debating societies, literary societies, like the Phoenixian Society, and even a women's group designed to raise money for Free African Schools, the Dorcas Society. Literacy was so impor-tant to bonding the community in 1837 that the Dorcas Society raised money for Cornish's editing salary. These efforts showed that blacks could think and that they could create institutions designed to elevate the care of society as a whole above one individual's needs. The hope even inspired what in hindsight looks like a flight of fancy. "Our infant sons, should we give them suitable advantages," proclaimed one *Colored American* writer on a column about education, "will be as eligible to the Presidency of the United States, as any other portions of the community."[25]

But the black editors did more than state their philosophy, form societies, and create schools to show that blacks could serve in a republic. They attempted, in their profiles of important figures, to create a change in their readers' thinking on the subjects of black virtue, labor, and race. They used these stories as an education for their audience that would directly counter and remake the dominant discourse on who could succeed. For example, *The Colored American* plastered the success story of former Kentucky slave Henry Boyd across its pages as a lesson in the mental abilities of black workers. The black papers in the 1830s and 1840s ran the narrative of Boyd's life repeatedly, and William Nell included his biography in *Colored Patriots of the American Revolution*. As a slave, Boyd performed double duty with his ax to earn the wages that bought his freedom. Once free, he stayed in Kentucky to learn the skilled trade of a carpenter and then headed for Cincinnati. There no one would hire him for fear that the white workers would all walk off the job. The narrative presents this abandonment as a crushing blow, the low point of the capable Boyd's young life. But Boyd was not to be kept low for long, the story assured readers. Boyd "recover[ed] from his dejection. [He] surveyed the brawny muscles that strung his herculean limbs, and a new design rushed into his mind."[26]

Boyd headed for the docks and found work unloading pig-iron from the boats that cruised down the Ohio River. The merchant who hired him to handle the pig-iron soon got into a jam when he couldn't find a carpenter to finish work on his shop. The ever-willing Boyd used his carpentry skills and so impressed the merchant that he set Boyd up in the building business. "Thus," the story informs readers, "Henry Boyd found himself raised, at once, almost beyond the reach of the prejudice which had well nigh crushed him." His skills, mental as well as physical, separated him from racial attacks. Boyd reigned as one of Cincinnati's premier craftsmen and ruled over a large shop that included white workers.

Boyd emerges from these tellings as a reading of the Channing myth of elevation applied to a black man, especially when we consider that the story was reprinted for the benefit of *free* blacks. Here, the worker isn't trying to elevate himself into wealth and power. First, he has to elevate himself into *liberty* and buy himself from slavery. Next, the worker still cannot pursue society's traditional rewards; he must contend with prejudice against blacks that blocks them from higher jobs. Even as this story worked to refute the notion that blacks can't move to higher employment, the language used by the writer draws on the old prejudices. Boyd "surveyed [his] brawny muscles," yet he was transformed not when he performed some feat of strength—but when he took stock in his strength and got "a new design" for a livelihood. In the end, Boyd's mind rescued him, but instead of finding a hero who merely performed mental work, this writer fused the mental and the physical.

Another favorite was the tale of St. Louis resident John Barry Meachum, who demonstrated how a skilled job made him a citizen ready to put the needs of the community above those of the individual. Like Boyd, Meachum earned his way out of slavery by "his own industry." Like Ben Franklin, he arrived in his new home nearly destitute, landing in St. Louis with three dollars in 1825. There he formed a successful business in the skilled trades of cooper and carpenter. He earned the money to buy his wife and children from slaveowners and then used his business earnings to buy twenty more slaves out of bondage.[27]

While mainstream America had made the focus of self-help the money and power that it brought, Meachum was thinking not about his own riches, but about community well-being. Meachum could never change the slave system by fiat. Yet he worked toward changing slavery by using money as a tool for all. "His method is to place [slaves] at service, encourage them to form habits of industry and economy, and when they have paid for themselves, he sets them free," reported the story. Once freed, slaves worked to repay him only to refill the coffers so that Meachum could begin the buying process again and set still more slaves free. Meachum's program to buy back slaves linked him to the collective black identity. The slaves' "habits of industry and economy" earned their freedom for them. Meachum's virtue elevated others and, in the end, modified the slave system.

And Meachum also spent some of his money to institutionalize this moral improvement just as one early American philosopher of virtue, Ben Franklin, had: he built a library. Meachum's story is intended to show readers white and black that African Americans did not simply see themselves as individuals. He saw his duty as living out the revolutionary rhetoric that required citizens to help not just themselves but also their community. In the process, they shape their society. Virtue, elevation, political participation, and labor take on new meaning. Meachum and the tellers of his story took the terms of the mainstream, mined its original intent from history books, and infused it into a political climate where it staked a claim for free blacks' rights.[28]

The philosophy embedded in these stories became doctrine in the form of resolutions at the black conventions in the 1830s and 1840s. Cornish and Smith attended these meetings and published the results in their newspapers. The conventions, like the newspapers, sought to exhort young black males to gain a trade. The Colored National Convention in 1848 created a resolution that set out the stakes involved: "Every blow of the sledge-hammer, wielded by a sable arm, is a powerful blow in support of our cause. Every colored mechanic is by virtue of circumstances, an elevator of his race. Every house built by Black men, is a strong tower against the allied hosts of prejudice. It is impossible for us to attach too much importance to this aspect of the subject."[29] Skilled labor here, wielded by a sable arm, restores the nation to its highest ideals.

This promise of more, of a new status and civil rights in America, threatened some white observers, who sought to maintain the divide that "whiteness" created; moreover, some whites wanted a ready supply of cheap labor for the worst jobs. Evidence to support this appears in reaction to the 1848 Colored Convention. James Gordon Bennett, the *New York Herald* owner who believed that "Puritan" abolitionists trafficked slaves overseas and would bring both the northern and southern economies crashing down, did not miss the implications of African Americans moving into higher-skilled jobs. "Hereafter the white race will have to wear their beards at full length, and to black their own boots, or let them remain dirty," the writer complained about the Colored Convention resolutions. "A revolution is threatened by the new movement, therefore, not only political, but social, personal, extending from the crown of the head to the sole of the foot, including boots, breeches and beards." *The North Star*, where Smith worked as an editor with Frederick Douglass, took pleasure in reprinting *The Herald*'s fears without further comment. The editors knew just how much their plans would revise society's rules of race, labor, and citizenship, and they needed to say nothing more.[30]

These words also prepare us for Frederick Douglass's abolitionist movement fifteen years later. James McCune Smith, writing the introduction to Douglass's *My Bondage and My Freedom*, complains that even the Garrisonians had merged skin color with menial jobs and mental capacity. Yet he tells us that Douglass performed his manual work with pride and also used the experiences to transform both his position in society and society itself. Douglass emerged from the drudge labor of slavery "conscious that he was wronged out of his daily earnings."[31] His passage is worth quoting at length, for it shows Smith's diagnosis of even progressive white thinking about blacks.

> Yet, these gentlemen, although proud of Frederick Douglass,
> failed to fathom, and bring out to the light of day, the highest
> qualities of his mind; the force of their own education stood in
> their own way: they did not delve into the mind of a colored
> man for capacities which the pride of race led them to believe
> to be restricted to their own Saxon blood. Bitter and vindictive
> sarcasm, irresistible mimicry, and a pathetic narrative of his
> own experiences of slavery, were the intellectual manifestations
> which they encouraged him to exhibit on the platform or in the
> lecture desk. (xxii)

This "pathetic narrative," as scholar Robert B. Stepto points out, in turn required authentication of Garrison himself to be taken seriously. Douglass broke free from Garrison to demonstrate that the black man could think for himself and write on his own.[32] Smith presented Douglass as the icon not just for slaves seeking freedom, but also for elevation among free blacks who felt only "half-freedom" (xx). Douglass demonstrated that a worker could move from the muscular to the mental, a process that allowed him to demand political rights. The former property of Thomas Auld "at his daily labor . . . went with a will; with keen, well set eye, brawny chest, lithe figure and fair sweep of arm." Here Douglass used his physical powers, but his "well set eye" looks beyond the skills of brute labor, while his "fair sweep of arm" prefigures the orator he would become. And brute labor did not distinguish

Douglass. Smith made the driving force of his sentence—and of the physical labor—Douglass's "*will.*" Douglass's mind, his vision and imaginative reach, drove his work.

Smith here inverted the old conventions of manual labor. He showed that Douglass accomplished what thousands of free black manual laborers, near poverty, could do. The physical labor did not act as an impediment; indeed, it was itself a tool. And Smith used the actions of manual labor to describe mental work. "What he needed was facts and experiences, welded to acutely wrought up sympathies, and these he could not elsewhere have obtained," said Smith (xix). Douglass needed the physical labor as *data* for his brain to craft its argument. In the forge of manual labor Douglass wrought the elevation that made him a contributor to American society.[33]

Smith saw far-reaching implications for this elevation. Because Douglass performed his manual work with pride—but also used those experiences to transform his position in society—he served as an icon of all black elevation. And he transformed the country. "To no man did the people more widely nor more earnestly say, '*Tell me thy thought!*'" proclaimed Smith. "And, somehow or other, revolution seemed to follow in his wake" (xxv). For even mainstream newspapers frequently mentioned the former slave and drudge worker, and "his name glided as often—this week from Chicago, next week from Boston—over the lightning wires, as the name of any other man, of whatever note" (xxv).

Douglass's persona was the culmination of Cornish and Smith's work. The public saw Douglass as neither the slave nor the laborer he had been but as both these things, distilled by a powerful intellect into the model of true republican virtue and success. In Douglass, nearly thirty years after Cornish and Russwurm founded *Freedom's Journal*, blacks saw payoff for their work on elevation. "His were not the mere words of eloquence which Kossuth speaks of, that delight the ear and then pass away. No! They were work-able, do-able words, that brought forth fruits in the revolution in Illinois, and in the passage of the franchise resolutions by the Assembly of New York" (xxv). As the 1853 Colored Convention predicted just two years earlier, "the ringing blows of the anvil and the axe, and the keen cutting edge of the chisel and the plane" symbolized "rough-hewn excellence . . . fashioned into models of beauty by reflection and discipline." Rough-hewn labor and intellectual reflection merge to create a model of beauty dedicated "to the cause of freedom."[34]

The northern blacks, led by James McCune Smith and Samuel Cornish, crafted notions that purposely cast these ideas together to intervene in the culture of whiteness that held them back. Black skin had become linked with slavery and with the worst manual labor, and hence to be black was to be more like a beast of burden than a thinking human being, fit for freedom and citizenship. The free black editors, creating a more democratic ideology that linked self-improvement with republican virtue and natural rights, both undid this old association and preserved older ideals of citizenship in an age when the mainstream had bent them to rationalize economic discrimination. Their stories, launched as entertaining legend, landed as a force that redefined antebellum labor, race, and, ultimately, the nation as a whole.

Notes

1. The number of surviving papers, of course, is much smaller. I draw this number from James McCune Smith, "Introduction," in Frederick Douglass, *My Bondage and My Freedom* (1855; reprint, New York: Dover Publications Inc., 1969), xxiv.
2. I use elevation here to denote an antebellum form of "uplift." This "uplift" is different from that defined by Kevin K. Gaines for postbellum blacks in *Uplifting the Race: Black Leadership, Politics, and Culture in the Twentieth Century* (Chapel Hill: University of North Carolina Press, 1996). Antebellum blacks used elevation to denote the variety of means, such as schools, reading societies, and jobs, that would give free blacks a stronger role in shaping of the country. Indeed, I show here that antebellum blacks carried a much broader definition of uplift—one that tied together the entire community—than did postbellum blacks.
3. Arthur M. Schlesinger, Jr., *The Age of Jackson* (1945; reprint, Boston: Little, Brown, 1950), 273. For a review of the literature about antebellum elevation, see Todd Vogel, *Staging Race and Sabotaging Whiteness* (forthcoming).
4. "African Free Schools In The United States," *Freedom's Journal*, 1 June 1827.
5. For background on Cornish, see David E. Swift, *Black Prophets of Justice: Activist Clergy Before the Civil War* (Baton Rouge: Louisiana State University Press, 1989), 23–27. For state by state comparisons, see United States, Bureau of the Census, *Negro Population in the United States* (1918; reprint, New York: Arno Press, 1968), 57.
6. From his post at the *Colored American*, Cornish lambasted Russwurm for joining the colonists. See "Take Care of Number One!," *The Colored American*, 27 January 1838. For more on the Cornish and Russwurm split, see Floyd Miller, *The Search for Black Nationality*," in *The Search For A Black Nationality: Black Emigration And Colonization, 1787–1863* (Urbana: University of Illinois Press, 1975), 82–90.
7. I draw biographical information on Smith from *The Colored American, The North*

Star, and David W. Blight, "In Search of Learning, Liberty, and Self Definition: James McCune Smith and the Ordeal of the Antebellum Black Intellectual," *Afro-Americans in New York Life and History* 9, 2 (July 1985): 7–25;
Crummell quote is on 7. "The Eulogy on Henry Highland Garnet" (New York:
Np, 1882), 6, in Vernon Loggins, *The Negro Author: His Development in America
to 1900* (1931; reprint, Port Washington, N.Y.: Kennikat Press Inc., 1964), 182.

8. Frederick Douglass, *The Life and Times of Frederick Douglass* (1892; reprint, London: Collier Books, 1962), 467–68; quote on 468.

9. "Great Anti-Colonization Meeting in New York" (from the *Emancipator*), *The
Colored American*, 19 January 1839. Compare this and other comments by Cornish with abolitionists' call for blacks to face prejudice "with the true dignity
of meekness." Quote from William H. Pease and Jane H. Pease, "Antislavery
Ambivalence: Immediatism, Expediency, Race," *American Quarterly* 17 (Winter 1965): 689 and passim.

10. See Thomas Jefferson, *Notes on the State of Virginia* (1787; reprint, *Writings* (New
York: Library of America, 1984), 211. This discussion of virtue and Republi-
canism draws heavily on Bernard Bailyn, *The Ideological Origins of the Ameri-
can Revolution* (Cambridge: Harvard University Press, 1967); Gordon S. Wood,
The Creation of the American Republic, 1776–1787 (New York: W.W. Norton &
Co., Inc., 1972); Wood, *The Radicalism of the American Revolution* (New York:
Vintage Books, 1991); and Drew R. McCoy, *The Elusive Republic: Political
Economy In Jeffersonian America* (Chapel Hill: University of North Carolina
Press, 1980). The terms *republican* and *virtue* can be fraught in historical study,
as Daniel T. Rodgers shows in "Republicanism: The Career of a Concept," *Journal of American History* 79, 1 (June 1992): 11–38. I use the terms here in the
tradition of Wood in *Creation* and *Radicalism* and Stanley Elkins and Eric
McKitrick, *The Age of Federalism* (New York: Oxford University Press, 1993),
as concepts that do not organize all of revolutionary life, but explain important social reforms that the Founding Fathers believed they accomplished by
writing the Constitution. Jacobson takes up republican ideology and whiteness
in *Whiteness of a Different Color*. For a take on how republicanism showed up
in the Founding Fathers' notion of self-help and how the definition of virtue
changed over time, see John Cawelti, *Apostles of the Self-Made Man* (Chicago:
University of Chicago Press, 1965). On Franklin's notion of virtue, see Cawelti;
Donald Meyer, *The Democratic Enlightenment* (New York: Capricorn Books,
1976), 61–81; and Joseph Fichtelberg, *The Complex Image: Faith and Method in
American Autobiography* (Philadelphia: University of Pennsylvania Press, 1989),
83–115.

11. Massachusetts Colonization Society, *American Colonization Society and the Colony
at Liberia* (Boston: Printed by Perkins & Marvin, 1832), 14.

12. The black press fiercely protested against the Colonization Society. See "Great
Anti-Colonization Meeting in New York," *The Colored American*, 19 January
1839. Revolutionary War veteran and Connecticut preacher Lemuel Haynes
may have been the first to touch these chords. See John Saillant, "Lemuel
Haynes's Black Republicanism and the American Republican Tradition, 1775–
1820," *Journal of the Early Republic* 14 (Fall 1994): 293–324. *The Colored American* reprinted a Haynes sermon, and other comments on Haynes in the 12
December 1840 and 8 April 1837 issues.

13. David Brion Davis notes that Jacksonian Americans evoked republicanism even
more strongly than the Founding Fathers had. See his *The Problem of Slavery
in the Age of Revolution, 1770–1823* (Ithaca: Cornell University Press, 1975),
275. Of course, in some cases, wage work improved some workers' freedoms.

For a fuller discussion of these issues, see Sean Wilentz, *Chants Democratic: New York City and the Rise of the American Working Class, 1788–1850* (New York: Oxford University Press, 1984), and Jonathan A. Glickstein, *Concepts of Free Labor in Antebellum America* (New Haven: Yale University Press, 1991).

14. Glickstein's *Concepts of Free Labor* presents a staggering amount of detail about ideologies surrounding antebellum labor, including the split between manual and mental labor; his is the definitive text to consult. Nicholas K. Bromell, *By the Sweat of the Brow: Literature and Labor in Antebellum America* (Chicago: University of Chicago Press, 1993), devotes a chapter to the differences between manual and mental labor and offers an inspired treatment of manual labor and the slave song. Cawelti, *Apostles*, and Wood, *Creation*, show how the definition of virtue changed in early America.

15. For a discussion of using race as a marker for freedom, see Edmund S. Morgan, *American Slavery, American Freedom: The Ordeal Of Colonial Virginia* (New York: W.W. Norton & Co., Inc., 1975), and David Roediger, *The Wages of Whiteness: Race and the Making of the American Working Class* (New York: Verso, 1991). Jonathan Glickstein complicates this whiteness argument by showing that white *skilled* workers did not react against race alone but also against age, ethnicity, and gender. See "Pressures from Below: Pauperism, Chattel Slavery, and the Ideological Construction of Free Market Labor Incentives in Antebellum America," *Radical History Review* 69 (Fall 1997): 114–59. For a more thorough discussion of this literature, see Vogel, *Staging Race*.

16. Philip S. Foner, *The History of Black Americans* (Westport, Conn.: Greenwood Press, 1975), 517–20; statistics on 520. Ohio General Assembly, Senate Select Committee on the Petitions of Sundry Citizens, Praying the Repeal of Certain Laws Restricting the Rights of Persons of Color and for Securing All Persons Within the Jurisdiction of the State the Right of Trial by Jury, *Report*, 3 March 1838, 11.

17. Samuel Ennals and Philip Bell, *A Voice from New York and An Address to the Citizens of New York*, 26 January 1831, 16. In *Black Abolitionist Papers* (hereafter referred to as *BAP*), Reel 1, Frames 21–23.

18. Douglass, *My Bondage and My Freedom*, 310–15.

19. *The Life of William J. Brown* (Providence, 1883), reprinted in *The Black Worker: A Documentary History From Colonial Times To The Present, Vol. I: The Black Worker to 1869*, ed. Philip Foner and Ronald L. Lewis (Philadelphia: Temple University Press, 1978), 56.

20. Leon F. Litwack, *North of Slavery*, 155–59; statistic on 155. See Foner and Lewis, *The Black Worker*, 116–34, to compare the occupational profile of free blacks in New York, Philadelphia, and Boston. The link between race and job was so strong that workers in some fields, like chimney sweeping and bootblacking, were assumed to be black. See, for example, the 1846 series in the Library of Humorous American Works on African Americans, "The Shakspearian Boot Black," in *Pickings from the Picayune*. Library of Humorous American Works (Philadelphia: T. B. Peterson & Brothers, 1846), 37–39. See also in this volume, "A Trial of Skill—The Rival Boot Blacks," on 68–69, and "Boot Blacks and Bad Times," on 126–28. Eric Lott deftly shows how blackface minstrelsy in the 1830s and 1840s offered white workers—as victims of a growing capitalist system—the chance to identify with slaves to lament the impact of capitalism even as they asserted their racial superiority. See *Love and Theft: Blackface Minstrelsy and the American Working Class* (New York: Oxford University Press, 1993).

21. "Letter to the Editor," *The Colored American*, 5 August 1837.

22. John F. Watson, *Annals of Philadelphia, Being a Collection of Memoirs, Anecdotes and Incidents of the City and Its Inhabitants From the Days of the Pilgrim Founders* (Philadelphia: E. L. Carey & A. Hart, 1830), 479, 483.

23. "Brethren, we have much to do," *The Colored American*, 6 October 1838. Italics in the original. "Bone and sinew" was Andrew Jackson's phrase for what he called the "producing class." See Alexander Saxton, *The Rise and Fall of the White Republic* (New York: Verso, 1990), especially 127–51, for a discussion of race and class in Jacksonian politics.

24. For an example of Jefferson's views on education, see his letter to John Banister, Jr., 15 October 1785. *The Papers of Thomas Jefferson*, ed. Julian P. Boyd, Mina R. Bryan, and Elizabeth L. Hutter (Princeton: Princeton University Press, 1953), 8: 635–37, and his 1818 "Rockfish Gap Report" to fix the site of the University of Virginia reprinted in *Theories of Education in Early America*, ed. Wilson Smith (Indianapolis: Bobbs-Merrill Co., Inc., 1973), 319–39. Also see Saillant's discussion in "Lemuel Haynes's Black Republicanism."

25. *The Colored American*, 24 June 1837. See also "Almanacks," *The Colored American*, 4 November 1837; "Notice," *Freedom's Journal*, 1 February 1828, for the Dorcas society contribution of clothing for the school. Also "New York African Free School," *Freedom's Journal*, 9 November 1827, for Russwurm's gift of free newspapers to the Free School. Elizabeth McHenry argues that these newspapers serve as formal and informal textbooks to foster literary communities. McHenry, *Forgotten Readers: African-American Literary Societies, 1830–1940* (Duke University Press, forthcoming).

26. Through repetition, Boyd's story became legend. Black papers in the 1830s and 1840s reran the same story on Boyd twice, and Martin Delany mentioned him as a model in one other story. See, for example, "Henry Boyd—The Carpenter," *The Colored American*, 17 August 1839; "Henry Boyd," *The North Star*, 11 February 1848; M. R. D. (Martin R. Delany), "Cincinnati, May 20, 1848," *The North Star*, 9 June 1848. Foner and Lewis, *The Black Worker to 1869*, credited this article as coming from the pen of William C. Nell in *Colored Patriots of the American Revolution*. Nell's story says, "This account is taken from the lips of a friend who resided in Cincinnati, and had good opportunity to know the facts" (265). Nell, however, took this section of his book verbatim from the article that ran in *The Colored American* and *The North Star*. See William Nell, *Colored Patriots of the American Revolution* (1855; reprint, New York: Arno Press and The New York Times, 1968), 265–70. See Foner and Lewis, *The Black Worker to 1869*, 62–63.

27. *The Colored American*, 11 March 1837, 4. Although this article originally ran in *The Liberator*, the fact that *The Colored American* chose to run the story with the headline "Capacity of Negroes to take care of themselves," shows that its editors intended to hold Meachum up as a model of the African American who has the power to help himself and the community.

28. This process of rebroadcasting a mainstream story resembles the "enunciation" that Homi K. Bhabha describes between the colonized and the colonizer. The colonizers need to remind themselves that they are in control and superior to the colonized. They keep repeating their superiority, as in popular tales of great men risen from the ranks. But in the "enunciation" of this superiority and the inevitable response by the colonized, the story takes a different turn. The rhetoric that created supremacy changes, and the colonizers' power leaches from it. The colonized—or the marginalized people—now take part in the world that

the colonizers had sought so hard to seal off. For Bhabha's thinking on "enunciation," see his "Commitment to Theory," in *Location of Culture*, especially 32–38.

29. "An Address to the Colored People of the United States," *Report of the Proceedings of the Colored National Convention, 1848* reprinted in Howard Bell, *Minutes of the Proceedings of the National Negro Conventions, 1830–1864* (New York: Arno Press, 1969), 7. See also Bell's *A Survey of the Negro Convention Movement, 1830–1861* (New York: Arno Press, 1969). *The Colored American*, in the tradition of the manual labor movement, linked physical strength with a strong mind. See "Colored Students," *The Colored American*, 2 September 1837. See Abzug, *Cosmos Crumbling*, 116–24, for a discussion of the manual labor movement.

30. "From Bennett's N.Y. Herald," *The North Star*, 10 November 1848. For Bennett's views on slavery, see Gary Whitby, "Economic Elements of Opposition to Abolition and Support of South by Bennett in New York Herald," *Journalism Quarterly* 65, 1 (1988): 78–84.

31. Smith in Douglass, *My Bondage and My Freedom*, xx. Future references appear parenthetically in the text.

32. Robert B. Stepto, *From Behind the Veil: A Study of Afro-American Narrative*, 2d ed. (Urbana: University of Illinois Press, 1991), 3–6. See also Eric Sundquist, *To Wake the Nations* (Cambridge: Harvard University Press, 1993), 83–93, on the differences between Douglass's autobiographies. On Douglass in England, see William S. McFeely, *Frederick Douglass* (New York: W.W. Norton & Co., 1991), 136–42.

33. Nicholas Bromell's treatment of Smith and Douglass in *My Bondage* interprets the *slave* experience as key to the freedom. Here I build on Bromell to argue that the history of manual and mental labor along with elevation makes its applicability still broader. We must remember that Smith also talks to all those free blacks in "half-freedom."

34. The mention of Kossuth refers to the short-lived liberal revolutions taking place in Europe during the 1840s. The political reformer Lajos Kossuth led Hungary's fight for independence from Austria. Kossuth took power, only to be crushed by the Russian army in 1848 and 1849. Douglass sought to act on the labor beliefs, but none came to fruition. In 1847 he tried to form the American League of Colored Laborers. For mention of the American League of Colored Laborers, see Benjamin Quarles, *Frederick Douglass* (New York: Atheneum, 1969), 125.

Chapter 3

Frederick Douglass's "Colored Newspaper"

ROBERT FANUZZI

Identity Politics in Black and White

THE SCHISM BETWEEN William Lloyd Garrison and Frederick Douglass provides us with an enduring image of a unique collaboration done in by the pressures of antislavery politics, racial tension, and conflicting ambitions. From 1841 to 1847, Douglass toured the abolitionist lecture circuit as one of the most prominent representatives of the Massachusetts Anti-Slavery Society (MASS), but when Garrison and his allies objected to Douglass's journalistic venture, the *North Star*, the black orator became convinced that the white-dominated abolition movement was resistant to the advancement of a former slave. Having been told that his best service to the abolition movement was to "'Be yourself . . . and tell your story,'" Douglass found himself forced to relinquish the "slavish adoration of my Boston friends," as he noted ironically in *My Bondage and My Freedom*, and to betray "what seemed to be a reckless disregard of their sage advice" (220, 241) in order to pursue his own antislavery agenda.[1]

From 1847 until 1853, a tentative peace existed between Garrison and Douglass until disagreements over a pro- or antislavery interpretation of the Constitution and the use of the elective franchise finally spilled over into an ugly war of words. In the abolitionist press, Garrison's surrogates questioned the loyalty, integrity, and character of the former slave while Douglass aired his suspicions that the "sycophantic followers" of Garrison and perhaps even Garrison himself were out to destroy him because he had dared to be independent.

The conflict between Douglass and Garrison was bitter; it was inflammatory; it was undoubtedly racial. But was it also personal? This essay hopes to displace this climactic dispute from the structure of personal relations and at the same time to displace the meaning of race in the antislavery struggle from the sphere of private identity by proposing that Douglass and Garrison, in the midst of their most bitter recriminations, fought over nothing more or less than newspapers. The grounds for their conflict, in other words, can be found in the print marketplace of the public sphere.[2] To be sure, each sought advantage over the other in a market of reform newspapers, but in this competition, personal invective was neither intended personally nor even intended to be true. Rather, it was a conventional weapon in a newspaper war, used for the strategic purpose of positioning. For both Douglass and Garrison, the authenticity of identity in fact mattered less than the thrusts and counterthrusts of what Gramsci would call a "war of position" over what mattered most for both combatants in the antislavery struggle: the historic title of a people.

Douglass spurned advice to "be himself" when he decided to publish the *North Star* for this same reason: through his affiliation with the newspaper, he could gain an editorial persona that was closely associated with a public voice and therefore with the prospect of an informed citizenry. In the African-American political culture that Douglass joined when he became an editor, the press organ was valued on this basis— as the bulwark of a free people—in accordance with the tradition of Anglo-American libertarianism. The public attribution of the *North Star* derived also from the egalitarian republicanism of printers and artisans, who preserved an ideal of rational progress or "mental liberty" well into the nineteenth century.[3] Both these influences can be heard in the signal declamation of James McCune Smith at the 1847 National Convention of Colored People and Their Friends: "The first step which will mark our certain advancement as a People, will be our Declaration of Independence from all aid except God and our souls. . . . And such conviction can only be produced through a Press . . . [which] will tell the world of our position in the path of human progress . . . [and] wholly controlled by colored men."[4] For Smith, Douglass, and other leaders of freemen communities in the antebellum era, the virtues of a press could be transferred to "colored men," who then were to be known "as a People." The authenticity of their collective racial identity in turn seemed to derive from the fact that it was found in print.

In the antebellum era, the institution of the "colored newspaper" did have the effect of giving race, even color itself, a public attribution in keeping with the authority and associations of the printed medium. Unfortunately for Douglass, color could be determined through and in this medium, which is why his decision to publish a colored newspaper brought him into direct conflict with Garrison, who also claimed to be the editorial voice of the people of color. The newspaper that he edited, *The Liberator*, was founded in 1831 as the avowed "organ" of free blacks and the enslaved, and over the next decade the newspaper became emblematic not only of the New England abolition movement but of politically organized African Americans, who composed its original and most loyal readership. In this capacity, the newspaper also became emblematic of the public identity declaimed by Smith, for those same African-American readers kept alive an increasingly anachronistic ideology of civic republicanism in the midst of a partisan, acquisitive, and racially stratified Jacksonian society. Garrison welcomed their patronage, but, more important, he welcomed the association with the idea of virtuous, active citizenry that their patronage gave *The Liberator*. In an antebellum version of what we might call the "Elvis syndrome," the white abolitionist gained a public identity for his editorial voice and by extension his own renown by adopting a theory and practice of African-American identity that was based on collective self-recognition in print.[5]

As an abolitionist orator, Douglass had solicited subscriptions for *The Liberator*, but as the editor of the *North Star* he wanted what Garrison had: a public attribution for his editorial voice. More to the point, he wanted the identification of color that a black reading public had bestowed on *The Liberator*. In *My Bondage and My Freedom*, he deemed the establishment of a "tolerably well conducted press, in the hands of the persons of the despised race" to be absolutely essential to the improvement, service, and national purpose of what he called pointedly the "colored people of the United States" (237). He deemed it so essential that we might have to rethink the distinction between the abstract, universalized subjectivity of liberal democracy and the materiality or corporeality of racial identity in order to understand the stakes in Douglass's and Garrison's dispute. Indeed, both editors vied to represent a colored people under the assumption that "persons of the despised race" could adopt what Lauren Berlant has called "the privilege of abstraction" through the mediation of a press organ.[6] Under these terms, the determination of color and perhaps even race turned on the deceptively simple question of which newspaper was colored. *The Liberator* and the *North Star* could both offer competitive claims precisely because antebellum racial identity was linked by tradition, practice, and particularly the print culture of newspapers to the republican ideal of a virtuous citizenry. In this form, the attribute of color betrayed an interracial lineage that bore witness to its origins in a fundamental conception of democracy.

In the second issue of the *North Star*, Douglass confronted the misgivings of his readers, who feared that their patronage of a colored newspaper would "keep up a wicked distinction between white and colored persons." Making a racially essentialist claim for the printed medium, he proclaimed baldly, "Facts are facts; white is not Black and Black is not white."[7] However, the facts were not that simple, and Douglass had to remind his readers that they did not have to subscribe to *The Liberator* to read a colored newspaper. Of course, Douglass's insistence on this point meant that he and Garrison were competing for the same subscribers, but before we examine their dispute in detail we must account first for the currency of printed articles as a medium of color and second for the standing of *The Liberator* as colored. The first assumption seemed to have succeeded almost too well (or at Douglass's expense), and so one of the issues that we should have to consider in the conclusion is the proposition of a black public sphere. The difficulty Douglass had in attracting subscribers from Garrison, combined with the patronage that he accepted from white abolitionist supporters such as Gerritt Smith, suggests that a racial identity that was based on institutions of print culture not just subject to dispute but configured in and through a public sphere of disputation.[8]

Although we might celebrate Douglass the orator according to Emersonian standards of self-identity, self-expression, and self-reliance, Douglass seemed to gain an equal but opposite renown from being an editor, especially among African Americans. In his introduction to *My Bondage and My Freedom*, the same James McCune Smith who had proclaimed "our certain advancement as a People" called Douglass "a type of his countrymen" whose "proclivity or bent, to active toil and visible progress, are in the strictly national direction." Smith found this direction and proclivity in Douglass's new career as an editor, which he claimed was the "highest position in society" (17). In the first issue of the *North Star*, Douglass made the same distinction by announcing with great fanfare, "In the grand struggle for liberty and equality now waging, it is meet, right and essential that there should arise in our ranks authors and editors, as well as orators."[9] His own advancement therefore represented nothing less than the progress of people toward freedom and enlightenment, a vision of racial improvement that reiterated the most expansive republican vision for an American citizenry.

As Robert Levine has shown, many such visions were offered over the course of the colored convention movement, which gathered leaders of free black communities through much of the 1830s and 1840s to proclaim the progress and fitness of the race. At nearly each gathering, a call was made such as Smith's for a colored press, reminding us that many African-American leaders of that period— including David Ruggles, James Forten, William C. Nell, Samuel Cornish, and of course, David Walker—came from the ranks of printers, editors, agents, or patrons of newspapers.[10] Douglass joined their ranks, but, more important, he joined the spectacle of racial improvement to the promise of a progressive Enlightenment when he committed himself to his journalistic venture. While preparing for the first issue of the *North Star*, he interrupted his efforts to tell the assembled audience at the 1847 colored convention that "this world is to be ruled, shaped and guided by the *marvelous might of the mind*. The human voice must supersede the roar of the cannon. . . . Free speech—free discussion—peaceful agitation . . . will subvert the giant crime."[11] Early the next year, he refined his statement to clarify the service of the *North Star* to the cause of rational progress. "The prospects are already brightening . . . ," he proclaimed in a March 1848 speech, "improvements are visible in several northern states; colored men and women are becoming *readers and thinkers*."[12]

Like any other newspaper editor, Douglass staked the success of his venture on the numbers of "readers and thinkers," but as the editor of a colored newspaper, he had extra reasons to hope that his subscribers would compose an enlightened public. The *North Star* was intended to play a featured role in a larger project of "mental culture" and "mental liberty," goals that black leaders inherited from the most radical aspects of the Enlightenment. David Walker, for one, was serving as an agent for *Freedom's Journal*, a New York-based black newspaper, when he wrote his famous "Appeal to the Colored Citizens of the World" in 1829. Included in the "appeal" were exhortations for freemen to educate themselves and *then "go to work and enlighten your brethren."*[13] The same message can be found in the first issue of *Freedom's Journal*, whose editor, Samuel Cornish, called forth a largely obsolete image of an impartial readership when he stated his intention to "come boldly before an enlightened public." The appearance of the newspaper, he claimed, proved that "knowledge and civilization are shedding their enlivening rays over the rest of the human family."[14] In its earliest incarnation, the black press and particularly its printer class indeed represented an image of a colored race discarding the taint of its inferiority in accordance with the progress of reason. Making special reference to the "mechanic arts," William Whipper told an 1835 colored convention of the need for the "extinction of mental thralldom" and admitted that "we are unable to conceive of any better method by which we can aid in the cause of human liberty, than by improving our general character, and embracing within our grasp the liberated slave for moral and mental culture."[15]

Douglass signed on to this project of "mental culture" when he claimed in *My Bondage and My Freedom* that the "best means of emancipating the slaves of the south is to improve and elevate the character of the free colored people of the north" (248). What was needed for the progress of the colored people was a colored newspaper, which he said would "demonstrate their capacity for a more exalted civilization than slavery and prejudice had assigned for them" by "calling out the mental energies of the race itself; by making them acquainted with their own latent powers" (237). The *North Star* would spearhead a counter-publicity campaign to end the widespread defamation against the morals, spirit, and capabilities of black people, but its most conclusive counterargument against inferiority, Douglass believed, was to be found in the paper's own success. Indeed, Douglass's advocacy of the colored newspaper had the effect of making the fitness, the equality, even the essence of the race dependent on either the support of black readers or the existence of a reading public. The failure of the colored newspaper, however, testified to a collective tendency toward regression, willing ignorance, and inconstancy, which is what he saw, fairly or not, in the history of past African-American journalistic ventures. In his inaugural editorial heralding the appearance of the *North Star*, he warned darkly, "Our race must be vindicated from the embarrassing imputations resulting from former nonsuccesses."[16]

The high stakes that Douglass placed on the success of the *North Star*—that is, the very existence of a colored people—drove him into the arms of the Liberty Party and the patronage of Gerritt Smith; he was so determined to signal the advancement of the race toward its mental liberty that he accepted a white subscription base. Until the *North Star* became *Frederick Douglass's Paper* in 1851, however, Douglass addressed himself largely to black readers, whom he was determined to present in the image of an enlightened reading public. Toward this end, he was willing to adopt the role of taskmaster, which he performed with relish in the startling editorial, "What Are the Colored People Doing for Themselves?" In a tweak at Martin Delany and the legacy of Primus and Prince Hall, Douglass condemned the "the weak and glittering follies of odd-fellowship and free-masonry," fraternal institutions through which African Americans historically created their public culture. He implied even that the great Bethel Church of Philadelphia had failed the race for failing to speak "the right word—the word for progress—the word for mental culture—[and] encourage reading." "We may read and understand," he continued, "we may speak and write—we may expose our wrongs—we may appeal to the sense of justice yet alive in the public mind" and achieve all these ends, he did not have to add, by subscribing to the *North Star*.[17]

Published in 1848, "What Are the Colored People Doing for Themselves" looked toward the events of European revolutions for the spectacle of an insurgent, liberty-loving people. "The oppressed of the old world are . . . making their wishes known to the world," he claimed. But "we confess, with the deepest mortification, that out of the five hundred thousand free colored people in this country, no more than two thousand can be supposed to take any special interest in measures for their own elevation; and probably not more than fifteen hundred take, read and pay for an antislavery paper. . . . But here we are mortified to think that we are now speaking to tens where we ought to speak to thousands."

Douglass made his appeal for a colored people to play their role in the universal progress of liberty in the name of the *North Star*, whose demise he evidently foresaw and feared. By the end of 1848, he was already envisioning the possibility of marketplace failure by telling his readers "we tremble at the reproach which would fall upon us, should this effort fail. . . . We therefore call upon our old subscribers . . . act at once to renew their subscriptions." He reminded his recalcitrant subscribers at nearly every opportunity that the "emancipation, improvement and elevation of the oppressed and disenfranchised of this land" were dependent on their support of the colored newspaper, as was "a complete contradiction of the charge of natural inferiority universally preferred against us at the North."[18] Nothing less than a subscription drive, led by black readers, would demonstrate the equality of the race.

Douglass's partner in his journalistic venture, Martin Delany, was more sanguine in the midst of the newspaper's tribulations. Conducting a typically thorough inspection of subscriber rolls, he concluded that it was "morally impossible" for the *North Star* to become self-sustaining.[19] But Douglass never wavered in his conviction that black readers could and should announce themselves to world and manifest their innate capacities. In an 1855 address, Douglass posed the question, "have [colored people] within themselves—enfolded within their organization, within their own brain—those germs of civilization, exalted character supposed to be within the reach of other men? . . . Can he rise from degradation to respectability, from ignorance to intelligence [?] . . . The answer to these questions cannot be answered by the white race."[20] Douglass seemed still to be coveting the answer he had sought through the *North Star*, which was to demonstrate the standing of the colored race not merely as a people but as a people engaged in its self-liberation through the "marvelous might of the mind." Of course, this was a destiny that might be ceded to an invisible historical agent: reason, civilization, perhaps modernity itself. For Douglass, however, the progress of history toward emancipation could be measured materially, in the black race, and even more critically, in the colored newspaper, which shared all its attributes. This was how he made the press an essential attribute of color: as an index of progress, often judged comparatively. In his apologia for the colored newspaper, he had made sure to remind his prospective subscribers, "The white man is only superior to the Black man when he outstrips him in the race of improvement. . . . We must stand side by side with our white fellow countrymen, in all the trades, arts, professions and callings of the day."[21]

The only trouble with Douglass's ambition was that Garrison had already accomplished what he wanted the *North Star* to accomplish—and with the support of black readers, too. Indeed, nothing would vindicate and at the same time upset Douglass's project for racial elevation like the attachment of freemen subscribers to *The Liberator*. Douglass knew full well its appeal; in his first autobiography, he proudly counted himself as one of its subscribers and credited his conversion to the principles of abolition to the newspaper.[22] Although he would later attribute his attachment to "hero-worship," the fact remains that there was something to *The Liberator* or to the assumption that a press organ could abstract an individual or community from the particularities of their situation and render them a free people. This assumption held true especially among black communities of the North, for they prized a tradition of colored newspapers in which the properties and qualities of the race were synthesized with the political ideal of progressive enlightenment. Garrison understood this tradition as well as the potential of a black subscriber base; he established *The Liberator* as an abolitionist press especially suited to the self-recognition of a black reading public. So if Douglass were going to succeed, he would have to imitate the success of Garrison, who had in turn imitated the principles of freemen newspapers.

The early years of *The Liberator* do reveal the crucial support lent by prominent African Americans. In the freemen community the subsidy and attendant approbation of James Forten—"May the 'Liberator' be the means of raising up friends to the oppressed People of Color"[23]—lent the newspaper a credibility that its leaders were eager to recognize. Writing in 1831, William Watkins declared, "We recognize *The Liberator* as the friend of bleeding humanity, the faithful representatives of our sentiments and interests, our uncompromising advocates of our . . . rights."[24] For his part, Garrison, eager to return the recognition, included a letter "to our free colored brethren" in the first issue of *The Liberator*. In that letter he promised them that "your moral and intellectual elevation, the advancement of your rights, and the defense of your character will be a leading object of our paper."[25] In keeping with the aims of Walker and Cornish, the agent and editor of *Freedom's Journal*, he interpolated a reading public—*The Liberator* was "their organ," he said—and then watched as the support of black subscribers made the newspaper nearly self-sustaining, justifying his claims for its partisan independence in the process.

As scholars of the abolition movement have shown, Garrison and Boston's black community developed a political partnership that brought a distinctively anticolonizationist agenda, a patriotic language of civic virtue, and a well-organized network of improvement societies into the New England abolition movement.[26] But perhaps most useful to Garrison was the precedent of colored newspapers like *Freedom's Journal*, *Rights of All*, and the *Colored American* in the 1820s and 1830s, all of which addressed readers as model citizens in the artisan republican mold. Linking the advancement of the race to their ascension as a virtuous people, the inaugural editorial of *Freedom's Journal* sought to inculcate thrift, "habits of industry," and "useful knowledge" into its would-be citizens. A short-lived newspaper simply called the *American* promised "to stimulate [our colored brethren] in the paths of education and virtue." An editorial in *Rights of All* sought to simplify the demands of the "free colored population" when it stated that its object was to pursue the path of education "such as are mechanics encouraged in their several branches of business."[27]

Emerging from a mechanic tradition himself, Garrison adopted this latter-day republican agenda from freemen newspapers and then made it an abolitionist imperative. Appearing before a gathering of African-American leaders in Philadelphia in 1831, he spoke the language they recognized. "Multiply periodicals among yourselves, to be conducted by men of your own color," he advised and added simply that parents should "put your children to the trades." However, the editor of *The Liberator* was there to solicit subscriptions, and so he did not shrink from presenting the nascent newspaper as the signal manifestation of republican progress. "I know that without the powerful energies of the press, every cause must languish. It was this engine which produced and tri-

umphantly effected the American Revolution, it has two times over-
thrown the despotism in France. . . . The press is the citadel of liberty—
the palladium of a free people."[28] Subscribing to *The Liberator*, as many
in the audience no doubt did, henceforth made the "free colored population" the agents of democracy, for it could bypass the manifest limitations on black citizenship and assume the title of a "free people."

The Liberator was recognized as colored only to the extent that it
signified the progress of a people, but to that same extent it was colored in the only sense that mattered. It is true that several freemen activists sought to publish a colored newspaper in Boston and that, had
it not been for the mysterious death of Walker, a rival to Garrison's ini-
tiative might have emerged sooner. Yet all efforts, including Douglass's,
would have to lay claim to the political tradition of the freemen newspaper through *The Liberator*, which is why Douglass was compelled to
travel to the heart of Garrison's subscriber base, Boston itself, to argue
the legitimacy of his colored newspaper. He had started his journalistic
enterprise by stating plainly, "Facts are facts; white is not Black and
Black is not white," but in the course of his dispute with Garrison, he
was confronted with a rather tortured racial politics that demonstrated
the affinity, if not the crossing over of white and black identity in and
through the printed medium.

Although there was little to Douglass's and Garrison's dispute that
did not directly concern the fate of their respective newspapers, the
competition between colored newspapers offered them the opportunity
to articulate a racial identity that, while not given in advance, nonetheless reflected the traditional political symbolism of a black reading
public. Garrison would have considered the initial appearance of the
North Star as a threat to his black subscriber base, so when Douglass
announced his conversion to a political, or partisan, interpretation of
abolition and endorsed the Constitution as an antislavery document at
the 1851 convention of the American Anti-Slavery Society, Garrison
seized the opportunity to remove the institutional support for Douglass's
press, striking it from a list of preferred abolitionist publications. For
this and other departures from Garrison's orthodoxy, Douglass was as-
sailed in the reform press for having had the temerity to have "expected
the Anti-Slavery sentiment to converge to his paper, the Anti-Slavery
patronage to widen its circulation," ambitions that were translated into

racial defects. A publicity campaign reached its peak in 1853, when the *Pennsylvania Freeman* editorialized that the black editor's purported desire to publish "the only newspaper devoted to the interests of the colored people" betrayed the "avarice," "love of dominion," the "fierce impatience opposition" of the former slave. Besides, the *Freeman* sniffed, "We had thought *The Liberator* devoted to 'the interests of the colored people.'"[29]

Exactly. Douglass recognized the import of this criticism, which was to present him as the incarnation of racial inferiority so that *The Liberator* might have a clear field. In his exhaustive defense of himself and his motives, "A Review of Anti-Slavery Relations," he noted that his character had been good enough for white abolitionists until *Frederick Douglass's Paper* had departed from their principles and become the organ of the rival Liberty Party. His opponents' interests would be advanced, he warned, by his "consenting to leave the field, giving up my mission in the world, abandoning my paper, flinging down my pen," which would leave Garrison to edit a colored newspaper without competition or contributions from people of color.[30]

In the same essay, Douglass sought to expose the pretension of the white editor: "Abolitionism does not change the color of the skin, so that while theoretically and abstractly the cause of antislavery is the cause of universal man, it is practically and peculiarly the cause of the colored man—and any attempt . . . on the part of Mr. Garrison . . . to lift this holy cause into a sublimity, beyond the comprehension of the colored men, as a class, deserves to be branded by every colored man with the reprobation due to so stupendous an insult."

Here was a definitive blow to the purported colored properties of *The Liberator,* a reminder that black was not white and white was not black. But in the interest of *Frederick Douglass's Paper*, Douglass seemed also ready to destroy the pretensions of African Americans to abstract citizenship and to define race "peculiarly" or "as a class." What then remained of the historic purpose of the colored newspaper, which had been to present race as the sign of a people, in the form of a universal aspiration toward progress?

Douglass attempted to introduce the fact or particularity of race into the public medium of print when he appeared before a gathering of Boston freemen in 1853 to solicit subscribers for *Frederick Douglass's Paper*.

In the exchange, his long-festering resentment at black subscribers, or at the lack of them, was combined with his resentment at Garrison's success in representing black interests and identity. His unfortunate target was William C. Nell, who had returned to manage *The Liberator* after a brief stint with Douglass's paper; he carried with him not only the interracial lineage of the colored newspaper but also, as the author of *Colored Patriots of the American Revolution*, the transracial ideal of a virtuous citizenry so prized by freemen. So when Nell rose up before the audience and maintained that Douglass's published remarks disqualified him for its support, his destruction at the hands of Douglass was, by Douglass's own reckoning, thorough, premeditated, and perhaps vindictive. In August 1853 he wrote, "William C. Nell rose, to put them on their guard against subscribing for a paper, the editor of which he charged with ingratitude and unkindness toward William Lloyd Garrison!! [Contemptible tool.] . . . He would doubtless be very happy to see my paper destroyed—and destroyed it may be, but while it lives, it will be a free and independent sheet."[31]

As always, Douglass sought to expose the threat to the colored newspaper, but in the course of amplifying his report he could not disguise his zeal for a publicity war:

> Wm. C. Nell with a harmless stir, a bowed down look, and a
> cat-like step arose to put the colored people on their guard
> against sustaining a paper, inimical, as he alleged, to Mr.
> Garrison. Believing him to have acted as a *"tool"* in this matter,
> we called him a *"tool,"* and being warm at the moment of
> writing, we called him a *"contemptible tool."* Well, now the
> battle commences. *The Liberator*, the most warlike chief of all
> its tribe . . . [will] exhibit the editor of *Frederick Douglass's Paper*
> to the worst possible advantage before the readers of *The
> Liberator.*[32]

Perhaps we should ask again: Was this dispute personal? Both Garrison and Douglass claimed to represent a colored people with a colored newspaper, but in the midst of their competition, that public attribution seemed less secure than ever or perhaps more dependent on personal qualities and properties. The complicated question of which newspaper was colored indeed became linked to the equally complex question of whether an editor represented the public, giving rise to charges and countercharges of personal ambition. Douglass mocked Nell's charge of ingratitude for this reason: it exposed the tie of personality that bound black readers to a white editor. Garrison's surrogates found equal advantage in exposing Douglass's purported ambition—it made him unfit to represent the colored people. A language of racial difference became the norm, as one side sought to uncover an inherent flaw and the other tried to address the race "peculiarly." And yet what they both wanted still was for their newspaper to be colored.

The overdetermined status of the colored newspaper does seem to leave us wondering whether it could convene or represent a public sphere in the form that Douglass, Garrison, and their predecessors imagined it. In the final analysis, the colored newspaper seems to have sponsored a conflicted sphere of debate over racial identity, not necessarily a body of black readers, and while this may have simulated the working of democracy, neither Douglass nor Garrison were willing to surrender the symbolic connection of a black readership to expansive, progressive democracy. Douglass's plans for his newspaper seemed to propose an alternate incarnation for the public that recognized its merely proximate relation to black readers—the paper was neither self-supporting nor subsidized by a black organization—but that also presented signal public attributes—rational self-determination, a capacity for self-perfection, and civic virtue—into particular, even inherent properties of the race. He presented this plan in "A Liberal Offer to Subscribers," printed shortly after the debacle in Boston. In return for the "names of three new yearly subscribers," Douglass offered the black icon Madison Washington, the protagonist of the short story "The Heroic Slave," which was included in a collection called Autographs for Freedom.[33] In "The Heroic Slave," Madison Washington was endowed with corporeal aspects of race; he possessed "arms like polished iron . . . a brow as dark and glossy as a raven's wing;"[34] but in committing that representation to the benefit of *Frederick Douglass's Newspaper*, Douglass was attempting to continue what he avowed to be in his "Liberal Offer": "our mission of the Slave's freedom and of the free colored man's elevation" through and in the particularity of race. This had been how he presented the colored newspaper to his freemen audience in Boston, presenting, it was said, the newspaper's "peculiar claims upon them."

This seemed also to be the "peculiarity" of Douglass's public sphere, which surrendered the conceit of a body of citizen in order to make printed medium itself the equivalent of a distinct racial identity.

Notes

1. Frederick Douglass, *My Bondage and My Freedom*, ed. William Andrews (Urbana: University of Illinois Press, 1987), 220, 240.
2. The tension caused by Douglass's plan to publish a newspaper is described in William McFeeley, *Frederick Douglass* (New York: Norton, 1991), 246–50. Many accounts, however, see only an ideal of self-identity at stake in his relation with Douglass. See Peter Walker, *Moral Choices: Memory, Desire, and Imagination in Nineteenth Century American Abolition* (Baton Rouge: Louisiana State University Press, 1978), 244–45; and James Olney, "'I Was Born': Slave Narratives, Their Status as Autobiography and as Literature," in *The Slave's Narrative*, ed. Charles T. Davis and Henry Louis Gates, Jr. (New York: Oxford University Press, 1985), 150–67.
3. The eighteenth-century tradition of libertarianism is explicated in Richard D. Brown, *The Strength of a People: The Idea of an Informed Citizenry in America, 1650–1870* (Chapel Hill: University of North Carolina Press, 1996), 28–84. The radical republicanism of artisans and printers is described in Daniel Schiller, *Objectivity and the News: The Public and the Rise of Journalism* (Philadelphia: University of Pennsylvania Press, 1981), 36–51; Sean Wilentz, *Chants Democratic: New York City and the Rise of the American Working Class, 1788–1850* (New York: Oxford University Press, 1984), 69–94.
4. Howard Holman Bell, ed., *Minutes of the Proceedings of the National Negro Convention*, The American Negro: His History and Literature (New York: Arno Press and New York Times, 1969), 19.
5. Garrison's attempt to present his editorial voice as a public property through the management of his newspaper is described in Fanuzzi, "'The Organ of an Individual': William Lloyd Garrison and the *Liberator*," *Prospects* 23 (1998): 107–27.
6. Berlant, *The Anatomy of National Fantasy: Hawthorne, Utopia and Everyday Life* (Chicago: University of Chicago Press, 1991), 13.
7. Douglass, "Colored Newspapers," *North Star*, 7 January 1848.
8. Critical interventions in the Habermasian concept of a public sphere appear in Elisa Barkley Brown, "Negotiating and Transforming the Public Sphere: African-American Political Life in the Transition from Slavery to Freedom," *Public Culture* 7 (1994): 107–46; Steven Gregory, "Race, Identity and Political Activism: The Shifting Contours of the African-American Public Sphere," *Public Culture* 7 (1994): 147–64.
9. Douglass, "Our Paper and its Prospects," *North Star*, 3 December 1847.
10. See Robert Levine, *Martin Delany, Frederick Douglass and the Politics of Representative Identity* (Chapel Hill: University of North Carolina Press, 1997), 22–30.
11. Bell, *National Negro Convention*, 31.
12. Douglass, "The Folly of Racially Exclusive Organizations," in *Frederick Douglass Papers: Speeches Debates, Interviews*, vol. 2, ed. John Blassingame (New Haven: Yale University Press, 1979), 111.
13. Sean Wilentz, ed., *David Walker's Appeal* (New York: Hill and Wang, 1995), 28.
14. Martin Dann, ed., *The Black Press, 1827–1890: The Quest for National Identity* (New York: Putnam, 1971), 34, 36.

15. C. Peter Ripley, ed., *The Black Abolitionist Papers*, vol. 3 (Chapel Hill: University of North Carolina Press, 1991), 149.
16. Douglass, "Our Paper and Its Prospects."
17. Douglass, "What Are the Colored People Doing for Themselves?" *North Star*, 14 July 1848.
18. Douglass, "The First Volume of the North Star Completed," *North Star*, 22 December 1848.
19. Delany, "Highly Important Statistics," *North Star*, 13 April 1849.
20. Douglass, "These Questions Cannot Be Answered by the White Race," in *Frederick Douglass Papers: Speeches, Debates, Interviews*, vol. 3, ed. John Blassingame (New Haven: Yale University Press, 1979), 86.
21. Douglass, "Colored Newspapers."
22. Douglass, *Narrative of the Life of Frederick Douglass, an American Slave, The Classic Slave Narratives*, ed. Henry Louis Gates, Jr. (New York: Signet, 1987), 325.
23. Ripley, *Black Abolitionist Papers*, 3:95.
24. Ibid., 3:92.
25. Quoted in Donald M. Jacobs, "David Walker and William Garrison: Racial Cooperation and the Shaping of Boston Abolition," *Courage and Conscience: Black and White Abolitionists in Boston*, ed. Donald M. Jacobs (Bloomington: Indiana University Press, 1993), 12.
26. See ibid. 1–20; James Oliver Horton and Lois E. Horton, *Black Bostonians: Family Life and Community Struggle in the Antebellum North* (New York: Holmes and Meier, 1979), 46–95; Horton and Horton, *In Hope of Liberty: Culture, Community and Protests Among Northern Free Blacks, 1700–1860* (New York: Oxford University Press, 1997), 212–40.
27. Dann, *Black Press*, 34, 42, 300. For the artisan republican values of African-American urban communities, see Horton and Horton, *In Hope of Liberty*, 167–200.
28. Garrison, *An Address Delivered Before the Free People of Color* (Boston, 1831), 9.
29. "Frederick Douglass vs. Robert Purvis, Wendell Phillips, and C. L. Remond," *Frederick Douglass's Paper*, 9 December 1853.
30. Douglass, "Review of Anti-Slavery Relations," *Frederick Douglass's Paper*, 9 December 1853.
31. Douglass, "Letter from the Editor," *Frederick Douglass's Paper*, 4 August 1853.
32. Douglass, "Opposition from Professed Friends," *Frederick Douglass's Paper*, 9 September 1853.
33. Douglass, "A Liberal Offer to Subscribers," *Frederick Douglass's Paper*, 13 January 1854.
34. Douglass, "The Heroic Slave," in *The Oxford Frederick Douglass Reader*, ed. William Andrews (New York: Oxford University Press, 1996), 134.

Chapter 4

SHELLEY FISHER FISHKIN
CARLA L. PETERSON

"We Hold These Truths to Be Self-Evident"

The Rhetoric of Frederick Douglass's Journalism

ON 22 AUGUST 1844, the young Frederick Douglass wrote to J. Miller McKim: "Though quite unaccustomed to write anything for the public eye, and in many instances quite unwilling to do so, in the present case I cannot content myself to take leave of you . . . without dropping you a very hasty, and of course very imperfect sketch of the Anti-slavery meetings."[1]

Little did Douglass then suspect that over the next fifty years he would do little else but "write for the public eye" on antislavery and other related topics. Indeed, under the aegis of such white abolitionists as William Lloyd Garrison, Douglass had started what would become a long and illustrious career in journalism in the early 1840s, writing for *The Liberator* as well as other antislavery newspapers. Chafing under constraints imposed by the white abolitionist leadership, however, Douglass gradually broke away to create his own journalistic organs: first *The North Star*, followed by *Frederick Douglass' Paper* and still later by *Douglass' Monthly*. After the Civil War, Douglass maintained his prolific journalistic output, writing on all the major issues confronting blacks in postbellum America for *The New National Era*, as well as such mainstream journals as *The North American Review*, *The Atlantic Monthly*, and *Harper's Weekly*.

How did a piece of property transform himself into a speaking subject?

How did a young man who had spent the first twenty-odd years of his life in slavery become the most articulate spokesman for his race and the foremost black journalist of the nineteenth century? In his auto-biographical *Narrative*, Douglass tells his readers that "you have seen how a man was made a slave; you shall see how a slave was made a man" and proceeds to locate this transformative moment in an act of physical resistance, his battle with the slave breaker, Covey.[2] And yet, the events of Douglass's life that frame this moment make it clear that for Douglass, manhood and freedom could not be purely physical states of being, just as resistance could never simply be of a physical nature. Indeed, Douglass's language specifies that his emergence into manhood was not a new event in his life, but rather a revival of feelings formerly felt, of thoughts formerly held: "This battle with Mr. Covey was the turning-point in my career as a slave. It rekindled the few expiring embers of freedom, and revived within me a sense of my manhood. It recalled the departed self-confidence, and inspired me again with a determination to be free" (74).

Douglass locates these earlier intimations of freedom and manhood in his acquisition of reading skills and in the act of reading itself, in particular in his reading of a volume titled *The Columbian Orator*. Compiled by Caleb Bingham and first published in 1797, *The Columbian Orator* contained a variety of pieces designed to instruct "in the ornamental and useful art of eloquence";[3] and, according to Douglass, it was these pieces that first "gave tongue" to thoughts that Douglass himself did not yet have the language to articulate (42). From them, Douglass was for the first time exposed to contemporary notions of oratory—both to the Enlightenment discourse of freedom and independence, and to the oratorical situation itself established between speaker and audience—which would greatly influence his antebellum journalism. Indeed, from these pieces Douglass first became familiar with the rhetoric of John Locke and the Founding Fathers, which invokes the inalienable rights of man to freedom and happiness; appeals to the natural principles of liberty, equality, and justice; and inveighs against all forms of tyranny and oppression. In the speeches the oratorical voices of national leaders—Roman, English, and American—ring out with great authority. These men were able to assert themselves self-confidently as speaking subjects because they spoke both out of personal experience and on behalf of an entity larger than the individual "I," be it an entire nation, an oppressed group within the nation, or a broad principle such as freedom.

Most important, perhaps, the pieces in *The Columbian Orator* underscored for Douglass the importance of the orator's relationship to his audience. In his introductory remarks, Bingham offers his readers some "particular rules for the voice and gesture" (24). But he focuses especially on the movement of the eyes as the "most active and significant" part of the body because, according to Cicero, "'all the passions of the soul are expressed in the eyes, by so many different actions'" (22). More than any part of the body, the orator's eyes express the passion of his convictions. How to direct one's eyes upon one's audience in order to catch *its* eyes and compel *its* attention becomes, then, a crucial question for the orator. For Douglass this question would in later years become that of translating this visual strategy into a verbal one, of figuring out how to direct the writing eye of the journalist most effectively to the reading eye of public newspaper readers.

The most prominent oratorical devices used to attract the public eye in *The Columbian Orator* are techniques of the dialogic that, as Bakhtin has pointed out, most often function as a subversive strategy designed to undermine the monologic official discourse of the dominant class.[4] In many of the reproduced pieces, the orator appeals directly to his audience by asking rhetorical questions that he then proceeds to answer himself. In addition, however, many pieces are actual dialogues that stage a confrontation between two antagonists who hold opposing points of view and must use their rhetorical skill to persuade the other of the rightness of his position. The "Dialogue between a Master and Slave," singled out by Douglass in his *Narrative*, exemplifies many rhetorical strategies that he was to make good use of in later years. In it, master and slave confront one another directly, face to face, making eye contact. The master, who prides himself on being kind and humane, berates the slave for having attempted to run away for a second time. The slave construes the mere fact of his master's talking to him as an acknowledgment that he is a man and, taking full advantage of this admission, constitutes himself as a speaking subject in order to press home his points. Speaking from his own experience as a man, he argues that liberty and the full exercise of his free will are the values most precious to him. Constituting himself as spokesman for all other slaves, he assures his master that they will not hesitate to resort to violence in order to obtain these same rights. He decries the injustice of slavery and points out that no man has the right to dispose of another man. When the master attempts to argue that it is the order of Providence that one man be the slave of another, the slave skillfully points out that the argument in favor of providential design can be made for just about any situation, to the point where Providence simply becomes another form of human agency: "'Providence . . . gave my enemies a power over my liberty. But it has also given me legs to escape with; and what should prevent me from using them?'" (241). The entire dialogue thus constitutes a bold assertion of the power of human agency through both physical and verbal resistance.

Douglass's antebellum journalism owes much to his reading of *The Columbian Orator*. For, as a result of this reading, Douglass was able to create what Foucault has called a "counterdiscourse," by means of which an oppressed minority begins "to speak on its own behalf," demanding "that its legitimacy or 'naturality' be acknowledged."[5] As Foucault has pointed out, the oppressed group most often asserts itself, not by creating a new discourse, but by "using the same categories [of the dominant discourse] by which it was . . . disqualified" and simply reversing these categories or the values that had been assigned to them. In addition, as we have seen, the dialogic can function as an important element of a counterdiscourse as it creates a variety of other voices—parodic, ironic, and so on—designed to subvert the official monologic discourse of the dominant class. In his early writings, Douglass relies heavily on such techniques of reversal and of the dialogic to fashion a powerful counterdiscourse for black Americans. He does so by forcing his opponents to enter into dialogue with him, by wresting the principles of the Declaration of Independence out of the exclusive possession of the dominant class and applying them to oppressed African-Americans, and finally by repeatedly and subversively reversing the categories that this class had so carefully assigned both to itself and to those it held in bondage. With emancipation and the acquisition of citizenship, however, Douglass would be forced to rethink the effectiveness of such rhetorical strategies and to recast them in new ways.

From his earliest days in the abolitionist movement, Douglass recognized the particular difficulty of constituting himself as a speaking and writing subject because a major goal of slavery had been to reduce the slave to the level of animal or property by denying him all sense of humanity and moral life. In an article published in *The North Star* on 29 September 1848, Douglass lamented that "shut up in the prison-house of bondage—denied all rights, and deprived of all privileges, we are blotted from the page of human existence, and placed beyond the limits of human regard. Death, moral death, has palsied our souls in that quarter, and we are a murdered people" (1: 332). And ten years later, he was to complain that "*slavery has bewitched us* [the American people]. It has taught us to read history backwards" (5: 402). The pressing question facing Douglass in the antebellum period was, then, how to raise a murdered people, how to reinsert blacks—both slave and free—back on the page of human existence, how to rewrite history so that it could once again be read forward. And Douglass knew that he could do so only by asserting himself as a man, that is, as a speaking and writing subject.

To do so, Douglass had, first of all, to prove that he was literally—biologically and physiologically—a man. In his early years of lecturing and writing in England, he made this argument by contrasting British recognition of his manhood to American ignorance. He sarcastically commented that even British dogs recognized him to be a man and wondered why the American people were unable to do so. When the *New York Sun*, in a hostile article of 13 May 1847, referred to him as a man, he ironically complimented the newspaper for having perceived that he was indeed a man as opposed to a monkey. Even as late as 1855, Douglass found it necessary to defend his manhood. In an article published that year, Douglass demonstrated the archimedean nature of his claim to being a man: He might be regarded as either a man or a thing, an object of property, but he could not be regarded as both. If a person, he maintained, he was entitled to all "the rights sacred to persons in the constitution" (2: 368). Following the example set by the slave in *The Columbian Orator*'s dialogue, Douglass, asserting an existential claim to manhood, argues that the mere fact of being addressed constitutes evidence of his manhood, as it implicitly recognizes his ability to talk back. To illustrate his point, he makes use of the incident on board the *Cambria* in which "mobocratic" American slaveholders had attempted to deny him the right to speak. He insists that the passengers on board the ship had every right to ask him to speak on the subject of slavery because "to deny that they had such right, would be to deny that they had the right to exchange views at all," a point that not even the slaveholders would uphold. Thus, Douglass continues, "if they had the right to ask, I had the right to answer, and to answer so as to be understood by those who wished to hear." Again following the lead of the slave in the dialogue, Douglass claims the right to speak on the subject of slavery; he himself has been a slave and can thus effectively represent not only himself but "three million of my brethren . . . in chains and slavery on the American soil" (1: 124, 189). Douglass's claim to speak on behalf of his enslaved brethren rests on memories of his own enslavement, as well as on his acute awareness that the prejudice under which they labor extends to free blacks as well.

Having thus asserted his manhood, Douglass then appropriated the Enlightenment discourse of liberty and equality—the discourse of the dominant culture—to shape it into a powerful counterdiscourse that would challenge the proslavery arguments of the period. He grounded the force of his argument and the sweep of his eloquence on a vision of human rights—self-evident, universal, and inalienable—that he had first come across in the pages of *The Columbian Orator* and later found in the rhetoric of the Declaration of Independence. As political theorists like Harry Jaffa have suggested, the Declaration is a clear embodiment of Locke's philosophy in *The Second Treatise of Civil Government*, which argues that all men are naturally in "a state of perfect freedom to order their actions . . . without asking leave, or depending upon the will of any other man. A state also of equality, wherein all power and jurisdiction is reciprocal, no one having more than another; there being nothing more evident than that creatures of the same species and rank . . . should also be equal one amongst another without subordination or subjection."[6] Jaffa further suggests that the Founding Fathers intended the Declaration to be a universalistic document and the American Revolution a war that was to secure these inalienable rights for some men while holding out the promise that they would one day be enjoyed by all.

Douglass understood the Declaration in just such a sense as well and felt that the time had finally come for these promises to become realities. In a speech reprinted in the 2 August 1858 issue of the *New York Times*, Douglass affirmed that the Declaration of Independence was the great act that gave the American republic its existence. In it the Founding Fathers asserted that "all men are entitled to life, liberty, and to an equal chance for happiness." They regarded slavery as a transient rather than a permanent feature of American society and nowhere made provision for blacks to be enslaved or for the principles asserted in the document to be unequally applied: "They nowhere tell us that Black men shall be slaves and white men shall be free They say, 'we, the people,' never we, the white people" (5: 402).

By midcentury, Douglass had further extended his interpretation of the Declaration of Independence to include more revolutionary and self-empowering efforts to achieve black liberation and independence. In the aftermath of the raid on Harper's Ferry, Douglass praised John Brown's heroic actions as perfectly consistent with the principles of the Declaration of Independence: "He believes the Declaration of Independence to be true; and the Bible to be a guide to human conduct, and, acting upon the doctrines of both, he threw himself against the serried ranks of American oppression" (2: 459–60). And in increasingly militant terms, Douglass exhorted blacks to work for their own elevation and that of their enslaved brethren: "We must rise or fall, succeed or fail, by our own merits" (1: 314). In so doing, Douglass, like the slave in *The Columbian Orator's* dialogue, was affirming his belief in the power of human agency over that of Providence. In this he differed quite strikingly from other black leaders of the period, particularly clergymen, whose liberatory rhetoric was at all times interwoven with appeals to Providence and divine intervention. Although never totally abandoning the rhetoric of providentiality, Douglass remained more suspicious of the promiscuous uses to which it had been put over time and more inclined to rely on the power of human agency to achieve the goals of freedom and full citizenship.

In further analyzing the historical situation of the Declaration of Independence, however, Douglass found that he had good reason to reproach the Founding Fathers, for he came to believe that the very men who had framed the document were at the same time "trafficking in the blood and souls of their fellow men" (1: 207). To Douglass, then, America was one great falsehood, fashioned on a fundamental contradiction: On the one hand, it professed equality and liberty for all people; on the other, it practiced slavery, thereby denying those rights to many. To illustrate the extent to which slavery perverts the ideals on which the Republic was founded, Douglass repeatedly resorts to rhetorical schemas of antithesis. He asserts that slavery "has given us evil for good—darkness for light, and bitter for sweet" (5: 402) and underscores the contradiction between America's "profession of love of liberty" and its "statute-book so full of all that is cruel, malicious, and infernal" (1: 212). In fact, Douglass argues, slavery has replaced the Declaration of Independence as "the only sovereign power in the land." It has so permeated the entire fabric of American society that it "gives character to the American people. It dictates their laws, gives tone to their literature, and shapes their religion" (1: 168).

To reinforce his condemnation of proslavery discourse and practice, Douglass relied on a wide variety of techniques of reversal. These techniques were designed to show that the "reality" asserted by the dominant class is in fact often the exact opposite of that claimed and that, similarly, the effects sought by this dominant class often result in the exact opposite, thereby reversing the system of values it has tried so hard to impose and maintain. Thus Douglass mocks the use of such "honeyed words" as the "peculiar" or "patriarchal" institution to describe the slave system. In particular, he calls attention to the sexual abuses created by the slave system; a slaveholder is not an uncle or brother but rather "a keeper of a house of ill-fame," and his "kitchen is a brothel" (1: 271). Douglass shows that the system of slavery works not because it is "benevolent" but because it relies on the cold fact of "the whip": "To ensure good behavior, the slaveholder relies on *the whip*; to induce proper humility, he relies on *the whip*; to rebuke what he is pleased to term insolence, he relies on *the whip*" (2: 135). After the passage of the Fugitive Slave Act, he repeatedly refers to slaveholders as robbers, manstealers, highwaymen, and kidnappers. Tearing away their mask of gentility, he mocks southern gentlemen and ladies who appear at Saratoga Springs, New York, "arrayed in purple and fine linen . . . covered with silks, satins and broadcloth," but who are in reality "naked pirates before God and man" (2: 242). And he sarcastically refers to those politicians in the federal government who have southern sympathies as highwaymen, thieves, and robbers.

Returning to the analogy of blacks as animals, Douglass once again manages to reverse the terms of the dominant discourse to point out how slavery's dehumanization of slaves dehumanizes slaveholders even more. He shows how, under the slave system, slaves are "registered with four footed beasts and creeping things" and are reduced to a level of brutishness that justifies the accusations of degradation so often leveled against them (1: 282). Through skillful manipulation of rhetoric, however, he also illustrates how the slaveholders themselves become animals. He likens their cruelty toward their slaves to "the kick of a jackass, or the barking of a bull-dog" (3: 182) and asserts that, in their greed, slaveholders have become worse than pigs, for "your genuine American Negro hater surpasses the pig in piggishness" (4: 229). To entrust the well-being of slaves to slaveholders is, finally, tantamount to suggesting that "wolves may be trusted to legislate for themselves and . . . for lambs" (2: 329).

In yet another ironic reversal, Douglass shows how supposedly tyrannical countries are in fact resolutely advancing the causes of liberty and equality while democratic America is eagerly trampling on the principles of the Declaration of Independence: "The fact is, while Europe is becoming republican, we are becoming despotic; while France is contending for freedom, we are extending slavery. . . . While humanity, justice, and freedom are thawing the icy heart of Russia into life, and causing, even there, the iron hand of despotism to relax its terrible grasp upon the enslaved peasantry . . . we of the United States are buried in stone-dead indifference" (1: 305; 2: 440). And of all ironies, England, the erstwhile oppressor, has now become the champion of the slave. "Monarchical freedom," Douglass bitterly concludes, "is better than republican slavery" (1: 172).

The most important rhetorical strategy of Douglass's counter-discourse in the antebellum period was, perhaps, his use of dialogic techniques that allowed him to make eye contact not only with his audience but with his opponents as well, with those "masters" from whom he had had to wrench his freedom. In particular, he made use of the form of the "open letter" to engage in dialogue some of the most important men of his time. Although the term "open letter" did not come into use until the 1860s and 1870s, the form had existed for hundreds of years, in kind if not in name. It was most often used by a society's elite to challenge an opponent's point of view in a political or religious controversy. Probably the first black American to make use of this form, Douglass fashioned it into a particularly effective counterdiscourse, claiming as his own a form that had proven useful to popes, bishops, noblemen, and political leaders throughout the last three hundred years. By adopting this form, Douglass was implicitly asserting his claim to equal status with all those who had used it before him.

As the most personal of literary forms, the letter implies by its very nature a back-and-forth, a give-and-take, a dialogue between two parties. With few exceptions, Douglass's open letters are addressed to individuals who would never deign to engage him in conversation, let alone answer him by letter. By means of this technique, Douglass was able to create hypothetical dialogues in which he invented his opponents' speeches or letters so that he could respond to them. The open letter thus became yet another effective means of entering into dialogue with those who wished to blot blacks from the page of human existence. Moreover, although each of Douglass's open letters is addressed to a particular individual, each is also addressed to a larger public concern, allowing Douglass to personify and make concrete larger issues that his readers might remain insensitive to in the abstract. By adopting the open letter format, then, Douglass used it, much as the slave in *The Columbian Orator* used the dialogue form, to constitute himself as a speaking and writing subject, engage his opponents in dialogue, and concretely claim for himself and for all blacks the principles of liberty and equality inscribed in the Declaration of Independence.

Douglass makes use of the open letter as early as 1846 in a series of letters to Garrison in which he diverges at given points from addressing his antislavery friend in order to address an antislavery opponent. Thus, in a letter dated 27 January 1846, Douglass turns away from Garrison to enter into dialogue with Mr. A.C.C. Thompson of Wilmington, who had attempted to invalidate Douglass's testimony against those slaveholders whose names were mentioned in the *Narrative*. Much like the slave in *The Columbian Orator*'s dialogue, Douglass responds to Thompson, thanking him profusely for the attention he has paid him, which proves that he is in fact the man he claims to be, "an *American slave*," rather than an imposter. He then proceeds ironically to compliment Thompson for doing "a piece of anti-slavery work, which no antislavery man could do" (1: 131). In another open letter, this one addressed to Samuel H. Cox, Douglass once again takes advantage of the fact that Cox has addressed him to engage him in dialogue, this time reclaiming Cox's words of insult and turning them into words of praise. In particular, he redefines the term "*abolition agitator and altruist*" to mean "simply . . . one who dares to think for himself—who goes beyond the mass of mankind in promoting the cause of righteousness—who honestly and earnestly speaks out his soul's conviction" (1: 192).

Douglass's boldest use of the open letter form may be found in two letters written in the late 1840s: one to Henry Clay, published in *The North Star* on 3 December 1847, the other to his former master, Captain Thomas Auld, published in *The Liberator* on 14 September 1849. In his letter to Clay, Douglass incorporates Clay's language into his own discourse, by quoting from it at length, and then proceeds to answer his points on the spot. The letter itself thus constitutes a kind of dialogue between master and slave. In it Douglass points out Clay's ideological inconsistencies. On the one hand, Clay calls slaves "unfortunate victims," but on the other, he continues to call for the perpetuation of slavery. Likewise, he purports to be a lover of liberty, but at the same time he insists that each state should have the power to decide whether it wants slavery within its borders or not. Faced with such an intellectual muddle, Douglass feels compelled to offer Clay advice, something that he would never have the opportunity to do in person; and his advice is "emancipate your own slaves" (1: 290). In his letter to Auld, Douglass adopts a more informal tone, audaciously asserting his intellectual and moral superiority over his old master. Intimating that his own antislavery activities have influenced Auld, he graciously compliments the latter on his emancipation of his slaves and then suggests that he make his conversion to antislavery public. In effect, in this open letter Douglass recreates the scene between master and slave in *The Columbian Orator*, in which the slave, having gained his freedom, turns around to lecture and warn his master.

In the 11 March 1853 issue of *The North Star*, Douglass published a short story entitled "The Heroic Slave," which also appeared the same year in Julia Griffith's *Autographs for Freedom*. Based on events surrounding the slave revolt on board the *Creole* in 1841, the story is important for the ways in which Douglass both continues and extends the themes and strategies of his antebellum journalism; in particular, he turns to techniques of fiction to accomplish what factual writing would not allow him to do. Douglass was already aware of the power of fiction when, in his "Farewell Speech to the British People," published in *The London Times* in 1847, he imputed certain statements to Daniel Webster concerning Madison Washington, which then allowed him to underscore the basic contradictions at the heart of the slave system. In Webster's hypothetical speech, he praised Washington's courage and nobility, while at the same time he demanded that the slave be returned to the chains of slavery. In fictionalizing Washington's story in "The Heroic Slave," Douglass took full advantage of the freedom that fiction allowed him further to point out the contradictions inherent in the slave system and to press home the abolitionists' cause.[7]

Many themes and rhetorical devices that Douglass employs in the story continue those of his journalism. In particular, Douglass is most effective in adapting certain of his journalistic techniques to the manipulation of voice and point of view in the story. First, he creates a powerful black hero who, through soliloquy, speeches, and storytelling, is granted full status as speaking subject. In addition, Douglass's technique of the hypothetical dialogue comes into its own here, as Douglass is able to create not only dialogues but full-blown characters—black and white—who interact dramatically in scenes spun from his imagination. In Part 3, for example, Douglass's narrator moves the action to a tavern in Virginia and creates a series of dialogues between a white proslavery "loafer" and the abolitionist Listwell as well as conversations among the loafers themselves. The main point of these dialogues is to expose the foolishness of the loafers' perceptions, their inability to read Listwell properly, and ultimately their failure to achieve any semblance of narrative authority. They are reduced to telling each other "stories" that the narrator, as controlling authority, refuses to record because he considers them unworthy of the reader's attention. Listwell, in contrast, remains very much in control, able both to withhold information about himself and to achieve an invisible, omniscient perspective so that, unknown to them, he may learn a good deal about them. When Listwell disappears in Part 4 of the story, it is so that the narrative may record a second conversation among a group of white men, this time southern sailors. Amplifying once again the technique of the hypothetical dialogue, Douglass's narrator creates a conversation between a sailor and the first mate of the *Creole*, who, goaded by the former, ends up praising Washington's heroic act of self-assertion, defending his essential dignity and nobility, and unwittingly underscoring the contradiction inherent in white America's refusal to apply the principles of 1776 to the black man.

In "The Heroic Slave" Douglass also extends the narrative techniques of his journalism in his efforts both to transcend the highly personal perspective of the "I" and to develop the broader perspective of a third-person narrator. In portraying Madison Washington, Douglass creates a character who, although a fictional projection of himself in many ways, is nonetheless historically distinct from him. In so doing, Douglass initiates a process whereby he attempts to distance himself from his autobiographical and factual "I." Moving beyond the autobiographical "I," Douglass creates a third-person narrator who is especially important to the development of the Washington-Listwell relationship. A primary function of Listwell, who is converted to abolitionism after hearing Washington's soliloquy in the forest, is to *listen well*. He listens well to both Washington and the white loafers at the Virginia tavern. This is clearly the role that Douglass, the journalist and public speaker, wants white abolitionists to play: to listen well to what the black slave has to say. But Listwell's function as listener has other implications as well. For without Listwell's position as overhearer of Washington's soliloquy or as recipient of his stories, Washington would not be able to tell his tale. A mutual interdependence is thus established between Washington and Listwell, between slave and abolitionist: Without Washington, there is no story to tell; without Listwell, there is nobody to receive and relay the story. Most important, however, both Madison and Listwell depend on the narrator, the controlling authority of the story, who organizes, shapes, and comments on it according to his own ideological perspective. Douglass here creates in his fiction a narrative situation that he must have desired in his journalistic career both before and after the Civil War: an interdependent relationship between the black slave as a speaking and experiencing subject, on the one hand, and the white abolitionist, who both listens well and takes an active role in his cause, on the other, guided by an authoritative black leader whose role it is to write the black back onto the page of human existence.

Although Douglass would never again experiment with writing fiction, his achievement in this story marks a key transitional phase in his rhetorical stance as a journalist. Just as his third-person omniscient narrator in the story moves back and forth from one point of view to another, Douglass the journalist would soon allow his own work to move back and forth between several points of view—those of black and white, of "we" and "they"—as the exigencies of the Civil War, Reconstruction, and the post-Reconstruction debacle demand departures from the rhetorical strategies that had proven so effective before the war.

During the Civil War, rapid shifts in political events gradually came to dictate shifts in Douglass's journalistic rhetoric. In one article, for example, Douglass follows a dramatic, searing condemnation of government policy toward slaves who escape across Union lines with a retraction based on just-received information that reflects a change in policy. Given such rapid changes of events, generalizations and abstract explanations were perhaps a wiser rhetorical strategy than an invocation of specific charges and *ad hominem* attacks. In addition, Douglass found that he could rely less frequently on his own experiences in slavery as the foundation on which to ground his arguments and instead had to find ways to broaden both his perspective and the issue of slavery itself. Thus the brutal facts and concrete metonyms of Douglass's journalism of the 1840s give way to such abstract comments as "self-deception is a chronic disease of the American mind and character. . . . We are masters in the art of substituting a pleasant falsehood for an ugly and disagreeable truth, and of clinging to a fascinating delusion while rejecting a palpable reality" (3: 126).

Looking ahead to the end of slavery and the beginning of a new social system, Douglass suddenly found himself confronted with the question of how those who had for so long been outside of the social system could now become part of it. He alternates between his earlier rhetorical mode of castigating the federal government for its complicity with slavery, rebuking it for its hypocrisy, dishonesty, and failure of nerve, and a new impulse to see himself and other blacks as part of the government, which he now sometimes refers to as "we" and "our rulers" instead of "they." Shifting between references to *the* government and *our* government, Douglass's stance is more constrained than it was in the antebellum period, when the interlocutor of his dialogues was clearly the slaveholding class and the government that supported it. As Douglass's own view of his place—and the place of other blacks—in America's democratic experiment changes, his strategies as a journalist change as well.

In this period, for example, Douglass still occasionally reverts to the form of the open letter, but with less and less frequency. The difference between his open letter to Postmaster General Blair, dated October 1862, and the earlier ones to Henry Clay and Thomas Auld is instructive: The Blair letter is a response to an actual letter sent to Douglass by a person in a position of power, who addresses him with respect and courtesy. Responding to Blair's arguments in favor of colonization and appealing to analogies from abroad to drive home his point, Douglass argues that if the free colored populations of Cuba and Brazil are not being subjected to expatriation schemes, why should the free black man in the United States be? The most interesting part of the letter is, however, the epistolary situation itself, in which Douglass is acutely aware that a man of Blair's stature has actually written to him and given him the occasion to respond. To underscore his sense of its importance, Douglass in the letter self-consciously places himself in a tradition of black men who have been addressed by great national leaders, recalling, for example, Jefferson's letter to Benjamin Banneker, in which the president "warmly commend[ed] his talents and learning" (3: 284).

During the Civil War period, buried among articles addressed to specific issues, such as black enlistment or colonization schemes, are several articles in which Douglass looks ahead to what lies in store for black Americans. In 1863, he had referred to "slavery and its twin monster prejudice" (3: 38). But although exposing slavery was something Douglass had honed into a highly developed art, exposing its "twin monster"—especially after Reconstruction—proved to be more complicated. Douglass may well have sensed this fact when in 1862 he pondered the question: "What shall be [the slaves'] status in the new condition of things? Shall they exchange the relation of slavery to individuals, only to become slaves of the community at large, having no rights which anybody is required to respect, subject to a code of Black laws, denying them school privileges, denying them the right of suffrage, denying them the right to keep and bear arms, denying them the right of speech, and the right of petition? Or shall they have secured to them equal rights before the law?" (3: 40–41).

After the Civil War, with slavery officially abolished, Douglass struggled to reframe this question. It was a troubling and difficult task. Whereas slavery was a clear and present evil, the postwar evil was often too murky and complex to name: "The thing worse than rebellion is the thing that causes rebellion," he wrote. "What that thing is, we have been taught to our cost. It remains now to be seen whether we have the needed courage to have that cause entirely removed from the Republic" (4: 201). The "we" that Douglass invokes here is an inclusive "we," a "we" that situates itself squarely among the citizenry that gives the government its legitimacy and its power. Douglass often employs this "we" to shame his fellow citizens into sharing his revulsion at the activities of former rebels. For example, in 1871 he writes: "The spread of the lynch law at the South, the wholesale slaughter of loyal men, the open defiance by the people of the General Government, the organization of secret bands sufficiently powerful in every rebel State to control its policy and defeat the ends of justice, prove how foolish and practically wicked has been the impunity with which we have treated their crimes" (4: 258).

From the end of the Civil War until his death, Douglass struggled to find ways to describe and expose the realities of postwar race relations in America. In a series of articles in mainstream, predominantly white publications, such as *The North American Review* and *Harper's Weekly*, Douglass endeavored to explain the current state of blacks in America by reminding his audience of the degradation of a slave system from which blacks had so recently been liberated.

Much of Douglass's writing during this period gives policy advice and social analysis of the kind he had given in the past. But there is often a restraint, keyed perhaps to his efforts to withhold judgment during a period of enormous transition. Although the articles are clear and well argued, they lack the passion of his antebellum writing. Much of the fire that characterized his earliest triumphs as a journalist is absent. His analysis is often more abstract than previously, such as his vague recommendation that "time and endeavor must have their perfect working before we shall see the end of the effect of slavery and oppression in the United States"(4: 227).

In his most important articles, however, Douglass was able once again to find his stride as a masterfully eloquent journalist when he reclaimed as fact and metaphor the subject that had fueled his writing from the start: slavery. That which he had expressed as a hypothetical fear in 1862 had come to pass by the end of Reconstruction: black people had exchanged slavery to individuals for slavery to "the community at large." As he claimed slavery both as symbol and as reality, and retold the horrors of the past to reframe the horrors of the present, Douglass broadened his perspective on his country's social ills and ascended to new heights of rhetorical intensity and passion. He achieves his effectiveness of old when he recalls and extends those images that had served him in the antebellum period. He reminds his audience that slavery still scars the free black and does not hesitate to detail its brutal and gory facts: "he has scarcely been free long enough to outgrow the marks of the lash on his back and the fetters on his limbs. He stands before us, today, physically, a maimed and mutilated man. Slavery has twisted his limbs, shattered his feet, deformed his body and distorted his features" (4: 194). Douglass is also compelling in his use of slavery as a metaphor, as he reminds his audience that slavery is not only a bondage of the body, but an even "more terrible bondage of ignorance and vice" (4: 224).

In article after article, Douglass reaches new heights of moral indignation as he effectively shows how slavery has left a legacy of barbarism hanging like a black cloud over the slave states. This legacy, Douglass claims, burdens former slaves and slaveholders alike. Slave labor has been replaced by cheap labor that is motivated by "the same lust for gain, the same love of ease, and loathing of labor, which originated that infernal traffic." Like slave labor, cheap labor brings "ease and luxury to the rich, wretchedness and misery to the poor" (4: 264–65). For slaveholders, the barbarism of slavery has left a "brutalizing, stupefying, and debasing effect upon their natures" (4: 243). Blind to their own interests, slaveholders are expelling northern emigrants from the South, engaging in burnings, lynchings, and wholesale murders. Such is the legacy of "besotted madness" that slavery has pinned upon the former slaveholding oligarchy of the South.

Douglass is equally effective in his postbellum journalism as he intensifies his efforts on behalf of women's suffrage. Aware that all his prior actions have been either on behalf of himself or his people, Douglass notes that in supporting women's suffrage "self [is] out of the question" and that a broader perspective than that of the personal "I" is necessary (4: 452). Douglass achieves this broader perspective as he once again reclaims the arguments and images of his antislavery journalism and applies them to women's causes. He asserts that women are human beings and do not need "protection" in the ways that animals do; he insists that if women are indeed human beings, then they must be intellectual and moral and therefore capable of making their own choices; finally, he argues that the true doctrine of American liberty demands that women, like blacks, be allowed to represent themselves.

Throughout his journalism of this period, then, Douglass's "I" is at its most authoritative when he once again positions himself as an outsider and presses arguments for reasons why blacks—and women—should become part of the "we." His rhetoric is most effective in those instances when he is most acutely aware that blacks still remain outside the "we" and must continue their fight to become a part of it, to break down the "color line" whose origins are rooted in the slave system. Against those who assert that race prejudice is both universal and natural, Douglass retorts that it is neither. In a tightly reasoned article entitled "The Color Line," he argues that prejudice is in fact a learned response that exists neither worldwide nor at all times. In the United States it is the result of a social system that had effectively sought "to enslave [the black man], to blot out his personality, degrade his manhood, and sink him to the condition of a beast of burden" (4: 347). The shadow of this system, still lingering over the country, poisons the moral atmosphere of the Republic and prevents genuine emancipation.

The "we" who hold those famous "truths to be self-evident" is, in several ways, a different "we" after the war than before. This "we" now includes millions of former slaves, and this "we" is sobered and chastened by the pain and death of strife. But rather than abandon the habits that animated his antebellum journalism, Douglass now recasts them in a new light. The dialogic power of his rhetoric is now trained not on one class and the government's support of it, but on the society as a whole. For the new "we," as Douglass well understands, embraces not only former slaves but also the forces of history that allowed them to be enslaved. Facing up to that history requires a constant vigilance toward all people and institutions that exploit, defraud, and degrade in the name of "civilization." The society Douglass wants to bring into being is a self-reflective political culture in which first principles are frequently invoked, deep questioning is both accepted and expected, and probing the gaps between the country's stated ideals and the actual condition of its people is the responsibility of every citizen. It is to membership in this new "we" that Douglass would have all of us aspire.

Notes

This essay first appeared, in slightly different form, in *Frederick Douglass: New Literary and Historical Essays*, ed. Eric J. Sundquist (Cambridge: Cambridge University Press, 1990). Reprinted with the permission of Cambridge University Press.

1. Philip S. Foner, *The Life and Writings of Frederick Douglass*, 5 volumes (New York: International Publishers, 1950–1975), 5: 3. All further references to Douglass's journalism are to this edition and are cited parenthetically in the text.

2. Frederick Douglass, *Narrative of the Life of Frederick Douglass, an American Slave, Written by Himself* (New York: Anchor Books, 1973), 68. All further references to *The Narrative* are to this edition and are cited parenthetically in the text.

3. Caleb Bingham, *The Columbian Orator* (New York: E. Duyckinck, 1816), title page. All further references to *The Columbian Orator* are to this edition and are cited parenthetically in the text.

4. M. M. Bakhtin, *The Dialogic Imagination*, trans. Michael Holquist (Austin: University of Texas Press, 1981), 324–35.

5. Michel Foucault, *The History of Sexuality*, 3 vols. (New York: Vintage Books, 1980), 1: 101.

6. Locke quoted in Harry V. Jaffa, *Crisis of the House Divided* (Seattle: University of Washington Press, 1959), 314–15.

7. For another analysis of "The Heroic Slave," see Robert B. Stepto, "Storytelling in Early Afro-American Fiction: Frederick Douglass's 'The Heroic Slave,'" in *Black Literature and Literary Theory*, ed. Henry Louis Gates (New York: Methuen, 1984), 175–86.

Part II

After the Civil War

Chapter 5

Black Separatism in the Periodical Writings of Mrs. A. E. (Amelia) Johnson

WENDY WAGNER

M<small>RS</small>. A. E. (A<small>MELIA</small>) J<small>OHNSON</small> is best known today as the author of two nineteenth-century Sunday school novels, *Clarence and Corinne; or, God's Way* and *The Hazeley Family*, recently reprinted as part of the Schomburg Library of Nineteenth-Century Black Women Writers.[1] In addition to *Clarence and Corinne* and *The Hazeley Family*, Johnson wrote a third Sunday school novel, *Martina Meriden; or, What Is My Motive?* and several stories and sketches for such extant Baptist periodicals as *The Ivy, The Joy, Our Women and Children,* and *Sower and Reaper.*[2] Tempting though it may be to read Johnson as a stereotypical minister's wife, writing inoffensive children's stories for the Baptist women's press while her husband dealt with denominational and political issues, a series of articles published by Johnson in the black press during the 1890s suggests otherwise. In these articles, unlike her novels and children's stories, Johnson directly confronts racial issues by calling attention to her identity as a black woman and espousing her belief in the institutional separation of the races as a solution to the problems of racial discrimination.

The difference between Johnson's fiction and nonfiction may be explained in part by the politics that pervaded her immediate surroundings. Johnson's husband, Harvey Johnson, a Baptist minister in Baltimore, was well known for his advocacy of civil rights causes and his identification with black separatist ideology. It is likely that Amelia Johnson was involved in her husband's work because she has been described, in her son's words, as Harvey Johnson's "best friend, and his

93

chief comfort, his guide in all his business matters."[3] But the best argument for Amelia Johnson's engagement with her husband's political views comes in her own writings. In addition to writing the introduction to her husband's 1901 book, *The Nations from a New Point of View,* Johnson published articles in the black press reinforcing black separatist ideology. In two articles written by Johnson during the 1890s ("Afro-American Literature," published in the *New York Age* in 1892; "How I Wrote a Story for the *Youth's Companion,* and Why It Has Not Been Published," published in the *Richmond Planet* in 1896), Johnson reveals her increasing anger at the failure of white-run publishers to publish black authors. Her 1899 article, "Some Parallels in History," published in the *National Baptist Magazine,* takes a more expansive approach and locates the black separatist movement in the tradition of other revolutionary political movements.

In her nonfiction writings, Johnson is a voice for both black cultural pride and separatism: she defends black authors' literary value, calls for separate black publishing houses, and affirms the right of African Americans to break away from white-run institutions that keep them in a permanent condition of subservience. Johnson thus does not serve as an example of Penelope Bullock's claim that blacks used the periodical press "to serve their needs in segregated communities and to agitate for integration into American society."[4] Instead, she exemplifies Evelyn Brooks Higgenbotham's observation that "the church-sponsored press played an instrumental role in the dissemination of a Black oppositional discourse and the creation of a black collective will."[5]

Amelia Johnson was born Amelia Etta Hall in 1858 in Canada (it is likely that her parents were free blacks who had fled from Maryland to Canada to escape the consequences of the Fugitive Slave Law of 1850) and moved to Maryland in 1874. In 1877, Amelia Hall married the Rev. Harvey Johnson, the minister of the Union Baptist Church in Baltimore. Harvey Johnson was born a slave near Richmond, Virginia, in 1843. He graduated from Wayland Seminary in Washington, D.C., in 1872, when he also became pastor of the Union Baptist Church. Under Johnson's leadership, the membership of this church expanded almost tenfold within twenty years.

Johnson's influence, however, extended beyond his daily duties as minister. Johnson helped form black Baptist institutions statewide, served in various capacities with Baptist (white and black) organizations, and was active in civil rights causes; he also attended the Niagara Convention, the forerunner of the National Association for the Advancement of Colored People (NAACP), in 1901. In 1885, Johnson and four fellow Baptist ministers in Baltimore formed the Mutual United Brotherhood of Liberty of the United States of America (MUBL), an organization that devoted itself to civil rights for blacks. One of the MUBL's first major initiatives was to advocate for Everett J. Waring, one of Johnson's parishioners to be admitted to the bar—the first African American to be admitted to the bar in Maryland.[6]

Reverend Johnson was also well-known for his sermons, several of which were published and one of which, *The Hamite* (1889), was widely read. *The Hamite* is typical of the type of black nationalist discourse that used religious motifs and appealed to a shared racial past to promote unity and pride among black Americans. In *The Hamite* Johnson refers to the biblical story of Ham, the son of Noah, who was believed to be the ancestor of the black race. Johnson derives from this biblical history an Afrocentric view of history, one designed to foster race pride by pointing to the accomplishments of the descendants of Ham: "[the Hamite] founded the first government, built cities, established kingdoms, built the first monuments and pyramids; and raised the first temple to the gods that men served." Johnson ends his affirmation of Africans' role in world history by suggesting that the term *Negro* is inaccurate and offensive and should be replaced with the term *Hamite*, a term more respectful of the spiritual and cultural past of African Americans than superficial characteristics such as physical appearance.[7]

Another aspect of nineteenth-century black nationalism that Johnson identified with was black separatism. In *The Golden Age of Nationalism*, Wilson J. Moses writes that "in its extreme form, [black separatism] advocated the perpetual physical separation of the races, but usually referred only to simple institutional separatism, or the desire to see Black people making independent efforts to sustain themselves in a provenly hostile environment."[8] Johnson's separatism occasionally did take radical form, as in his support of a plan known as the "Texas Purchase Movement." This plan called for all African Americans to move to Texas to form their own sovereign nation.[9] However, for the most part, Johnson concentrated his efforts on developing separate black institutions for black Baptists. In an 1895 article for the *National Baptist Magazine*, Johnson called upon his fellow Baptists to take steps toward complete separation of the races: "the time is fully come for us to establish and maintain institutions of our own."[10] The National Baptist Convention and the Colored Baptist Convention in Maryland represent the fruits of these efforts.

In 1890, Amelia Johnson was thrust into the middle of the debate over separatism as not only a partner to her husband and a Baptist but also a writer. When the white-run American Baptist Publication Society bowed to pressure from the Southern Baptist Convention and reneged on a promise to include essays by three prominent black Baptists in *Baptist Teacher*, the foremost journal of Baptists nationwide, it aggravated an already existing rift between black and white Baptists.[11] Harvey Johnson was among several black Baptist leaders who responded to this rejection by calling for the establishment of a separate black Baptist convention and an accompanying separate black publishing house. Amelia Johnson found herself in the center of this controversy because her first novel, *Clarence and Corinne*, was the first novel by an African American to be published by the American Baptist Publication Society. Johnson's novel was promoted by supporters of cooperation with the American Baptist Publication Society as an example of the gains made by blacks in the Baptist church. Cooperationists also argued that the American Baptist Publication Society supported black Baptist leaders and published their works as monographs. Separatists, however, insisted that because the white Baptist leadership refused to grant black Baptist leaders equal standing in nationwide organizations and equal opportunities to publish in the denomination's national periodicals, black Baptists needed to form their own organizations to provide sufficient leadership and publishing opportunities for black Baptist writers.

Johnson was drawn into this conflict between cooperationism and separatism because of not only her husband's involvement but also her engagement with these issues as a writer herself. Johnson had been writing and publishing since the 1880s; her work appeared in several Baptist women's and children's publications, and she even founded and edited a short-lived periodical, *The Joy*. One of her children's stories, "Nettie Ray's Thanksgiving Day," was published (and according to Irvine Garland Penn, republished annually) in the *National Baptist*, a

Baptist periodical distributed nationwide.[12] Johnson's Sunday school novels—*Clarence and Corinne* (1890), *The Hazeley Family* (1894), and *Martina Meriden* (1901)—are distinguished by their moral didacticism and their lack of pointers to the author's racial identity; thus, these books have been read as exemplifying Johnson's assimilationist beliefs.

Johnson's novels were ignored for many years by scholars of African-American literature because her characters do not have any identifying racial characteristics and thus did not appear to belong to an identifiably African-American literary tradition. Recently, however, scholars such as Hortense Spillers and Claudia Tate have argued that the absence of race in the novels does not necessarily mean that Johnson was accommodating white publishers' racism. Spillers, for example, turns to contemporary reviews of Johnson's work to suggest that "the situation of Black women's writing, even the very act of writing itself, is far more important than any particular aesthetic outcome." In addition, Spillers claims that Johnson's novel *Clarence and Corinne* was significant to Johnson's readers for being the first work of its kind published by white publishers.[13]

Furthermore, by foregrounding not racial difference but the similarities of beliefs and Christian values held by Johnson and her primarily white readership, these scholars argue, Johnson was asserting her equal standing as a member of American society and appealing to the shared humanity of her audience. Tate argues that this strategy was effective in marketing Johnson's work to her white readers, who sympathized with the racially indefinite but religiously devout characters stigmatized because of their social class position; Johnson's black readers, however, undoubtedly understood the need for Johnson to silence and displace racial discourse and thus appreciated Johnson's novel as a form of racial protest: "Such a displacement [of a discourse of racial difference in favor of one of social class] would be ineffective as a strategy of social intervention if Johnson's readers had not already been conditioned to regard this form of displacement as a mode of racial affirmation (and by implication of racial protest) as well."[14]

Yet Tate and Spillers do not satisfactorily account for the confrontational tone of Johnson' s nonfiction articles written in the black periodical press. These essays appear to contradict the message of assimilation implicit in her fiction. Rather than displacing or silencing the discourse of race, Johnson's articles foreground it while focusing in particular on the problems facing writers who are black. In these articles, Johnson analyzes these problems not as a politician or as a religious leader but as a writer interested in the craft of writing and the institutional mechanisms by which writers' work would be published, distributed, and read. She shows herself to be a persuasive spokesperson for African-American writers: challenging depictions of black writers as derivative, fighting for equal treatment by publishers, seeking positive portrayals of African Americans in literature, and using her rhetorical skill to situate the black Baptist separatist movement in the context of past revolutions in history, such as the American revolution.

One of Johnson's first known essays, which appeared in the *New York Age*, a black newspaper,[15] confronts criticisms of African-American writers and defends their talent. This essay, "Afro-American Literature," takes on critics who claim that black literature is not "original." While conceding (wrongly) the point that there is no indigenous African literature, Johnson nevertheless refutes this criticism by pointing out that many writers considered "original"—even Shakespeare, Milton, and Longfellow—drew on previously written works but have not been similarly criticized for being "unoriginal." Johnson argues that this is a double standard. "These men could attain greatness with a very substantial prop to support themselves upon," she writes, "but the poor colored writers . . . must base their remarks actually upon nothing or be told that they are not original."

Johnson also compares the writings of African Americans in the twenty-nine years since emancipation to the early writings of the white colonists in America. Johnson observes that the first book was not published in the colonies until nineteen years had passed, and then, when white colonists did write, their work was primarily theological. Wondering why theological writings by African Americans are not similarly valued, Johnson asserts that the twenty-nine years since emancipation have produced "many books of different kinds" written by African Americans.

Johnson ends her essay with the complaint that there are no publishing houses supportive of black writers that "can give us money and reputation and at the same time relieve us of the petty worry of trying to place our literature," as the white publishing houses do for white writers. She thus sounds a theme that resonates throughout her nonfiction writing: white publishers discriminate against black writers, and the only way for African-American writers to achieve the recognition they deserve is to establish and support black publishing houses and other black-run venues for African-American writers.

Johnson explains her bitterness toward white publishers in an article written four years later for the *Richmond Planet*.[16] In this article, which appeared in two parts over two weeks, Johnson details her correspondence with the editors of the *Youth's Companion*, a nationally known children's magazine. Claiming a desire to expand her portfolio and reputation by publishing a story with the magazine, Johnson submitted a story along with a letter addressed to an editor she knew to be a fellow Baptist. In the letter, she identified herself as "a colored woman, and proud of it." When her story was rejected, she took the editors to task for rejecting her story while publishing other stories containing racist depictions. After a series of letters back and forth, in which the *Companion*'s editors denied her charges of racism, one of her stories, "Dr. Hayes' Wire Fence," was accepted, and she received a check for twenty dollars. However, several years passed, and the story never appeared; this absence led Johnson to renew her correspondence with the *Companion* and discover that her story would, in fact, never be published.

Johnson's article describing this incident reveals not only the difficulties she faced in getting her work published but also the failure of shared religious beliefs to transcend racial differences; this turn of events reinforces her turn toward racial separatism. Knowing that Johnson shares the editor's religion but not his race, the editor rejects Johnson and leads her to conclude that racial prejudice is stronger than a shared religious identity. Johnson's article thus cleverly argues against racial integrationists who believed that African Americans needed to emphasize the common beliefs and values whites and blacks hold instead of focusing on racial difference. Johnson's essay provides a case study of how such an approach is doomed to failure.

Johnson's response to the rejection by the *Youth's Companion* is also interesting in the light it sheds on her perception of herself as an African-American writer. When Johnson began her quest to publish for the *Companion*, she denied an interest in speaking to a white audience and spoke only of expanding her resume: "It was not my desire to get before the white public, for I have but small dealings with them, and they with me." After her initial rejection, however, her letters indicate that she is committed to writing stories to counter negative representations of African Americans in the white-authored literature of the *Companion*. In one letter she writes, "I thought that if you would permit me to write as other people write, while you allow others to write as they wish it to appear, that my people look and act, it would help me bear it better." Later, when she is informed that her story will not be published after all, she writes that "while the *Companion* with its half million subscribers must be bigger than the desires of any one of its contributors, I was a representative of eight million people in whose interest I was making the effort." Johnson clearly saw herself as a spokesperson for her race, as an author by whose works the entire race would be judged, echoing Anna Julia Cooper's famous words of 1892: "Only the BLACK WOMAN can say when and where I enter, in the quiet, undisputed dignity of my womanhood, without violence and without suing or special patronage, then and there the whole Negro race enters with me."[17]

Johnson's narrative of rejection was intended to symbolize to readers the ultimate failure of reaching out to whites and achieving integration and to suggest the need for the formation of black-run institutions (like the *Richmond Planet*) that would give African Americans a voice. One such institution was the *National Baptist Magazine*.[18] First established in 1895, the *National Baptist Magazine* became the voice of black Baptists nationwide. Johnson contributed two essays to the *National Baptist Magazine* during the 1890s: an 1895 article, "What Is Originality?" a variation on the primary theme of her 1892 *New York Age* essay, and an 1899 essay, "Some Parallels in History."

In this latter essay, the lead article of the July 1899 issue, Johnson indirectly addresses the concerns of those anxious about the ultimate success of the separation of black Baptists from the white-run national organization by situating this societal change in the context of past political conflicts over nationhood.[19] Beginning with the axiom "history repeats itself," Johnson demonstrates that the current movement within African-American society for separation has historical parallels in the conflicts between the Saxons and the Normans in the eleventh century and between the British and the American colonists in the eighteenth century. The Saxons rose up against the conquering Normans, Johnson says, because "it was the love of liberty and independence . . . that made it impossible for them to content themselves under the despotic rule of their conquerors, and they were determined to win back their birthright." Similarly, according to Johnson, this rebellion of the tyrannized against the tyrant is played out again in the American Revolution of the eighteenth century. Like the Saxons, the American colonists were oppressed, and they fought back against that oppression by casting out the oppressors and forming their own nation, the United States.

These historical parallels lead into Johnson's discussion of the situation between blacks and whites in the United States in her time. Johnson observes that though African Americans were brought to America in the slave trade and eventually freed during the Civil War, white Americans have not allowed blacks to take their place as equal citizens of the United States. Thus, Johnson argues, it is only natural that blacks will do as the Saxons and the American colonists did. Although she stops short of speaking directly of rebellion, using instead an injunction that blacks should "refuse to be set aside by their white brethren," Johnson adeptly makes a case for black nationalism by linking the cause of blacks in America to that of other groups that have formed nations. In light of Harvey Johnson's advocacy of the Texas Purchase Movement, to create a black nation in Texas, Johnson's article may have an ulterior motive—the promotion of her husband's (and presumably her own) political views.

Johnson's article also foregrounds the rhetoric of self-help influenced by Booker T. Washington, who called for the social separation of the races. Johnson formulates her call for self-help in reaction to the failure of whites to support integration: "if our white brethren close their avenues to us . . . , we must create avenues for ourselves." Also implicit in her writing is an emphasis on racial pride and a critique of those who look to whites for validation: "Let us cease trying to prove to the world that we were born into it for the sole purpose of admiring the white people of the United States," she writes sardonically. Only when blacks turn their attention away from whites and toward themselves and their race will they be able to "furnish our true and complete parallel to history."

Johnson's periodical writings thus stand in stark contrast to her fiction writings. When Johnson was writing to children and to whites (usually fellow Baptists), she practiced an integrationist approach designed to minimize racial difference and focus on the religious and moral beliefs she shared with or wished to transmit to her readers. However, when writing to her peers,[20] she took a starkly different tone. In her nonfiction articles for the black press, Johnson is clearly engaging in the "dissemination of a Black oppositional discourse and the creation of a Black collective will," as described by Higgenbotham. She challenges the restrictions on and negative representations of black writers. Her educational articles teach her readers how to respond to criticisms of black writers, inform them of the kinds of discrimination that lead to the absence of black writers from nationally recognized forums, and provide them with the historical justification for the undoubtedly risky and fearsome actions they were taking to form separate black institutions. Unlike her fictional writings, in which she implicitly argued that shared religious and moral beliefs should be the basis for blacks' integration into American society, Johnson's nonfiction contributions to the black press seem designed to motivate her readers to take political action toward separatism by expressing her anger and disbelief with the racism of whites.

Johnson expresses her identity as a writer even more forcefully than she does her Baptist beliefs. Although Harvey Johnson also wrote and published, Amelia Johnson's family thought of her as the author of the family: "We always kept our mother busy in telling us stories, fairy tales, etc. She was so interesting to us for she was a writer, you know," said Harvey Johnson, Jr.[21] Unfortunately, institutions did not exist to give Johnson the forum she deserved. Though the National Baptist Convention flourished (and still exists today), the *National Baptist Magazine* and the National Baptist Publishing Board never mustered the kind of support they needed to thrive and succeed. Despite the failures of black Baptist publishing, Johnson was in many ways prescient about the need for separate black publishing institutions. Within the following three decades, black publishing concerns would flourish, culminating in the rise and cultural power of black-run national periodicals such as the *Crisis* and *Opportunity* during the Harlem Renaissance.

Notes

1. Amelia Johnson, *Clarence and Corinne; or, God's Way* (Philadelphia: American Baptist Publication Society, 1890; reprint, New York: Oxford University Press, 1988); *The Hazeley Family* (Philadelphia: American Baptist Publication Society, 1894; reprint, New York: Oxford University Press, 1988).
2. Amelia Johnson, *Martina Meriden; or, What Is My Motive?* (Philadelphia: American Baptist Publication Society, 1901).
3. Azzie Briscoe Kozer, *Dr. Harvey Johnson: Pioneer Civic Leader* (Baltimore: [s.n.], [1957]).
4. Penelope Bullock, *The Afro-American Periodical Press. 1838–1909* (Baton Rouge: Louisiana State University Press, 1981), 11.
5. Evelyn Brooks Higgenbotham, *Righteous Discontent: The Women's Movement in the Black Baptist Church, 1880–1920* (Cambridge, Mass.: Harvard University Press, 1993), 11.
6. "A Long Full Big Life: Johnson's Political Activism," Maryland State Archives. http://www.mdarchives.state.md.us/msa/stagser/s 1259/121/6050/html/ 12414300.html. 21 April 1998.
7. Harvey Johnson, *The Hamite* (Baltimore: J. F. Weishampel, 1889).
8. Wilson J. Moses. *The Golden Age of Black Nationalism: 1850–1925* (Hamden, Conn.: Archon Books, 1978), 23.
9. "A Long Full Big Life."
10. Harvey Johnson, "A Fraternal Letter," *National Baptist Magazine*, 3 January 1896, 16.
11. James Melvin Washington, *Frustrated Fellowship: The Black Baptist Quest for Social Power* (Macon, Ga.: Mercer University Press, 1986).
12. Irving Garland Penn, *The Afro-American Press and Its Editor* (Springfield, Mass.: Wiley & Co., 1892. 2d rev. ed. Washington, D.C.: New York Publishers Co., 1969), 422–25.
13. Hortense J. Spillers, "Introduction," *Clarence and Corinne; or, God's Way* (New York: Oxford University Press,1988), xxix.
14. Claudia Tate, *Domestic Allegories of Political Desire: The Black Heroine's Text at the Turn of the Century* (New York: Oxford University Press, 1992), 104.
15. Amelia Johnson, "Afro-American Literature," *New York Age*, 30 January 1892.
16. Amelia Johnson, "The History of a Story: How I Wrote a Story for the *Youth's Companion* and Why It Has Not Appeared," *Richmond Planet*, 22 February 1896 and 29 February 1896.
17. Anna Julia Cooper, *A Voice from the South* (Xenia, Ohio: Aldine Printing House, 1892; reprint, New York: Oxford University Press, 1988), 31.
18. *The National Baptist Magazine*, published by the newly formed National Baptist Publication Board, is different from the *National Baptist*, mentioned earlier in this essay, which was published in Philadelphia.
19. Amelia Johnson, "Some Parallels of History," *National Baptist Magazine*, 7 (July 1899): 4.
20. As Evelyn Brooks Higgenbotham notes, the *National Baptist Magazine* not only published black male writers who had been excluded from nationally distributed white-run publications but also many black female writers, who "wrote from a gender conscious perspective" (*Righteous Discontent*, 79).
21. Kozer, *Dr. Harvey Johnson*.

Chapter 6

Poetics of Memory and Marginality

HANNAH GOURGEY

Images of the Native American in African-American Newspapers, 1870–1900 and 1970–1990

IN A 1995 ESSAY in the *New Yorker* magazine, Henry Louis Gates, Jr., merged the plight of two marginalized communities by referring to the inner cities as "urban reservations."[1] In *Black Looks*, bell hooks acknowledged a history of oppression shared by blacks and Native Americans that needs greater attention and recognition to cultivate a strong "political solidarity."[2] Both scholars praise the contemporary relationship between black Americans and Native Americans and suggest that by reaching back into the annals of history we find examples of a similar sense of solidarity and political purpose. Indeed, as early as 1827, African-American abolitionists and political activists such as David Walker sought to organize and unite "the colored peoples" against the institutionalized racism of American society. As promising as his endeavor may have been, it was never realized on a large scale during the nineteenth century.

This essay identifies certain rhetorical choices made by the black press that stymied solidarity in the nineteenth century and then emphasized and honored it some 120 years later. Through shifts in description and image-creation, the black press influenced the perception of the Native American over time. The 1990s celebrated the kinship between African Americans and Native Americans and expounded on the common past experiences of the two communities. But, the black press of the mid-to-late nineteenth century tells a very different story and reveals that the relationship between black Americans, who emerged from slavery, and Native Americans, who lost battles over land, may have been, at best, fitful. Indeed, these African-American newspapers and periodicals reveal a divisive consciousness that framed the Native American in terms of racist stereotypes.

There should be little surprise in this process. As Abdul JanMohammed and David Lloyd assert in the introduction to *The Nature and Context of Minority Discourse*, language produced in and through minorities is a "damaged" discourse, imbued with a sense of the material oppression experienced through history.[3] In other words, communities in the process of forming a sense of their own political awareness first attend to the mainstream language available to them. This language most often uses the same damaging frame that banishes them to the margins. During the latter half of the nineteenth century black newspapers constructed an image of the Native American that symbolically distanced these two communities. These images are examples of how language used by and against minorities establishes boundaries for their own evolving identities. This rhetoric, in turn, shapes the evolution of their political voices by comparing and contrasting their images with mainstream society and one another.

Understanding these different symbolic choices offers us not only a glimpse of the barriers to solidarity but also a chance to see how solidarity may grow and flourish in the quest for full public participation and political transformation. In the case of African-American and Native-American communities, this process has, in large part, begun. The first half of this essay describes the rhetorical walls created by the black press to build barriers between these two communities; the second half shows how language can tear those barriers down and in the process empower both communities. The fluidity of this language enables the creation of new political voices to join together in challenging the larger social order. Although such challenges must not remain in the realm of symbols, they are born and sustained in such locales of political awareness as the black press.

I should qualify that the political voice emerging in these papers represents one of many voices developing across regions, classes, and religions in black communities nationwide. To the extent that these papers influenced their readership and their own sense of marginality, it is important that we account for this representation. Furthermore, it is neither possible nor desirable to assume a single political voice; however, I use this term to describe an emerging identity set *against* images of the Native American. In the broad range of newspapers and periodicals I examined, there developed a common theme that consistently turned to the stereotype of the Native American. Although the scope and purpose of these papers varied, this theme articulated a single voice that set the African-American identity in opposition to the Native American. The salient issue continues to be the pervasiveness of this type of comparison. Its prevalence foreshadows an equally pervasive radical change that appears in the black press roughly one hundred years later.

In the process of developing a sense of political consciousness, marginalized communities become acutely aware of their existence on the edges of power, and this awareness charges their political expression with both a defiance of mainstream discourse and its reluctant adoption. What matters in this instance is the "position" at the edges of power. When determining who we are outside the mainstream, what parameters do we use? Stuart Hall argues that all identities—regardless of their relation to the center or margins—are in a constant process of negotiation with a series of *positionalities*.[4] Hall envisions a social constellation of public culture in which the varying positions of each community illuminate the other's in ever-changing patterns of relation. The complexity of negotiation derives from the many conversations occurring simultaneously to fix political identity and public voice. The early editors of the black press saw the purpose of their papers as "fixing" political identity for their communities and—in so doing—legitimating their public voice.

Many editors facing this challenge were ambivalent toward those other communities that operate outside the mainstream. JanMohammed and Lloyd observe that part of the trouble minority communities have in uniting against common institutions of oppression is their acceptance of the familiar, if distasteful, definitions of themselves and others.[5] Such was the case for editors describing Native Americans in the nineteenth century.

The Nineteenth Century: Reconstruction and Backlash

As the Civil War ended, black Americans embraced the opportunity to form their own political community and to participate in state and local governance. Reconstruction marked one of the most prolific eras in black history as an entire population emerged from the shadows of slavery to help construct an African-American identity. Yet, even with promise of freedom brought by the initial policies of Reconstruction, black Americans struggled against an increasingly hostile climate as they began to compete with poorer whites for jobs in both the South and the West.

In the South, a chief struggle for blacks and their representatives occurred over property rights. This failed contest on the part of the earliest black public officials eventually led to the dismantling of black public participation. Without legal ownership of land, black farmers remained wholly dependent upon an embittered and impoverished white population.[6] Such material dependence threatened to derail an emerging black political consciousness. The struggle over land also gave African Americans an additional competitor, particularly in the West—the Native American.

In addition to these economic pressures, which tended to impede the growth of black political identity, the introduction of a new kind of discourse on race and civilization into American society "scientifically" justified institutional racism. Shortly after the enfranchisement of black Americans and their introduction into the free market economy, American elites adopted a theory of human evolution that relegated those of African descent to positions of racial inferiority. *Eugenics* referred to a biological community with shared characteristics. Scientists ranked civilized races according to "progress" and placed the northwest European (Caucasian) at the top. "Negroes" and "Natives" vied for the bottom rung. Eugenics was readily adopted because it rationalized a backlash of race-related, exclusionary policies.[7] Legislation ranged

from immigration restrictions to overt segregationist practices. Fortified
by institutional legitimacy, eugenics pervaded all levels of American
society and left virtually no community untouched.

In the United States, black elites challenged the theory of eugenics by developing their own sense of race consciousness. W.E.B. Du Bois
is arguably the most enduring black voice on the issue of race in the
latter half of the nineteenth century and well into the twentieth. In
his most famous book, *The Souls of Black Folk*, published in 1903, Du
Bois inverted the race scale by arguing that it was up to black people
to "re-civilize" a white America and Europe obsessed with the false values of material wealth and racial superiority. Du Bois observed the close
relationship between material and racial oppression. In *The Souls of
Black Folk*, he created the term "double consciousness," which referred
to an awareness of being both included and excluded from American
society. Du Bois maintained that there were psychological differences
between races and that the "race spirit was the greatest invention of
human progress." But the reality of the nineteenth century controverted
this ideal. Even as African-American intellectuals embraced his theory
of race as a viable counterrhetoric to eugenics, their own language remained steeped in a eugenicist discursive quagmire.

Viewing themselves as the voices of the Negro community, editors
of the black press mapped out their own version of black identity as
they struggled for solvency and readership. As I. Garland Penn observes
in his 1891 history, *The Afro-American Press*: "The reader cannot fail
to recognize some achievement won by Negroes, the measure of whose
rights is yet being questioned, and will readily see that the social, moral,
political and educational ills of the Afro-American have been fittingly
championed by these Afro-American journals and their editors."[8] Despite an awareness of the political and social consequences of this new
theory of race, African Americans could not expunge the language from
their own discourse in relation to other communities. Editors from a
variety of periodicals including the *A.M.E. Church Review*, the *San Francisco Vindicator*, the *Negro World*, and the *Afro-Independent*, used language that perpetuated the mainstream stereotype of the Native
American.

On the banks stood the wigwam; in the boughs swung the rude
cradle of the papoose. The young Native American rejoiced in his manly

strength and the sisters of Pocahontas in their maiden beauty. Here in song and dance, to the sound of rattle and tom-tom, they worshipped the Great Spirit, and all felt the "wild joy of living." "A closer scrutiny of this apparently charming picture, however, reveals some somber tints. . . . Civilization only touched this savage tribe to render its degradation more abject."[9]

In July 1888, the Reverend L. J. Coppin, editor of the *A.M.E. Church Review*, introduced the merits of Methodist missionary work with this description of the Ohio Wyandott tribe. The admiring countenance of the Native American followed immediately by the denigration of the Wyandott culture exemplifies the predominant image of the Native American in nineteenth century black press and illustrates a complex relationship between competing images of the Native American during the latter half of the century. The essay also employs a hierarchy of race that sets the "Indian" apart from and below the "Negro."

The first major theme captured in this essay is the Native American *as child of nature*. This theme romanticizes the Native-American experience, glorifies the relationship to the earth, and equates that culture with nature. By viewing the Wyandott paternalistically, as "children" of nature, the language ensures a power inequity between the writer and the subject. In the *A.M.E. Church Review*, language such as "in the boughs hung the rude cradle of the papoose" implies that the child of the Indian is also the fruit of the tree. This theme becomes far more explicit in "Indian Cradles," an 1894 publication of the *Baptist Headlight* out of Topeka, Kansas. The writer described these cradles in the following manner: "One could have seen this kind of fruit hanging from a tree while the mothers are picking berries." Earlier in this same story, the author described the advantage of these cradles for mothers on the move: "It is an easy matter for her [to climb a tree] for all Indians can climb like squirrels."[10] The use of these analogies of "fruit" and "squirrels" suggests that Native Americans have more in common with these species of nature than with their own. The writer employs eugenics, applying its racism through the trope of nature.

Similarly, references to women in the *A.M.E. Church Review*, depict the "Indian maiden" in the images of pre-Eve innocence. The virginal quality to the nature of the Wyandott women is redemptive. Pocahontas, the historical figure, was "civilized" and considered a shining

example of the potential of this "savage" race. The Wyandott women
are her sisters, who promise that same potential. Coppin conflates the
disparate nations of Native Americans into one culture by referring to
the women as the sisters of Pocahontas. The taming of their "wild innocence" in emulation of Pocahontas becomes a primary theme in the essay.

In a November 1888 publication of the *San Francisco Vindicator*,
poet Charles Beattle writes an "Indian Girl's Reply" in which he says,
"My fair forest home is all Eden to me/ No snares for the soul, no for-
bidden fruit tree."[11] The suggestion is that the Indian woman is without Original Sin; she is pure, but she is also uncivilized. For in the
Judeo-Christian world the Original Sin marks the beginning of civilization. In a variation on this theme, a second article in the November
17 issue of the *Vindicator* recounts the story of a Native American spirit
who led a property owner to discover oil on his land. The article merges
the theme of Native American kinship to the land with these ghostly
encounters: a disembodiment that implies no real material need. The
article states, "The spirit of an Indian chief came and beckoned [the
old man]. He followed out into the open air over fields and through
the woods many miles, to where there was a hill in the midst of a big
field. . . . The spirit said that far down in the earth's crust there was water
that would burn."[12] This "soft" story blurs the spirit of the Native American, the spirit of nature, and the spirit of the entrepreneur. The con-
vergence of these three "spirits" exemplifies the modernist perspective
on industrial capitalism—the earth (in the spirit of the Native American) revealing herself for the purposes of resource production.

A second closely related theme found in the nineteenth-century
black press depicts the Native American as "exotic other," a primitive
anachronism. This second theme, used in contrast to black identity, suggests a willingness to acknowledge the primitivism of the "other" despite similar charges made against blacks by a dominant "white" culture.
To label the Native American as primitive is at once a denial of African-
American primitivism (that is, we are civilized enough to recognize
other primitive cultures) and an affirmation of the hierarchy delineated
by the theory of eugenics. The acknowledgment of this exotic other
suggests another common image used in contrast to both African-
American and white cultures—the Native American as wild and violent savage. In a Texas newspaper, *The Freeman's Press*, the editor wrote:

"Men must be either savages like the wild Indian, who knows no want but his appetite for the meat of the buffalo, and the gratification of his passions, or they must be civilized, Christian men."[13] Written just five years after the Emancipation Proclamation, Dr. Keith prescribed a way to improve the African-American community. By disparaging the Native American, Keith implied that the upstanding black man should define himself by *not* assuming the characteristics of the Native American. The negation of Native American identity was symbolically central to the formulation of a distinctly African-American consciousness. Keith's rhetoric suggested Hall's theory of marginal positionality in which the negotiated boundaries determine the formation of identity.

The theme of "exotic other" also appeared in the St. Paul/Minneapolis paper, the *Afro-Independent*. In an 1888 article reporting on negotiations with the Sioux Nation, the author observed: "Civilization, cruel though it may seem at times, has driven the Indian from the Atlantic to the Far West, and it will drive him still farther West, or perchance, exterminate him, unless he becomes civilized and lives as white men do."[14] The author, G.W.W., showed little remorse for the possible extermination of the "red man" because, for an uncivilized race, extinction was "inevitable." The Sioux represented an anomaly in time, a mark against the progress of civilization. Assimilation or annihilation seemed to be the "red man's" only choices. The appearance of this harsh condemnation of Indian culture in an African-American newspaper reflected the penetration of mainstream stereotypes into African-American thinking. By employing this rhetoric the black American press chose to align itself with dominant culture in an effort to gain legitimacy. The boundary set in the case of G.W.W. operated as a way to curry acceptance and to assert a right to participate in the larger polity. In Minnesota, the African-American community was small and earnestly sought a voice in the growing western frontier. By describing the Native American as an "other" in worse position to mainstream culture, black Americans allowed themselves to ascend the hierarchy of civilization. The price of this position was to partake in the dialogue of dominant culture: the cost—a lost opportunity for solidarity against a common oppressor.

The power of dominant discourse is that it prevents minority communities from developing a common front against institutional oppression because these communities readily accept definitions given them by the mainstream culture. In emerging sites of resistance, language is first borrowed before it is subverted. It is borrowed because other sources of description remain either mystified or beyond the immediate reach of those seeking new identities. In the case of black editors 120 years ago, this "borrowing" legitimated their role as shapers of black consciousness, and it prescribed progress for this developing community. The racist stereotype in this case included not only the rhetoric of eugenics but also the language of modern industrial capitalism: "With thousands of able-bodied men in search of rich soil, the Indian who uses immense tracts of rich land for hunting purposes does not deserve consideration—and he will not receive it."[15]

As the century ended, articles covering the American Indian appeared with less frequency. The violence of the 1890s ended the battle over land rights in the West. Indians either attempted to matriculate into American society, or they withdrew to the poor living conditions on the reservations. As a result, fewer newspapers, both mainstream and African-American, saw the need to cover Native-American issues. This is only part of the story. Ending here would leave the depressing impression that the divisive force of mainstream stereotypes and their power to penetrate all dimensions of discourse is inevitable and unending. But the image of the Native American in black newspapers changed dramatically during the 1970s. This next section describes this shift in the "negotiated" boundaries between the African and Native Americans as it unfolds in the *Chicago Daily Defender*, the *Amsterdam News*, and *The Negro History Bulletin*, particularly in consideration of the American Indian Movement's recapturing of Wounded Knee in 1973.

Michel Foucault argues that eras throughout history are demarcated by the discursive formations that govern the structure and production of knowledge.[16] These formations become the interpretive lens through which both individuals and institutions rationalize human experience and social relations. For marginalized communities seeking the creation of their own distinctive voice, the adaptation of certain discursive transformations can create new ways of negotiating for positionality. The master narrative becomes unfixed, challenging traditional notions of authority and power.

The social movements of the 1960s challenged the discursive formations that fostered racism, classism, and sexism in the United States.

For marginalized communities, civil rights and antiwar movements adopted new strategies with which to challenge authority. The language and actions of these two movements contributed to the production of a new discursive formation that contested "historical knowledge" as it had been written. By the end of the 1960s African Americans, Latinos, Native Americans, and women all embarked on practices of remembrance in order to "unforget" their own experiences in America's past. Through this process of "remembrance" African Americans were able to reject their former descriptions of the Native American and forge a new and promising relationship.

One of the most powerful strategies used to gain civil rights was to expose the social injustice that dominated the language of law and local government. By revealing the discursive formation of justice and governance as racist, the Civil Rights Movement directly challenged not only the policies that continued to oppress but also the knowledge produced from these discourses. This type of challenge questioned the accepted model of American history by declaring it abridged and linear. Freed from this linear and exclusionary methodology, the practice of remembrance focused on the value of shared experience. The emotional force of such experience became a way to build bonds in the present by revealing a common past of suffering.

Fueled by the language of civil rights, the antiwar movement of the mid and late 1960s changed old beliefs about the sanctity of American imperialism as "manifest destiny." Activists within this movement challenged the historical accuracy and validity of the "American Century." As Vietnam veterans returned with stories of war, the rhetoric of the antiwar movement openly vilified the institutions and administration that had trapped these soldiers into a no-win situation. Leaders of the movement pointed to class and race bias that sent more poor, black, and Hispanic soldiers off to the war.[17]

The rhetoric of the movement also denounced the authority of western history: "The rebel is someone for whom injustice and society are only different names for the same thing. . . . [The rebel] is unimpressed and grows apathetic toward Western grandeur. This [is] new consciousness, this radical alienation from past and present authority."[18] This 1967 essay, "The Revolted," decried the dangerous assumptions of western thought and politico-economic policies that fed on domination and violence. The history of the West became a master narrative by which its domination was justified and rationalized. Instead of history, black Americans turned to critical memory for their voice.

Houston Baker argues that, in looking at "property" as a key criterion for public participation, public sphere theorist Jürgen Habermas omitted from history huge populations who sought public expression by whatever means available. In the case of African slaves brought to America, public expression took a variety of alternative forms from spirituals to a kind of "public memory."[19] Baker documents the practical importance of memory to the slave as a means of conveying a public identity. This concept of memory versus history suggests a less causal approach to understanding and interpreting past experience. In the black press of the 1970s this practice significantly challenged accepted histories of the African-American and Native-American experience.

Memory, as opposed to history, makes conspicuous the institutions of oppression. By relying on shared consciousness and the emotional power of experience, memory converts affect into agency, into a trope for solidarity against those agents of oppression; therefore, memory becomes a critical tool for marginalized communities. Memory is also used by these groups to talk about one another. The African-American press of the 1970s was no exception. The following cases illustrate the extent to which marginal discourse employed the trope of memory to shape a new image of the Native American in black newspapers and periodicals. No longer was this community a measure of what not to be; rather, it became the most salient representation of the "colonization" of American society by "whitey": a violent pilgrimage of the center into the sacred realm of the Other.

The Case of Charley Cherokee in the Chicago Daily Defender

The most enduring emblem of the Native American in the black press is the *Chicago Defender's* still-running, politico-gossip column written under the pseudonym Charley Cherokee. Charley Cherokee has appeared most often on page four of the first section of the newspaper. His columns typically begin with his most national and controversial news and end with more local information: "Look for the lid to blow soon on a systematic pattern of eliminating jobs for blacks and demoting others in state government. Hundreds are being affected. The spotlight will be on Mary Leahy, the director of Children and Family Services. It is her department where the axe is really chopping, but she is trying to disclaim any responsibility."[20] Charley Cherokee's columns focus on exposure, on reporting the actions of public figures or law enforcers that hinder the growth of the African-American community. Thus, Mary Leahy's refusal to except the responsibility represents the individual's contribution to institutional forms of oppression that threaten the economic livelihood of blacks nationwide.

Charley's tone chastises scornfully, a reflection on the unfulfilled promises made by both black and white public figures. In the same column concerning the loss of jobs within the black community, Charley says: "Dr. Metz T. P. Lochard, our erudite editor, recalls that was he who saw promise in Deton Brooks [human resource official] years ago and took him off the playground where he was an instructor and brought him into the *Defender*. He gave [Dr. Brooks] his assignment as an overseas correspondent in World War II." In Charley's columns he serves as the "town crier," creating and maintaining a sense of "community" to blacks dispersed across cities nationwide. This "gossip" created a sense of communal feeling that transcends the physical distances.

As a symbol, Charley Cherokee, a rallying point for the *Defender's* readership, overcomes regional distance and political difference. "Charley Cherokee" is not black, but he is not white either. Operating from this liminal space between marginal communities, Charley can make more controversial claims, use more incendiary rhetoric, and expose more institutional hypocrisies than can a more traditional persona in this black public sphere. Charley's gossip becomes politically charged with the marks of institutional and community critique. His persona offers the editors of the *Chicago Defender* a power critical tool.[21] This persona provides enough rhetorical distance to create a political safety net for the editors; Charley Cherokee only "partially" reflects the opinions of the paper. The constant references to public figures and the quick changes from one public figure to the next create a sense of dynamic interaction, of many events happening all at the same time. The bustle of the language implies a thriving and vibrant public.

Charley Cherokee also represents a sense of shared past experience, an extant memory between blacks and Native Americans that began to emerge in the early 1970s. Charley Cherokee trades in shared purpose by providing the chance for political engagement with a measure of distance that enables a more unrelenting voice to emerge. Charley has turned the tables and is "scouting" for the African-American community while mapping out this increasingly populated discursive frontier. The cartoon turns textbook American history on its head and jettisons the given story of the past for the promise of a united present.

Charley as symbol is a mask for the *Defender* as well as emissary from his own community. The parody of stereotype is a parody of "otherness" that simply accentuates the proximity (on the margins) of these two communities. They identify with one another and in so doing, become equal in their solidarity. As a symbolic Native American with a voice in the black community, Charley becomes a conversation with Native Americans. His identity both closes the gap between these two communities and demonstrates the shifting meaning in the stereotype and signifier. His very unreality becomes a vehicle for proving his reality. The *Amsterdam News* flirts with this same slippage of stereotype in its coverage of the Wounded Knee occupation in 1973.

> Even in the midst of our own struggle for civil rights, we must take time to sympathize with and support the Native Americans fighting for their rights at Wounded Knee. These "first Americans," robbed of their property and their freedom, are responding to an oppressive and paternalistic government with the same militancy black Americans have exhibited in their fight for rights.[22]

During the first three months of 1973, members of the American Indian Movement (AIM) occupied the region around Wounded Knee, in memory of the massacre that had occurred there eighty-three years earlier. AIM "recaptured" Wounded Knee and proceeded to settle there despite attempts by the FBI and American troops to "retake" the battleground. The holdout lasted roughly three months.

In a series of editorials and political cartoons, the *Amsterdam News* strongly supported AIM. In one editorial, that paper invoked not a memory but a naming that reveals the difficulty in attaching any signifier to the native peoples of the western hemisphere. By calling the Native American the "first Americans" these editors challenge the historical claim that European settlers have previously been assigned. The historical meaning of "first Americans" chafes against the present and the U.S. historical policy of "manifest destiny." It stands as a critique of history when set against the memory of the Native-American experience. The irony of the name "first American" as a "site of shifting commentary" rewrites the master historical narrative.[23]

As the "history" of Wounded Knee is reexperienced by the members of AIM, the memory takes on a palpable texture for the African-American community in its own struggle against discrimination. This is a kind of amorphous awareness depicted in the mocking tone laden with the evidence of an "other" history exposed. The trope of memory is tangible here—a stark subjective critique of America's past. The incomplete past as it has been given to these communities, the "invisibility" of the experience makes the gap in the name, "first Americans" suddenly visible. The support of AIM's stand at Wounded Knee, the irony intoned in the editors' use of "first Americans," and their choice to link AIM's actions with the militancy of their own political purpose, begs this question: What feats of historical narrative had to be performed to erase US from the American experience?[24]

In an editorial cartoon during that same period, cartoonist Melvin Tapley depicts the stereotypical Native American in absurd exaggeration. Caricatured and mocking, the "brave" defiantly gazes at the American eagle whose feather now adorns his headdress. In the background cheering, a black man raises his fist in the sign of black power.

The drastic change in the image of the Native American in black newspapers and periodicals within a span of one hundred years can reveal the evolution—enabled by shifting material and political conditions—of a minority discourse from "damaged" to "subversive." In one hundred years the black press found its own language with which to challenge the master narratives that stunted solidarity. The press offered a means of negotiating political and social identity by seeking communion with other marginalized groups. In demonstrating the insidious nature of the discursive formations that undergird society, the black press "disciplined" the center and weakened the rationale behind many of its unjust policies.

By the 1970s black newspapers were openly calling for solidarity between other minorities using the trope of memory as the counter-narrative to accepted history. So bell hooks can say, "As red and black peoples decolonize our minds, we cease to place value solely on the written document. We give ourselves back memory. We acknowledge that the ancestors speak to us in a place beyond written history."[25]

Memory as a process of "revealing" in the black press's interpretation of Wounded Knee and the subverted stereotype of Charley Cherokee unhinged the master narrative and restored a sense of shared consciousness between the African American and the Native American. Memory provided a new means of framing the Native-American community to recognize the shared experiences and discover a common ground for communication. Memory as recall served as a construction of unity, an expression of experience that offers up the present—not the past—for its potential.

In the nineteenth century, as black Americans fought against the waves of hostility that rolled over every facet of society, the discursive formation that gave rise to the science of eugenics wrested away the possibility of counterdiscursive constructions within the pages of newspapers struggling for survival. Yet, these negative images were not without their own discursive force. They served as models of identity-building for not only the readership of these newspapers but the larger polity as well. In this case the "edges of power" functioned as a disciplinary power by showing what NOT to be. This is, in large part, how counterpublics operate—well, at least for a little while. Their subversive power lies in their ability to remain ever-changing and therefore uncolonizable.

The use of the stereotype in contemporary African-American newspapers shows the fluidity of the symbol when set against mainstream assumptions. The changes in the image of the Native American in these newspapers followed the emerging political consciousness of this community. The emergence of the Native-American voice in the discursive landscape of the 1960s enabled the rhetoric to create a shared consciousness between these two communities. This new awareness forms a different demarcation zone—between mainstream society and those living on the edges of institutional power.

Henry Louis Gates, Jr.'s reference to "urban reservations" arises from the work done by the black press in recasting the Native American. The metaphor strengthens the voices of both marginal communities and challenges the discourse of policy and knowledge still clinging to old modes of authority and power. Today the struggle for solidarity is no less important. The black press looms large in the evolution of consciousness that fosters this sense of solidarity not only for its own community but for others seeking a stronger voice in American culture.

Notes

1. Henry Louis Gates, Jr., "Thirteen Ways of Looking at a Black Man," *The New Yorker*, 23 October 1995, 26–34.
2. Bell hooks, *Black Looks: Race and Representation* (Boston: South End Press, 1992), 190.
3. Abdul JanMohammed and David Lloyd, *The Nature and Context of Minority Discourse* (New York: Oxford University Press, 1990), 4.
4. Stuart Hall, "The Toad in the Garden: Thatcherism Among Theorists" in *Marxism and the Interpretation of Culture*, ed. Lawrence Grossberg and Cary Nelson (Chicago: University of Illiniois Press, 1988), 61.
5. JanMohammed and Lloyd, *Minority Discourse*, ix.
6. Eric Foner, *America's Black Past* (Evanston, Il.: Harper & Rowe, 1970), 209.
7. Judith Stein, "Defining the Race: 1890–1930," *The Invention of Ethnicity*, ed.Werner Sollers (New York: Oxford University Press, 1989), 80.
8. I. Garland Penn, *The Afro American Press and Its Editors* (Springfield, Mass.: Willey & Co., 1891), preface.
9. Reverend L. J. Coppin, "GET TITLE," *A.M.E. Church Review* [Philadelphia, Pa.] 5, no. 1 (July 1888).
10. Editor unknown, "Indian Cradles," *Baptist Headlight* [Topeka, Kan.] 1, no. 31 (1 August 1894).
11. Charles Beattle, "An Indian Girl's Reply," *San Francisco Vindicator* 5, no.15 (9 February 1889), 3.
12. J. E. Brown, ed., "Old Tonahauqua's Spirit," *San Francisco Vindicator* 5, no. 6 (17 November 1988), 5.
13. Dr. M. Keith, "On Education," *Freeman's Press* 1, no. 6 (22 August 1868), 4.
14. G.W.W., "The Sioux Conference," *Afro-Independent* 11, no. 40 (22 September 1888); paper edited by J. C. Reid.
15. Ibid.
16. Michel Foucault, *The Archeology of Knowledge*, trans. A. Sheridan Smith (New York: Harper Torchbooks, 1972), 71.
17. Judith Clavir Albert and Steward Edward Albert, eds., *The Sixties Papers: Documents of a Rebellious Decade* (New York: Praeger, 1984), 322.
18. Carl Oglesby, "The Revolted" in *Sixties Papers*, 327.
19. Houston A. Baker, Jr., "The Black Public Sphere," *Public Culture* 7 (1994): 96–106.
20. Charley Cherokee, *Chicago Defender*, 6 September 1975, 4.
21. Edwin Black, "The Second Persona," *Quarterly Journal of Speech* 56, no. 2 (April): 111.

22. Editor, "We Support the Indians," *Amsterdam News* 63, no. 11 (17 March 1973), 4.
23. Kathleen Stewart, *Space on the Side of the Road: Cultural Politics in an "Other" America* (Princeton, N.J.: Princeton University Press, 1996), 144.
24. Trin T. Minh-ha, *When the Moon Waxes: Representation, Gender, and Cultural Politics* (New York,: Routledge, 1991), 197.
25. Hooks, *Black Looks*, 165.

The Harlem Renaissance and the 1930s

Part III

Chapter 7   Our(?) Country

ADAM MCKIBLE   *Mapping "These*
'Colored' United States"
in The Messenger

OVER ITS LIFE SPAN, *The Messenger* experienced a number of abrupt transformations, which prompted Langston Hughes to characterize the magazine's politics as "God knows what."[1] One of the most influential periodicals of the Harlem Renaissance, *The Messenger's* eleven-year history began in 1917, when A. Philip Randolph and Chandler Owen launched a black radical journal devoted to politics, economics, and the arts. After a few years, the magazine moved toward boosterism for the African-American bourgeoisie and "read more like sleek, snobbish *Vanity Fair* than a protest periodical."[2] Finally, in 1925, when Randolph became involved in the Brotherhood of Sleeping Car Porters, *The Messenger* transformed into an organ of trade unionism. Although the magazine went through some rather extraordinary changes in its editorial policies, thus provoking Hughes's bemused assessment, it did not do so primarily because "it reflected the policy of whoever paid best at the time" but because it remained intellectually engaged and politically committed to addressing its era's various formulations of race, class, and politics.[3] *The Messenger's* editors and contributors strove to define a national black identity at a time when Jim Crow laws and the Ku Klux Klan flourished and when one African American was being lynched every four days. According to Theodore Kornweibel, Jr., *The Messenger* tested a number of political options because it "was trying to chart the most viable, opportune, and productive course for blacks to follow through the hostile seas of American racism. The magazine's ultimate failure to find a sure course is indicative of the obstacles black Americans in the postwar years found in the path to first-class citizenship."[4] I would argue, following Houston Baker, that a better measure of an era is not its "failure" to reach certain goals, but the productivity of its engagements.[5]

One particularly sustained and productive engagement in the pages of *The Messenger* is the series of articles, "These 'Colored' United States," which ran from January 1923 through September 1926. Providing valuable readings of national identity, racial geography, and political possibility during the Harlem Renaissance, "These 'Colored' United States" attempts to survey the whole of a nation by exploring the dialectics between individual black experiences and those of a (perhaps putative) national community. Two years prior to Alain Locke's observation in *The New Negro* that African Americans were experiencing "a sudden reorientation of view . . . we have not been watching in the right direction,"[6] *The Messenger* had already begun the task of establishing new directions, of asking "where do we fit?" and of wondering what "we" consist of in "These 'Colored' United States." How the contributors to the series answer such questions challenges our own spatial metaphors for the creative energies of an era—our very understanding of the Harlem Renaissance—because in the series the "map" of America in the 1920s locates cultural and political possibilities well beyond uptown Manhattan.

Provoked by a 1922–1925 *Nation* series called "These United States," which claimed inclusiveness but which largely excluded black experience from American self-definition,[7] *The Messenger*'s "These 'Colored' United States" began in January 1923, when the magazine was still clearly radical. It continued through the editorial tenures of George Schuyler, Theophilus Lewis, and Wallace Thurman, who intensified *The Messenger*'s interest in the black bourgeoisie and also made the magazine more "literary." Finally, by the time "These 'Colored' United States" concluded, in September 1926, *The Messenger* had been engaged in the trade union struggles of the Pullman porters for more than a year.

Although the *Messenger* ran several series exploring black American life and locations during its eleven years,[8] nothing matched "These 'Colored' United States" in expansiveness, depth, variety, and length. The series is also remarkable for its interplay of discourses and genres. Largely historical and sociological in nature, "These 'Colored' United States" borrows from fictional and oral discourses, and the tones of its individual essays are just as often satirical, bitter, or optimistic as they are formal and removed.

And "These 'Colored' United States" is remarkable because it brought together so many disparate voices from America's black communities. Prefacing William Pickens's inaugural installment of the series, "Arkansas—A Study in Suppression," the editors write, "A brilliant representative from each state that has a goodly population of Negroes will speak out as Mr. Pickens had done and say to the world in plain language just what conditions they face."[9] These representatives were as brilliant as they were diverse. Among their ranks were college presidents, deans and professors, NAACP officials, editors, reporters and essayists, sociologists, authors, businessmen, schoolteachers, and a state legislator. Some were politically radical, others staunchly conservative, while still others seemed to have no interest in politics at all. Some contributors already were or would become known as African-American luminaries (i.e., Charles S. Johnson, George Schuyler, Roy Wilkins, E. Franklin Frazier, Wallace Thurman, and Kelly Miller), while others (but not many) were rather obscure. Most contributors were men, but a few were women.

While the focus and tone of each article reflects the specific concerns of its author, certain commonalties among the contributions arise that conform to generic conventions of the era; Tom Lutz writes that "by the mid 1920s, essays on individual states appeared not just in *The Nation* and *The Messenger*, but in *The New Republic, American Mercury,* and elsewhere" (11). The topics generally covered in *The Messenger's* essays include the state's history, particularly in relation to antebellum slavery and to the Reconstruction; educational opportunities available to African Americans at the secondary and college levels; *de jure* and *de facto* segregation; lynching; notable black figures past and present; economic life, sometimes focusing on labor, sometimes on business; religious life; and politics and publications. Usually the authors concentrate on one or two representative cities in their state. Comparing

"These 'Colored' United States" to other essays of this genre, Lutz calls
the series an intervention "in this important general debate about the
state of American civilization, from the perspective of, and in the interests of, African Americans in the 1920s" (9).

The "state of American civilization" was of particular interest to
African Americans at this time because the Great Migration was un-
derway, and the United States was rapidly being "colored" anew, a phenomenon that demanded extended efforts at cultural remapping. The
South's agricultural economy was reeling from bad weather conditions
and the boll weevil, while World War I had both spurred the North's
industries and had also led to a significant decline in overseas immigration.[10] This economic imbalance, coupled with the South's relentless racial oppression, propelled African Americans toward the greater
opportunities and justice afforded elsewhere in the nation. Locke characterizes the Great Migration as "a mass movement toward the larger
and the more democratic chance—in the Negro's case a deliberate flight
not only from countryside to city, but from medieval America to modern" (6). Kornweibel suggests that the influx of almost 1.5 million
Southern blacks into the North during the fifteen years leading up to
the Great Depression "created a situation ripe for new journalism" (43).

"These 'Colored' United States" constitutes one response to this
situation. The Messenger provided a map for African Americans that
charts a way out of the South. Several years before the series began,
the magazine ran an editorial, "Negroes, Leave the South," that urges:

> Fellow Negroes of the South, leave there. Go North, East, and
> West—anywhere—to get out of that hell hole. There are better
> schools here for your children, higher wages for yourselves,
> votes if you are twenty-one, better housing and more liberty.
> All is not rosy here, by any means, but it is Paradise compared
> with Georgia, Arkansas, Texas, Mississippi and Alabama. . . .
> Stop buying property in the South, to be burned down and run
> away from over night. Sell out your stuff quietly, saying nothing
> to the Negro lackeys, and leave! Come into the land of at least
> incipient civilization![11]

With "These 'Colored' United States" as a guide, The Messenger's readers might find where such "incipient civilization" could be found.

Understanding the significance of *The Messenger*'s project of African-American self-definition and self-location, William Pickens begins his essay on Arkansas by asking, "What is a state? Is it so many square miles, so many different kinds of minerals, breeds of hog, species of hardwood and types of factory? Do such statistics show the *character* of a state?" The answer to this rhetorical question is clearly "no." Enunciating the materialist politics of *The Messenger* at this time, Pickens writes, "The character of a state is not its mountains of quartz, its acres of cotton and its prized Hereford bulls. It is rather the relation of that state as an institution to its people and the relation of its people to each other."[12] Pickens thus underscores one of the basic concerns of the series: to explore African-American experience in terms of community, state, and citizenship. The series seeks ultimately to examine how the descriptors "'Colored'" and "United" simultaneously define, bind, and unravel both the states and The States. Where, the articles ask again and again, do African Americans fit in relation to America's social, political, and economic uncertainties? How should self-definition be pursued?

The Messenger was determined to find a livable space in America, and "These 'Colored' United States" constitutes a mapping of the United States that describes American regionalism and ideological discourse during a decade marked by both expanding possibilities and declining rights. Coming only sixty years after the Emancipation Proclamation, "These 'Colored' United States" not surprisingly establishes a fairly straightforward regional dichotomy: a South marred by the persistent legacy of slavery and a more liberal North characterized by greater justice and opportunity. In fact, the magazine seems to insist upon this dichotomy by starting the series with articles on Arkansas and then Pennsylvania. But on closer inspection, the dichotomy doesn't quite hold; race and region, black and white, are more complicated.[13] Instead of a bifurcated picture of America, *The Messenger* divides the nation into four regions—or, perhaps, four floating regionalisms—southern, northern, western, and "border."

There are both a "South" and a "Southernness" that one might expect to find. The region is oppressive, small minded, and overrun by "po' whites, " but it also has aspirations to a moonlight-and-magnolias tradition. Persisting through the gains of the Reconstruction, southern slavery has transformed into Jim Crow segregation, peonage, and lynchings.

"The astuteness of the Southern white man (aided and abetted by white men elsewhere)," writes Nathan Ben Young, "in no instance has expressed itself more emphatically than it has in his maneuvering himself into the position of guardianship of the emancipated Negro—a control well-nigh as complete as that of the old master over his slave."[14]

In fact, the southern states seem to be locked in a dire contest to outdo each other in barbarism. Young writes, "Florida is making strenuous efforts to win the pennant in the lynching league for 1923. It came to the end of the first half with a *terrible* lead that Georgia and Texas may not overcome" (91). A few months later, Clifton F. Richardson notes that Texas "won the pennant in the Lynching League of America during 1922."[15] "Yet this is a general Southern condition," Young explains in his essay on Alabama (Young is the only author to contribute twice to the series),

> not alone true of Alabama, but as well of her sister States in
> misery. The average American, it may be ventured, has the
> general picture of the South's criminal negligence towards half
> her population. Alabama is but a part of the picture, hardly any
> better than Georgia, Florida, Louisiana or Mississippi in the
> main. Let this sketch be more of a sightseeing trip, which for
> the lack of space can only be a peep here and there. If only a
> whiff of that nature-kindled flame that sears beneath the crust
> or a tang of the bitter-sweet of a viand that is human flesh, if
> you can register these you will have partaken of Alabama.[16]

"A civilized man cast among cannibals," writes E. Franklin Frazier, "would have a better chance of justice than a Negro in an Atlanta court where a white man is involved."[17]

Compared with the South, the northern "'Colored' United States" do offer relatively greater freedom, opportunity, and justice, but conditions there are hardly ideal—and they threaten to become worse. As in its articles on the southern states, the series explores the American history of slavery, and the North's abolitionist legacy does put it in a better light. But, again, this light is only relatively better. For, while there is the sense of a "North" that is antithetical to a "South," the northern states do not generally make good on the promises they seem to offer. For example, employment and business conditions, despite the boosterism of certain articles, are clearly constricted for most African Americans. To a large degree, "the North" functions as an ideal that few, if any, of the northern states in the series actually embody.

What's worse, the articles indicate a growing fear that the North is becoming more southern. Thus, while Ernest Rice McKinney describes Philadelphia as "the Negroes' *'cradle of liberty,'* " he also notes that Pennsylvania "is one of the few northern states having any distinctly colored schools. Such jim-crow schools are found in a few cities in the eastern part, notably Philadelphia."[18] In Connecticut and Minnesota, restaurants, soda fountains, and theaters are beginning to practice more aggressive forms of segregation and discrimination. Lionel F. Artis's March 1924 essay is entitled, "The Negro in Indiana; or, The Struggle Against Dixie Come North." And in Michigan, where a large number of newly arrived southern whites joined that state's police force, official and quasi-official violence against African Americans increased significantly.[19]

In his essay on "Minnesota: Seat of Satisfaction," Roy Wilkins voices an alarm shared by many of the series' writers about the northern states. Noting the growth of northern racism, Wilkins warns against northern blacks' "apathy and self-satisfaction" in the face of such changes: "the indifference of the colored Minnesotan is shown in his lack of resistance to restrictions that are creeping in upon him. He offers little or no resistance to the dangerous and often vicious propaganda of the press."[20] Wilkins warns his readers that a misplaced trust in the North's "Northernness" could lead to disaster: "While the forces of discrimination make inroads upon his freedom the Negro in the North Star state rests in satisfaction, contenting himself with the thought that Georgia is so many and so many miles away. His civil rights organizations are dead. The so-called leaders do not see the vanguard of proscription marching down upon them, or if they see it, they choose to ignore it" (173).

Warnings such as Wilkins's are found throughout the series' northern articles, and they underscore the tentativeness that pervades *The Messenger*'s imaginary map of "These 'Colored' United States." Only the more conservative writers in the series note the growing prevalence of Jim Crow conditions with anything like comfort. William Ferris, for example, ends his essay on Connecticut by noting that "the partial segregation in New Haven does not oppress the colored citizens. They are, for the most part, taking advantage of present opportunities and looking forward to the future with hope."[21] The majority of the articles, though, approach the North's waxing segregation and racism with alarm.

The "'Colored' United States" that most embody the ideals of justice and equality traditionally attributed to the North are the western states. The titles of the articles alone indicate the extensive praise these states receive: "California: The Horn of Plenty," "Oklahoma—The Land of the Fair God," and "Arizona and New Mexico—The Land of Esperanza." Notwithstanding the optimism of these articles, "the West" exerts little force on the imagination of the series as a whole. Despite the series' construction of a geography that complicates an easy North/ South dichotomy, this binary still does exert the greatest imaginative force in the series.

In "These 'Colored' United States," the region that offers the greatest latitude and promise is arrayed along the borders of the former Union and Confederacy. Seen as fluid mixtures of unmet northern possibilities and unrelieved southern inhospitality, the "border" states are characterized as sites of genuine potential. They have speckled histories concerning slavery, generally offer economic opportunities as limited as elsewhere in the nation, and to varying degrees they are all prone to Jim Crow segregation. But it seems to be their very uncertainty that makes these states attractive to their observers. In the 1920s, "These 'Colored' United States" argues, the possibilities of African-American identity formation are found at the "betwixt and between" of competing visions of American national identities.

Charles S. Johnson's "Illinois: Mecca of the Migrant Mob" exemplifies the complex possibilities of the border states. Johnson begins his article by describing Illinois as "one of those perplexing border countries which only by the most reckless interpretation of statehood can be referred to as a sovereign unit." While the state's "northern end is a polyglot of races, characters and cultures . . . [the] southern end is more homogeneous. Its first strata of population come from the contiguous south, cherishing the traditions of a system whose blind and brutal operation had driven them out."[22] Johnson notes the state's complicated historical relationship to slavery, which led to its being both Unionist and opposed to Lincoln's Emancipation Proclamation:

This conglomeration of vagrant and dissimilar strains and this lack of a common background no doubt account for the absurd contradictions in the life of the state: for Springfield, from whose soil both Lincoln and a bloody race riot sprang; for Chicago, where Negroes may hold responsible office, and Granite City where they by ordinance may not live within the city limits; for Brooklyn and Robbins in which only Negroes live and 200 other towns where they may not live at all; for a clause in the Constitution vouchsafing equal rights without respect to color and separate schools in every town south of Chicago; for the wanton bloodshed of East St. Louis, Springfield, Chicago and Herrin, in spite of God, and civilization. (109)

But these riots and bloodshed, Johnson argues, although "abominable," are attributable "not so much [to] the deep set, innumerable layers of carefully cultivated hatred [found elsewhere in the nation] as the raw nature of the savage. . . . They balance the throbbing animation of youth—the spirit that has fought its way to power and consequences in spite of its cultural backwardness" (111). Race relations might be strained, Johnson suggests, but they are also not carved in stone; there is room for negotiation at the borders.

While David Levering Lewis accurately describes Johnson as "doggedly optimistic" (47), Johnson's perspective was shared by many of the series' contributors writing about border states. T. G. Nutter, for example, notes both West Virginia's segregated school systems while also claiming that "the Negro in the state is fast solving his economic condition . . . and he is entering into every avenue of business. This group is being greatly encouraged in its upward stride by the happy relation existing between the races."[23] Writing about Delaware, Alice Dunbar-Nelson observes that state's segregation. "Yet," she claims "there is no city in the country, no state in the Union where there is more complete amity between the races, more apparent respect for the Negro by the white man,"[24] and she proudly calls Delaware "a right little, tight little state of surprises and inconsistencies, but like all inconsistencies, a jewel—and a jewel of a state she is, the veritable diamond center in the Atlantic seaboard circlet of states" (75).

In "These 'Colored' United States," then, it is at the borders between established southern "Bourbonism" and unfulfilled northern ide-
alism that the authors of the series find the surest footing. *The Messenger*
seems to suggest that the greatest possibilities are to be found in the
cracks between established concepts and discourses—and that these
cracks might not necessarily be where one might expect. This provides
us with a fascinating counter to contemporary suggestions during the
1920s that Harlem was black America's most promising locale. For,
while the magazine is one of the great achievements of Harlem during
"its" Renaissance, *The Messenger*'s vision of black America is clearly not
limited to the magazine's site of production. George W. Lee's conclusion to his essay on Tennessee perhaps best exhibits *The Messenger*'s vision of national possibilities:

> Tennessee is the battle ground where the practical solution of
> the race problem will be fought out. It smacks of just enough
> Southern sentiment to be followed by the whole South with
> confidence and appreciation. It imbibes just enough Northern
> liberal thoughts to temper that program with justice. There is
> enough free thought in East Tennessee together with the free
> thinkers in the Middle and Western sections to neutralize West
> Tennessee positive conviction, and where East meets west to
> determine the future of the South and call the free and inde-
> pendent Negro Leadership of the self sacrificing type to join in
> the deliberations, a better understanding of the Negro's aim,
> aspiration and where his progress leads to, will be obtained and
> the South, suffering from migration, will blossom like a rose.[25]

The interest of the series in borders leads to a rather startling equation, one that perhaps destabilizes our notions of American racial identities in the 1920s. As "These 'Colored' United States" makes clear again
and again, the histories of the United States and African Americans
are inextricably intertwined from their beginnings, yet at the same time,
the series also claims an affinity between the experiences of African
Americans and immigrants. Such an equation should come as no surprise. After all, "These 'Colored' United States" was a response to the
Great Migration; just like foreign immigrants, who by 1910 accounted
for as much as one-third of the U.S. population,[26] African Americans

were uprooting and relocating in response to shifting opportunities. However, while claiming immigrant status might constitute an attempted break with racist American ideologies, such a move also threatens to sever potentially sustaining ties with the centuries-long history of black America. Why should African Americans assert affinities with the nation's latest arrivals when they could lay claim to an American presence stretching back to the sixteenth century? Besides, despite (and because of) their huge numbers, immigrants were becoming unwelcome in the United States: "Restrictions on immigration grew tighter during the Twenties as first the Johnson Act of 1921 and then the 1924 National Origins Act imposed a quota system that drastically checked the migrant tide."[27] But as with border states, the series explores the possibility that the gaps between histories and national origins might offer the greatest potential.

Thus Johnson refers to Chicago's black population as "expatriates . . . adventurous, daring spirited and—raw" (111). Excited by the idea that these African Americans are testing their inherited regional histories, he writes, "The social set is still a bit promiscuous—vague and uncertain, lacking in definite standards of ancestry and culture and even wealth—a sort of one big union as contrasted with New York City's confederacy of small groups and Charleston's rigid color-caste lines. New countries are always democratic" (113). This new democracy applies both internally, among the African-American community, and to African Americans as one group of "foreigners" among many; "race relations are not fixed, and they are not fixed because Chicago is the open ground for myriad transplanted traditions" (113). So, while "economic competition is severe," this pertains not necessarily because of racism, but "because the groups in contact are so nearly equal" (114).

Johnson's embrace of an immigrant identity signals an engagement with the ongoing American debate concerning the "place" of the foreign inside the space of the nation. Today, we might even read Johnson's move as a startling formulation of the term "alienation," one quite different from either Marxist or literary modernist conceptions of that term. Rather than what Fredric Jameson calls the "'damaged existence' we lead in modern society, the psychological impairment caused by the division of labor and specialization, the general alienation and dehumanization of modern life in all its aspects" (61), we might see in "These

'Colored' United States" the willing embrace of ethnic differentiation
as potential, not failure. As Houston Baker points out, the "acknowledgment of radical uncertainty" is a chief characteristic of twentieth-
century modernity. "Where precisely anyone or anything was located
could no longer be charted on old maps of 'civilization,' nor could even
the most microscopic observation tell the exact time and space of day."[28]
Such uncertainty might lead white writers such as T. S. Eliot to despair,
but it could also represent new and better possibilities for nonwhite and
immigrant writers. The very "cracks and reforms and bursts" of Eliot's
Waste Land might, therefore, also represent the openings in American
culture that the condition of migrancy inhabits.[29]

   The influx of millions of "swarthy" immigrants from southern and
eastern Europe led to a widespread national debate on the nature and
fate of "the races." As the foreign population swelled in the United
States, so grew a whole new range of pseudosciences that were dedicated to codifying and establishing racial hierarchies. As Ann Douglas
explains, social scientists such as Madison Grant and Lothrop Stoddard
were redefining human biology in order to suit the classism and xenophobia of American hegemony:

> Their leading practitioners explained that "race" designated
> and included not just color but ethnicity, nationality, and, even
> by implication, class and language. The only really "white"
> people were the "Nordics" of northern Europe, the educated
> "pure Caucasians" whose ancestors had settled America in the
> seventeenth century. The rest were "Mediterraneans" and
> "Alpines," all of them, it was feared, far less intelligent and self-
> controlled than their Nordic rivals.[30]

   What this legal and cultural policing of race and nationality indicates is an extraordinary amount of anxiety on the part of "white"
America because "whiteness," as an identifiable and discrete category
during the era of both foreign immigration and the Harlem Renaissance,
had become severely unstable. Tom Buchanan's outburst in *The Great
Gatsby* makes this anxiety clear: "Civilization's going to pieces. . . . I've
gotten to be a terrible pessimist about things. Have you read 'The Rise
of the Colored Empires' by this man Goddard? . . . 'Well, it's a fine book,
and everybody ought to read it. The idea is if we don't look out the

white race will be—will be utterly submerged. It's all scientific stuff; it's been proved. . . . This fellow has worked out the whole thing. It's up to us, who are the dominant race, to watch out or these other races will have control of things."[31] Tom's pessimism and racism are fueled by the scientifically sanctioned suspicion that, as George Schuyler notes in *Black No More*, "Everything that looks white ain't white in this man's country."[32] According to Susan Marren, whiteness "became exceedingly rarefied" in the 1920s;[33] discourses on race were at least as (unintentionally) effective at unraveling white purity as they were at shoring it up. Consequently, the writers of "These 'Colored' United States" saw "white" anxiety as a chink in the armor of xenophobia, and they were able to at least conceptualize a livable national space that seemed unavailable through economic tactics alone.

This is hardly an unqualified success, as the contributors to "These 'Colored' United States" were usually quick to note. Cut through by a timeline that charts the intransigent racism of U.S. class politics, the map of America presented by "These 'Colored' United States" reveals the myriad injustices inflicted by an anxious culture that cannot accommodate its always inadequate languages of race, power, and history. Whether they write about North or South, West or the borders, whether they represent business or radical politics, the contributors to "These 'Colored' United States" compose their map of America with an ear to its languages and thus reveal the "cracks" and "bursts" that erupt between discourse and practice.

Special interest is paid to representations of patriotism. "There is no finer patriot anywhere," writes Ernest McKinney,

> than the industrial baron or the mayor of a small steel town in western Pennsylvania. They can stab unionism, annihilate free speech, declare a four hundred percent stock dividend, murder a miner's wife or rape his daughter, swear allegiance to the principles of Lincoln, steal elections, build playgrounds for the poor, and wave the flag all in the course of one day's work. It is a sort of dollar mark patriotism that has permeated the whole state. All who do not subscribe to it are in danger of the hell of fire and the state constabulary, affectionately known among the proletariat as the "Pennsylvania Cossacks." (236)

Patriots such as McKinney's are found throughout the series. In his "The District of Columbia—A Paradise of Paradoxes" (October 1923), Neval H. Thomas asserts that, "Every one of us from the cradle to the grave is the victim of these American skin specialists who can determine every person's deserts, character and ability by the color of his skin."[34] This observation begs the question whether "our democratic capital" (80) is either "ours" or "democratic." Or, as George Schuyler puts it, the United States is "our (?) country."[35]

But the evident distrust in the series of the language and trappings of patriotism is more than matched by its determination to struggle toward a greater realization of democratic principles. Although few articles equal Charles Johnson's almost unbridled optimism, many of them are informed by a sense that the United States might yet deliver on its promises. The authors of "These 'Colored' United States" write about human bondage, unspeakable cruelties, and institutional racism in installment after installment, yet they never surrender to self-pity or hopelessness. What ultimately arises from a reading of "These 'Colored' United States" is a chorus of voices, all asserting the determination of African Americans to make a place for themselves in the nation. Thus Thomas writes that, "the Negro is still determined to overcome his all but insurmountable obstacles. . . . We acquire culture, not *through* segregation and oppression, but *in spite* of them" (81–82). And Nathan Ben Young writes, "Some day ruddy young Birmingham, capstone of Alabama, will emerge, like Miriam, from the Red Sea of her struggles and a new era will begin. Some day! And as Birmingham emerges, Alabama will emerge" (24). And W. H. Twine writes: "In spite of the many obstacles in our way, we are determined to stand by our *guns and stay in Oklahoma*, and continue to battle for our rights. We are determined not to sacrifice our property and seek other climes, but rather stand and fight the scoundrels who deny us our civil and political rights. If necessary, we will fight until the Plutonian regions are congealed and continue the battle on the ice."[36] Even the acerbic George Schuyler writes that, "the United States with all its faults is heaven compared to most any other place on the planet" ("New York," 210); his article, although bitterly satirical, nonetheless encourages his readers to continue their struggle for inclusion in American democracy.

Finally, "These 'Colored' United States"—posing the questions, where do we stand? and what do 'we' consist of?—proposes no easy answers. What the series does offer, though, is the example of commitment, a spirit of experimentation, and a refutation of despair. Where did the readers of and contributors to "These 'Colored' United States" stand? That was hard to say because firm answers could be found in neither the language nor the history of American democracy. The past offered only the certainty of slavery and the brief glimmer of the Reconstruction, while contemporary discourses of freedom and patriotism were often thin veils for violence and exclusion. And who were these readers and contributors? Were they a potential vanguard—of the black proletariat? Of all workers? Of a new black bourgeoisie? These questions also remain largely unanswered.

What does remain from a reading of "These 'Colored' United States" is *The Messenger*'s determination to speak from, to, and about a people that had no choice but to negotiate the margins of a society. In the process of this enunciation, "These 'Colored' United States" tried to center the margin. Houston Baker's concept, "radical marronage" (75), which he applies to Alain Locke's project, also describes what is at stake in *The Messenger*'s sustained effort to situate the African-American experience. "These 'Colored' United States" "represents a unified community of national interests set in direct opposition to the general economic, political, and theological tenets of a racist land. The work is, in itself, a *communal* project, drawing on resources, talents, sounds, images, rhythms of a marooned society or nation existing on the frontiers or margins of *all* American promise, profit, and modes of production" (77). Writing from the borders of the putatively United States and publishing from Harlem, a marginalized center, *The Messenger* suggests that a sustained communal enunciation might just carve out for African Americans a communal identity and a place to stand in the nation.

Notes

1. Langston Hughes, *The Big Sea* (New York: Hill and Wang, 1993), 236.
2. David Levering Lewis, *When Harlem Was in Vogue* (New York: Oxford University Press, 1981), 109.
3. Hughes, *Big Sea*, 234.
4. Theodore Kornweibel, Jr., *No Crystal Stair: Black Life and The Messenger, 1917–1928* (Westport, Conn.: Greenwood Press, 1975), 222.
5. The most comprehensive treatments of *The Messenger* are by Abby Arthur

Johnson and Ronald Maberry Johnson, *Propaganda and Aesthetics: The Literary Politics of Afro-American Magazines in the Twentieth Century* (Amherst: University of Massachusetts Press, 1979); Kornweibel, *No Crystal Stair*; and George Hutchinson *The Harlem Renaissance in Black and White* (Cambridge, Mass: Belknap Press of Harvard University Press, 1995).

6. Alain Locke, *The New Negro*, with an introduction by Arnold Rampersand (New York: Atheneum, 1992), 4.

7. Tom Lutz, "Introduction: Diversity, Locality, and Ideology in 'These "Colored" United States,'" in *These "Colored" United States: African American Essays from the 1920s*, ed. Tom Lutz and Susanna Ashton (New Brunswick, N. J.: Rutgers University Press, 1996), 6–7.

8. Some notable series in *The Messenger* are "Eight Weeks in Dixie" (November and December 1922) and "The Mirrors of Harlem" (December 1922 through February 1923) by Floyd J. Calvin; and "The Eatonville Anthology" by Zora Neale Hurston (September through November 1926).

9. Editor's Note, *The Messenger*, January 1923, 565.

10. Lewis, *When Harlem Was In Vogue*, 21.

11. "Negroes Leave the South," *The Messenger*, March 1920, 2.

12. William Pickens, "Arkansas—A Study in Suppression," in *These "Colored" United States*, ed. Lutz and Ashton, 31–40; for the reader's convenience, all subsequent citations from "These 'Colored' United States" are from this edition. The 1996 republication of the series is a welcome addition to the study of the Harlem Renaissance, modernism, and modernity; Lutz's general introduction and the introductions to each essay are insightful and informative.

13. Alain Locke critiques oversimplified analyses of race and American regionalism in his essay, "The New Negro": "But while the minds of most of us, black and white, have thus burrowed in the trenches of the Civil War and Reconstruction, the actual march of development has simply flanked these positions, necessitating a sudden reorientation of view. We have not been watching in the right direction; set North and South on a sectional axis, we have not noticed the East till the sun has us blinking" (4).

14. Nathan B. Young, "Florida: Our Contiguous Foreign State," in *These "Colored" United States*, ed. Lutz and Ashton, 90.

15. Clifton F. Richardson, "Texas—the Lone Star State," in *These "Colored" United States*, ed. Lutz and Ashton, 257.

16. Nathan B. Young, "Alabama—Like Miriam," in *These "Colored" United States*, ed. Lutz and Ashton, 21.

17. E. Franklin Frazier, "Georgia, or The Struggle against Impudent Inferiority," in *These "Colored" United States*, ed. Lutz and Ashton, 102.

18. Ernest Rice McKinney, "Pennsylvania: A Tale of Two Cities," in *These "Colored" United States*, ed. Lutz and Ashton, 240.

19. Robert W. Bagnall, "Michigan—the Land of Many Waters," in *These "Colored" United States*, ed. Lutz and Ashton, 164–166.

20. Roy Wilkins, "Minnesota: Seat of Satisfaction," in *These "Colored" United States*, ed. Lutz and Ashton, 171.

21. William Ferris, "Connecticut: The Nutmeg State," in *These "Colored" United States*, ed. Lutz and Ashton, 58.

22. Charles S. Johnson, "Illinois: Mecca of the Migrant Mob," in *These "Colored" United States*, ed. Lutz and Ashton, 108.

23. T. Gillis Nutter, "West Virginia," in *These "Colored" United States*, ed. Lutz and Ashton, 298.

24. Alice Dunbar-Nelson, "Delaware: A Jewel of Inconsistencies," in *These "Colored" United States*, ed. Lutz and Ashton, 73.

25. George W. Lee, "Tennessee—the Last Stand of Justice in the Solid South," in Lutz and Ashton, 254.

26. Eliot Asinof, *1919: America's Loss of Innocence* (New York: Donald I. Fine, 1990), 243.

27. Burl Noggle, *Into the Twenties: The United States from Armistice to Normalcy* (Urbana: University of Illinois Press, 1974), 115.

28. Houston A. Baker, Jr., *Modernism and the Harlem Renaissance* (Chicago: University of Chicago Press, 1987), 3.

29. T. S. Eliot, *The Waste Land and Other Poems* (New York: Harcourt Brace Jovanovich, 1962), 44.

30. Ann Douglas, *Terrible Honesty: Mongrel Manhattan in the 1920s* (New York: Farrar, Straus and Giroux, 1995), 305–306.

31. F. Scott Fitzgerald, *The Great Gatsby* (New York: Scribners, 1953), 13.

32. George Schuyler, *Black No More: Being an Account of the Strange and Wonderful Workings of Science in the Land of the Free, A. D. 1933–1940* (Boston: Northeastern University Press, 1989), 56.

33. Susan Marren, "Passing for American: Establishing American Identity in the Work of James Weldon Johnson, F. Scott Fitzgerald, Nella Larsen, and Gertrude Stein" (Ph.D. diss., University of Michigan, 1995), 13.

34. Neval H. Thomas, "The District of Columbia—a Paradise of Paradoxes," in *These "Colored" United States*, ed. Lutz and Ashton, 80.

35. George Schuyler, "New York: Utopia Deferred," in *These "Colored" United States*, ed. Lutz and Ashton, 194.

36. W. H. Twine, "Oklahoma—the Land of the Fair God," in *These "Colored" United States*, ed. Lutz and Ashton, 233.

Chapter 8

"Bombed in Spain"

MICHAEL THURSTON

Langston Hughes,
the Black Press, and
the Spanish Civil War

In June 1937, Langston Hughes, poet and novelist, became for a short time Langston Hughes, reporter. Already interested in the Spanish Republic's struggle for its existence against the insurgent forces led by General Francisco Franco, Hughes arranged with two African-American newspapers, the *Baltimore Afro-American* and the *Cleveland Call and Post*, to act as their correspondent in Spain and write a series of articles on the conflict's significance for American blacks.[1] This essay examines Hughes's Spanish Civil War contributions to the black press and, based on that examination, reaches beyond Hughes to characterize the broader black press coverage of the war.

Essays like this one typically show the significance of their claims, their evidence, their readings, by pointing out differences, setting the objects of their scrutiny apart from other texts, occurrences, or movements. I will, however, do just the opposite. Where Arnold Rampersad, Hughes's biographer, writes that Hughes affects a new merger between the *Baltimore Afro-American*'s "narrowly racial . . . view" and his own "proletarianism and antifascism" to yield "excellent propaganda for the left, aimed directly at the black American world,"[2] I argue that Hughes's writings from and about the Spanish Civil War at once exemplify his writing of the 1930s and typify coverage of Spain in the African-American press. The first of these points requires no real demonstration; as not only the premier African-American poet of the 1930s but also the premier poet on the American Left in that decade, the single most frequent poetic contributor to the left-wing *New Masses*, Hughes predictably gravitates to Spain and writes about it in terms recognizable from his essays and poems about the Scottsboro case, the Soviet Union, and the conjunctions of race and class in the United States. The second point, though, enables us to see how editors and writers for the African-American newspapers understood the complex relationship between American race politics and the agendas of the international Left (agendas intimately bound up with the Spanish conflict). Like Hughes, the black press in general recognized that, to borrow Rampersad's terms, the way to the broad coalition suggested by proletarianism and antifascism lay precisely through the "narrowly racial." In their representations and analyses of the Spanish Civil War, the African-American newspapers, like Hughes, their most prolific correspondent from Spain, drew together matters both black and red, issues related at once to race in the United States and to socialism internationally.

In February 1936, the people of Spain elected a progressive, Popular Front government with many promises: land reform, which might ease the crushing poverty of the nation's many landless peasants; cultural reform, which would relax the Catholic Church's hold on most of the institutions of civil society; and military reform, which could ensure the democratic determination of national priorities and the peaceful exchange and exercise of state power. Although the government itself advocated a moderately left-wing agenda, the landowners, Church hierarchy, and military officers whose positions were threatened feared broader changes that might strip them completely of their power. Almost immediately, a group of military officers began to plan a coup. On 18 July 1936, they led the majority of the Spanish army against the five-month-old Republic. Joined promptly by Church leaders and landowners, the army of General Francisco Franco gained control of one-third of the country in less than a week.[3]

The regular Army had largely abandoned the Republic, but the government continued to be supported by both a majority of the Spanish

people and the progressive political communities of Europe and the
United States. The governments of Britain, France, and the United
States, however, maintained a neutral stance toward Spain and refused
(aside from minor assistance by France early on) to intercede on the
Republic's behalf. The defense of democratic Spain was left to the Spanish, at least at first. Local militias fought the rebels in the field and in
the streets, defended the mountain passes to Madrid, and finally
mounted the barricades to protect the city itself. International brigades,
organized by the Communist International (Comintern) in Moscow and
comprised of volunteers from Europe and the United States, arrived in
November 1936 to add their men and materiel to the defense of the
Republic, especially the defense of the capital, which managed to hold
off the rebels through intense street fighting and which, though heavily
bombarded by the rebels, stood for more than two years.[4] By early 1937,
the battle lines were drawn; the country lay divided, with Madrid and
Barcelona in Republican hands, but important territory possessed by the
superior forces and armaments of the right-wing rebels.

By 1937, as Arnold Rampersad writes, Langston Hughes "needed a
tonic, a restorative."[5] The Civil War in Spain offered a perfect opportunity to get away from divisive political and aesthetic debates in New
York and California and to participate more directly in the international
politics that had long captivated his attention. Hughes had, indeed, already responded to the war in print. When Nancy Cunard and Pablo
Neruda appealed to him for a contribution to their anthology of poetry
on behalf of the Republic's defenders, Hughes sent the poem, "Song of
Spain." He also signed (or was, at least, included as a signatory to) the
New Masses' "Manifesto and Call," which dubbed Spain the first site
of a "civil and international conflict that is certain to recur elsewhere."[6]
When André Malraux and Phillipe Aragon wired Hughes to urge him
to attend the Second International Writers' Congress in France (an
event Hughes had previously declined to attend), he decided to go and
proceed from Paris to Spain to see the war at first hand. Arranging with
the *Baltimore Afro-American* and the *Cleveland Call and Post* to send a
series of articles from Spain, Hughes left as a foreign correspondent in
June 1937.[7]

The mixed racial and political motives that came to define his reportage *from* Spain manifested themselves from the beginning in

Hughes's actions *in* Spain. When Hughes arrived at the *Alianza de Intelectuales* in Madrid, he carried a note of introduction from Bill Lawrence, chief American commissar in Spain at the time. The note, addressed to Edwin Rolfe, serving then as chief American commissar for Madrid, introduces "Comrade Langston Hughes" and asks Rolfe to help Hughes "in whatever way possible to get necessary information."[8] The note reflects an awareness on the part of both Hughes and the Communist Party that, as Cary Nelson writes, "Hughes was receiving Party cooperation in Spain and thus at the very least the Party considered him to be working on common interests."[9] Hughes worked on those common interests not only by writing both the articles he sent back to Baltimore (and to other periodicals) and the poems he would soon publish in the International Brigades' *Volunteer for Liberty*, *New Masses*, and *Esquire* but also by travelling to the front, giving poetry readings, and speaking on the radio.

Hughes began his series of weekly articles for the *Baltimore Afro-American* in the 23 October 1937 issue. Perhaps not accidentally, the initiation of the series coincides with the paper's announcement of the death of Milton Herndon, brother of activist Angelo Herndon. Of the two items on Spain, Hughes's receives much greater attention; his presence in Spain tops the front page: "EXCLUSIVE!!!—From war-torn Spain, Langston Hughes, celebrated American novelist and poet, brings exclusively to AFRO-AMERICAN readers a vivid and accurate picture of the bitter struggle that is now going on. This interesting series and the accompanying photographs will appear only in the AFRO-AMERICAN."[10]

Hughes's first article lives up to its headline, as the poet-cum-journalist recounts his experience of the bombardment that pounded Madrid during the fall of 1937. But the majority of the article focuses on Hughes's actions during the days before the air raid. He details his meeting and conversations with Nicolas Guillen, describes the city's plazas and facades, and rehearses the directions hotel clerks gave regarding conduct during air raids. Two aspects of the preraid text stand out as significant discursive strategies of both Hughes's reportage and, as I will show, black press coverage of Spain. First, Hughes spends several column-inches on an account of his and Guillen's evening at the Mella Club: "We were invited to a dance that afternoon given in honor of the soldiers on leave, and here we met a number of Cubans, both colored and white, and a colored Portuguese, all taking an active part in the Spanish struggle against the fascists. And all of them finding in loyalist Spain more freedom than they had known at home. . . . In Spain, as one could see at the dance that afternoon, there is no color line, and Catalonian girls and their escorts mingled gaily with the colored guests."[11] Suggested by neither the title nor the tease, and having little to do with the bombing raid supposedly at the article's heart, Hughes's visit to the Mella Club provides an opportunity to commend Spain's value. Hughes presents the example Spain can set for race relations before the bombs fall down and threaten to destroy it.

Another passage in the long buildup to the bombing raid evokes the remarkably normal life lived by many Madrileños in spite of the war and bombardments and elicits readers' sympathy for people whose lives might seem quite like their own until explosives and incendiaries shatter it. When Hughes and Guillen return to their hotel after the dance to have dinner, they discover that the most pressing privation wrought by the war, at least for international guests of finer hotels, is the limited menu; while the dining room remains "luxurious" and the waiters continue to wear their tuxedos, Hughes writes, "there was only one fixed dinner menu, no choice of food."[12] That said, though, he acknowledges that the available dinner is "good," with all the expected courses present and accounted for, but "nothing elaborate." And after dinner, the two writers stroll with the promenading citizens and take their coffee, "as one often does in Europe," in a sidewalk cafe (right out of Hemingway).

Hughes's evocation of everyday life in Madrid, so familiar even in its minor privations, makes the bombing, when it finally happens in the last third of the article, that much more shocking. It enables, in other words, Hughes's primary aim in the piece: the re-creation of the experience of bombardment in ways that draw readers' sympathy to the Madrileños through their recognition of similarity, shared lifestyles, and values even across the Atlantic. But no sooner does Hughes begin to undress than the night erupts in sirens. Just as he led readers through his day and evening, his experience of relative routine, now he recounts the confusion and fear, the utter departure from the normal, wrought by the air raid: "Suddenly all the lights went out in the hotel, but we heard people rushing down the halls and stairways in the dark. A few had flashlights with them to find the way. Some were visibly frightened. In the lobby two candles were burning, casting weird, giant-like shadows on the walls."[13] The fact that the raid does not materialize this time, that the only firing the guests hear as they huddle in the lobby is that of Republican antiaircraft, enhances rather than detracts from the moment's shock and strangeness. And the night has just begun.

Sleeping soundly after the false alarm, Hughes is jerked awake by a nearby explosion and quickly realizes that this bombardment is for real; there is "no foolin' this time": "The next thing I knew, the telephone was ringing violently in the dark, the siren screaming its long blood-curdling cry again, and the walls of the building shaking. BOOM! Then the dull roar of a dying vibration. And another BOOM! Through my window I saw a flash of light. I didn't stay to look again. Down the hall I went, clothes in my arms, sensing my way toward the staircase in the dark."[14]

In its descriptions of the bombing and of the citizens' reactions to it, Hughes's first communique back to Baltimore makes good on the headline's promise of "a vivid and accurate picture of the bitter struggle." More important, though, it humanizes the Spanish, especially the Republicans. And Hughes exploits the fact that, as Raymond Williams has argued, "to address an account to another is, explicitly or potentially, . . . to evoke or propose an active relationship to the experience being expressed."[15] The article at once shows the city's efforts to live normally and the impossibility of a life American readers would consider normal under the conditions of war; it renders and invites relationship. Although the article concludes with a comment about "getting used to air raids in Spain," it demonstrates through its representation of Hughes's own experience that air raids are not the sort of thing people get used to. In so doing, it grants readers a stake in what's at stake in Spain.

As "Madrid's Flowers Hoist Blooms to Meet Raining Fascist Bombs" shows, two months later, everyday life is grimmer still. In text surrounding a photograph of a shell-riddled Madrid apartment house, Hughes alternates descriptions of horrific shellings and the random rain of death ("there is no way of telling where the shells are going to fall—in the street or on the houses, on the east side of town or on the west side, in the suburbs or in the heart of the city") and examples of the citizenry's calm handling of the situation ("if the bombardment is a long one, and several guns are dropping missiles of death on the town, then people may get out of bed and seek the basement").[16] Amidst the bombings, death, and general suffering, which seems to have increased, or to have become more evident to Hughes in the weeks since his first article, the people of Madrid, Hughes assures his readers, "are calm, serene, even gay at times with flashes of the old gaiety for which Madrid was noted among the capitals of Europe before the war."[17]

It might seem strategically wrong-headed for a writer whose purpose is, at least in part, to elicit sympathy (and often funds) for the people undergoing the ordeal of daily bombardment to emphasize their calm, indeed, their continuing capacity for "gaiety." But by showing the Madrileños's smiling endurance, Hughes draws a stark contrast with the grim visage of Franco and his "fascists"; by showing the Republicans remaining cheerfully and steadfastly dedicated to their embattled government's ideals, he establishes a standard that Franco, with his conscripts and his terror campaigns, cannot meet. More than this, Hughes subtly criticizes the neutral governments of Europe and the United States. In a concluding peroration, he transforms Madrid's capacity to withstand privation and bombardment into the abstraction of "Time," which he allies with such universal goods as art and freedom:

> Time is with the people of Spain. Time, and the moral con-
> sciousness of the world. The Fascists who bomb women and
> children, who have put to death Garcia Lorca, Spain's greatest
> poet, who deliberately rained explosives on the art museum of
> El Prado and on the National Library with its priceless books
> and manuscripts, who use churches for arsenals and bring
> Mohammedans to battle for a "Christian ideal," and who fight
> for no cause at all except the forcing of the Spanish people
> back into economic and spiritual slavery for the sake of a
> handful of rich men and outworn nobles—these Fascists,
> Madrid feels, cannot win.[18]

Madrid endures because Madrid is right. Madrid holds out because it holds out against wrongs: destruction, privilege, closed-mindedness, and murder. And the African-American readers of the *Baltimore Afro-*

American can clearly see, through the lens Hughes polishes for them, their connection with Madrid's embattled citizens. Their families have been threatened, their spokespersons murdered, and their freedom, within distant memory, has been taken away by a state apparatus shielded by its own "Christian ideal."

"Hughes Bombed in Spain" and "Madrid's Flowers" put Hughes himself front and center. Through his experiences, readers experience the Spanish conflict. In his other articles, however, Hughes allots more space to stories about other blacks in Spain. By charting black soldiers' rise to command positions in the International Brigades and then setting such stories alongside accounts of the North African shock troops' devastating losses in the front lines, Hughes demonstrates the opposing racial policies of the Republic and its supporters on one hand and the Fascists on the other. Throughout the series, Hughes insistently explores the direct significance of the war for American blacks, but in "Hughes Finds Moors Used as Pawns by Fascists in Spain," one of his most important articles for the *Baltimore Afro-American*, he emphasizes the participation of blacks in the war, in actual conflict.

In "Hughes Finds Moors," Hughes draws the stark contrast between blacks in the International Brigades and their counterparts in Franco's army.[19] While blacks could (and did) rise to command positions in the Brigades, Hughes writes, North Africans served as shock troops, pressed to the front lines of offensives to absorb the highest casualties. Although service in the Brigades was voluntary, Spanish Moroccans were forced to fight for Franco; even when not directly conscripted, they were often lured by promises of good pay and then, as Hughes has it, "paid off in worthless German marks which they were told would be good to spend when they got back to Africa."[20] Moreover, the North Africans' participation in the war marks their return to a country they once conquered and ruled themselves. Their former status as rulers, Hughes implies, aligns the Moroccans with the Ethiopians recently defeated by Italy. The "Moors" are avatars, then, for Haile Selassie's kingdom, a nation with whom African-American readers deeply sympathized and whose defeat at Italy's hands provoked riots in American cities.[21] Their current status, as conscripts of poorly paid, duped shock troops, indicates the threat to blacks under the heel of fascism. Hughes bleakly concludes his discussion of the Moroccans by pointing out that most never live to return to Africa and try to spend the marks they have been paid. Indeed, as the war enters its second year, Hughes writes, the Moroccans "are no longer a potent force in Franco's army. Too many of them have been killed."[22]

To show the contrast between how Franco treats blacks and how the Republic does, he lists the many places from which blacks have come to fight for Spain: "Within the last year, colored people from many different countries have sent men, money, and sympathy to Spain." Josephine Baker has danced to raise money for the Republic, Hughes informs his readers. Paul Robeson has sung, a black band in the Moulin Rouge has played, and a large group of black writers from Africa, the West Indies, and Cuba have written and read for Spain. Cities all over the United States have sent black soldiers for the International Brigades and black nurses for the medical corps. More important, Hughes unites these disparate black volunteers under the shared recognition he attributes to them. Not only do all these blacks participate in order to "fight against the forces that have raped Ethiopia," but they also share a broader understanding of how race and the Republic's fate are intricated: "All of them [are] here because they know that if Fascism creeps across Spain, across Europe, and then across the world, there will be no place left for intelligent young Negroes at all. In fact, no decent place for any Negroes—because Fascism preaches the creed of Nordic supremacy and a world for whites alone."[23]

If the Republic loses to Franco and the imperial powers behind him, the world will be neither safe nor comfortable for any nonwhite peoples. Fascism, Hughes writes, assumes the supremacy of white Europeans and systematically institutionalizes that supremacy through laws governing all aspects of social life. In an America already inclined to separate the races and assume social superiority for whites, Hughes sees an analogue to the Fascists' racist codes. And the battle for Spain resonates back to the United States, for, once blacks have fought together with whites for the common cause, they will refuse to return to their former social position. This, at least, is Hughes's expectation as the war rages on.

Just as important, though, "Hughes Finds Moors" clearly articulates Hughes's aims for the reportage he is sending home: "Why had I come to Spain? To write for the colored press. I knew that Spain had once belonged to the Moors, a colored people. . . . Now the Moors have come again to Spain with the Fascist armies as cannon fodder for Franco. But on the Loyalist side there are many colored people of various nationalities in the International Brigades. I want to write about both Moors and colored people."[24] The second sentence here is crucial, for Hughes puts at the center of his Spanish mission his work for the "colored press." To help to construct the kind of collective necessary for victory in Spain, the kind of collective modeled by the International Brigades themselves, Hughes must reach key constituencies, especially his black readers. By bringing home to those readers the experience of Madrid's bombardment, Hughes elicits sympathy for those who are "bombed in Spain" and attempts to mobilize that sentiment in the service of a broadly socialist vision. At the same time, by exploring and explaining the role of blacks in Spain in the *Baltimore Afro-American*, a newspaper whose front pages were also filled with stories about Joe Louis and the Wagner Anti-Lynching Act, Hughes links American racism with international Fascism and forcefully consociates international left politics and racial equality. In so doing, he contributes to the African-American press's general aim: to raise the profile of race in the portfolio of interests at play in American attitudes toward the Spanish conflict.

Articles surrounding Hughes's pieces strengthen the connections he draws in the articles themselves. During Hughes's months in Spain, several issues dominate the news pages of the *Baltimore Afro-American*. Articles on aspects of the Scottsboro case, now six years old, appear in almost every issue. These short pieces deal with things like the mounting costs of continued appeals and the activities of the defendants in and out of prison. Longer articles appear on the progress of the Wagner Anti-Lynching law through the U.S. Congress and the probable appointment of Alabama Senator Hugo Black to the U.S. Supreme Court. Hughes's articles on Spain, broken up over several pages and columns, physically intertwine with the coverage of these issues; Spain's significance for American blacks is thus woven into the fabric of the news. Only one issue of great interest to the paper's readers fails to connect with Spain. In the November 13 issue, coverage of boxer Joe Louis's alleged infidelity eclipses all other news; for the first time since October 23, no article by Hughes even appears in the paper. The only item on Spain in the issue is a one paragraph article about a black volunteer's anger over a mistaken report of his death.

In poems and prose pieces he wrote for other periodicals, including the *Nation, Esquire,* and the International Brigades' magazine, *The Volunteer for Liberty,* Hughes deploys precisely the same representational strategies to elicit sympathy for the Republic, to link its fate with the fate of blacks in the United States, to laud the International Brigades, and to contrast them with Franco's Moors. Of the reportage Hughes published from Spain, his essay "Laughter in Madrid" reached the largest readership. Published in the *Nation* in January 1938, this essay, like the *Afro-American* articles, elicits readers' sympathies for Spain's civilians as they endure Franco's bombardment. Here, again, Hughes effectively transcends simple reportage and rhetorically establishes a relationship between the citizens of Madrid and the *Nation's* audience by equating them and opposing both to Franco's forces: "Imagine yourself sitting calmly in the front room of your third-floor apartment carefully polishing your eyeglasses when all of a sudden, without the least warning, a shell decides to come through the wall—paying no attention to the open window—and explodes like a thunder clap beneath the sofa."[25]

And, in "Air Raid: Barcelona," published in *Esquire's* October 1938 issue, Hughes casts into poetry the same sort of bombardment. Here, as in his newspaper articles, Hughes strives to draw readers into the war by making both the bombings and their human costs real to readers. Jerked awake in the dark, citizens must depend on their hearing as they scramble for safety while stumbling half-dressed down stairs. In a climactic moment of the bombing, Hughes breaks from the rhyme pattern he has established to elaborate this aural death as all other sounds are overcome by the falling ordnance:

> Then the BOMBS fall!
> All other noises are nothing at all
>   When the BOMBS fall
> All other noises are suddenly still
>   When the BOMBS fall
> All other noises are deathly still
> As blood spatters the wall.[26]

Moreover, Hughes appeals openly to readers' probable sympathy with "innocent" victims; children appear in three crucial moments as the emblematic victims of the bombardment. The poem seems calculated to draw on not necessarily the political sympathies of its readers in *Esquire*; rather, it seems pitched at almost any reader who might object to the indiscriminate murder of children under cover of darkness.

Hughes also explores the specifically racial significances of Spain in his magazine essays and poems. In "Negroes in Spain," a short essay he wrote for the *Volunteer*, Hughes once again elaborates his description of the Spanish Moroccans' plight: "Thus the Moors die in Spain, men, women and children, victims of Fascism, fighting not for freedom—but against freedom—under a banner that holds only terror and segregation for all the darker peoples of the earth."[27]

In this essay published for the International Brigades, Hughes used the economy of his newspaper articles to distill a keen political analysis of race politics on both sides of the war. The same analysis shapes a poem Hughes published in the *Volunteer*. In "A Letter from Spain Addressed to Alabama," Hughes frames his understanding of Spain's importance for African Americans in a form particularly well suited to his aims and his audience; the poem, appearing in the *Volunteer* in November 1937, features a dialect report of a black volunteer's encounter with a dying African. His confrontation with this living emblem of imperialism provokes a vision with geopolitical resonance; the foundations of the old order, shaken by a "workers' Spain" that elevates blacks to equal social status, draw the attention and defense of the world's imperial powers:

> I said, I guess that's why old England
> And I reckon Italy, too,
> Is afraid to let a workers' Spain
> Be too good to me and you.[28]

In the voice of an undereducated black man from the American South, Hughes demonstrates the interpenetration of imperialism, race, egalitarianism, and education; he articulates, thereby, the multiple grounds for the war's significance for American blacks.[29]

Hughes was the most prolific and, probably, the most effective African-American writer/journalist to cover the Spanish Civil War. But he was not the only one. It remains for me to show, briefly, how other black press coverage of the Spanish Civil War foregrounds the same issues, the same agenda, as Hughes's *Afro-American* articles and his other writings, how that coverage shared Hughes's thematic emphases, persuasive strategies, and political understanding.

As Robin D. G. Kelley has pointed out, black newspapers like the *Afro-American*, the *Pittsburgh Courier*, the *Atlanta Daily World*, and the *Chicago Defender* "unequivocally sided with the Spanish Republic."[30] The reasons for this are clear. Like many black volunteers, the editors of these newspapers saw Spain as a continuation of the Italo-Ethiopian conflict that had so enraged the African-American community. More than this, though, the black press had, since before the First World War, often made common cause with the American Left and, at key moments, with the international Left, including the Communist Party.[31] Black newspapers joined their voices with those of socialists and the International Workers of the World (IWW) in opposition to the First World War. The black press lauded Communist Party of the United States of America (CPUSA) funding and support for the International Labor Defense, which paid for the Scottsboro defendants' appeals after their conviction.[32] When the Popular Front Spanish Republic was attacked, black editors and writers acted on their historic sense of strategic connection with the Left.

As Lawrence Hogan writes, it was unfortunate that most African-American newspapers could not afford on-the-spot coverage of the war.[33] Even the *Afro-American* was only able to secure Hughes's services because he planned to be in Spain anyway and because he could procure his own passage to Europe.[34] Other papers could, occasionally, develop "stringers," people already in Spain who sent dispatches when possible. The Associated Negro Press (ANP), for example, benefited from the presence in Spain of Thyra Edwards, a Chicago social worker who had traveled to Spain as a delegate to the Social Workers' Committee to Aid Spanish Democracy and who sent a series of articles to the ANP.[35]

Edwards's coverage, like Hughes's, focused on the hardships suffered by ordinary Spanish citizens. In December 1937, for example, she wrote of refugees leaving bombed villages: "The huge square outside the station is crowded with some 1500 refugees sitting about on bales that hold their remaining goods. A curly haired lad of perhaps six years cradles in his lap a mite of perhaps two years while their mother, two others clinging to each hand, stands in line for the canteen from which she can get food for the whole brood without trying to find seats in the crowded canteen. There is talk, movement."[36]

Similar scenes are reported in articles published in the *Pittsburgh Courier* ("To Aid Spain," 31 July 1937) and the *Amsterdam News* ("Harlemites Taking Part in Conflict," 26 June 1937 and "Nurse Aids in Ambulance Drive," 20 August 1938), as well as in lengthier essays published in *The Crisis*. Among the latter, William Pickens's "What I Saw In Spain" is exemplary; after describing the Spaniards' suffering, Pickens concludes that "when there is a human fight going on, other humans cannot be neutral. . . . When a thug attacks the innocent, when a brute attacks the helpless, when a grown-up is beating a child, one certainly then is far from neutral."[37]

Stories of African Americans who did not remain neutral make up the majority of black press coverage of Spain. Oliver Law, the first African American to command a racially integrated American armed unit in combat, served in Spain for less than six months, from late January 1937 until his death at Brunete in July 1937, but, because he both rose so rapidly through Brigade ranks and exhibited real heroism in the field, he received a great deal of attention in black newspapers and was featured most prominently in "Negro Heroes in Loyalists' Gallant Stand" (*Richmond Planet*, 24 July 1937). The *Pittsburgh Courier*'s report of Law's death in battle is one of its most substantial articles on the conflict.[38] And Nancy Cunard's article on Law's death, published in the *Atlanta Daily World* (20 December 1937), is simply one of the most moving articles on Spain to appear in the black press. Also frequently featured was Dr. Arnold Donowa, a Trinidad-born physician who practiced in Harlem before joining the American Medical Bureau in Spain in 1937. The *Daily World* and the *Courier* covered Donowa's departure for Spain, the *Courier* published an article on his wounding in October 1937, and the *Afro-American*, in an article by Edwin Rolfe, among others, covered the time in between.[39] Several articles about the activities and finally the death in Spain of Milton Herndon, brother of American labor organizer, Angelo Herndon, appeared in the *Chicago Defender*. Like Hughes's articles, these demonstrate the progressive racial politics of the International Brigades as well as the commitment of many American blacks to the cause of the Spanish Republic and the broader international Left the Republic came to symbolize.

The oppressive race politics of Franco and his army also appear in black press coverage of the war. Richard Wright, writing for the *Daily Worker*, interviewed African-American activist Louise Thompson upon her return from a tour of Spain, and his reworking of Thompson's comments are typical, if a bit lengthier, of black press treatment of the North African troops. Thompson says that her "greatest interest was in the American Negro Volunteers fighting in the International Brigades and in the Moors fighting with the fascist Franco. I wanted to see with my own eyes the difference between these two dark-skinned peoples fighting on opposite sides of the struggle."[40] Thompson concludes, like Hughes, that the North Africans have been "duped" and "tricked" into fighting for Franco. Given the opportunity and the truth, she muses, the North Africans would join the likes of Vaughn Love, Oliver Frankson, and Oscar Hunter (African Americans in the International Brigades).[41] In its February 1937 article on a Republican attempt to draw African troops from Franco's army, the *Chicago Defender* emphasizes the Africans' powerlessness and ill-treatment.[42] By the next year, the North African soldiers themselves seem to realize their predicament, according to an *Atlanta Daily World* article; they face execution rather than continuing to fight and have deserted in such numbers that they no longer pose a threat to Republican troops.[43]

In its emphases and analyses, as these examples indicate, the black press's coverage of the Spanish Civil War aligns quite clearly with Langston Hughes's writings from Spain, prose and poetry alike. Describing the plight of Republican Spain so that readers might sympathize and see themselves, deploying the activities of African Americans in the Brigades so that readers might experience a connection to the war, and focusing on the contrasting race politics of the conflict's two sides, the black press as a whole constructs a common sense about Spain and black America, about leftist politics and race politics, that Hughes effectively encapsulates in his address to the Paris Writers' Conference. Identifying himself as "both a Negro and poor," as a member of "the most oppressed group in America, the group that has known so little of American democracy," Hughes first explicitly connects the treatment of blacks in the United States with international fascism: "We are the people who have long known in actual practice the meaning of the word Fascism—for the American attitude towards us has always been one of economic and social discrimination: in many states of our country, Negroes are not permitted to vote or to hold political office."[44]

The plight of southern sharecroppers, the refusals of public facilities to admit blacks, the treatment of the Scottsboro defendants, race riots, and lynchings all comprise, Hughes argues, "Fascism in action." And these aspects of American "fascism" resemble the operation of fascism in Italy, Germany, Japan, and, now, Spain. In a rhetorically brilliant maneuver, Hughes locates the racial heart of actually existing fascism; throughout the essay, he connects the murderous policies and practices of Franco's Spain and the treatment of blacks in the United States. The Spanish Republic is important, therefore, because it is both a "workers' Spain" and a racially egalitarian society. At the end of the essay, Hughes clarifies the race/class connection and its far-reaching implications: "We represent the end of race. And the Fascists know that when there is no more race, there will be no more capitalism, and no more war, and no more money for the munition makers, because the workers of the world will have triumphed."[45]

This essay's publication history is unique among Hughes's work. Delivered at the Second International Writers' Congress in Paris, published in the *Volunteer for Liberty*, the *Crisis*, and the *Negro Worker*, the essay reaches readers primarily concerned with Left politics and literature, with the Spanish Civil War, and with issues of interest to American blacks. In both its content and its circulation, Hughes's address brings together the components of Spain's significance and the constituents of his audience, an audience of which the black press, and its readers in turn, formed a crucial component.

Notes

1. Arnold Rampersad, *The Life of Langston Hughes*, Vol. 1: 1902–1946 (New York: Oxford University Press, 1986), 339.
2. Ibid., 339.
3. Histories of the Spanish Civil War are numerous. My account is informed by several, but especially by Gabriel Jackson, *The Spanish Republic and the Spanish Civil War, 1931–1939* (Princeton: Princeton University Press, 1965), and Hugh Thomas, *The Spanish Civil War* (New York: Harper & Row, 1977).
4. On the American and European responses to the Spanish Civil War, see Jackson, *Spanish Republic* 256–60, 354–56. See also Frederick B. Pike, "Introduction: The Background to the Civil War in Spain and the U.S Response to the War," in *The Spanish Civil War, 1936–39: American Hemispheric Responses*, ed., Mark Falcoff and Frederick B. Pike (Lincoln: University of Nebraska Press,

1982), 1–49. On the formation of the International Brigades, see Peter Carroll, *The Odyssey of the Abraham Lincoln Brigade: Americans in the Spanish Civil War* (Stanford: Stanford University Press, 1994), Arthur Landis, *The Abraham Lincoln Brigade* (New York: Citadel, 1967), and Robert A Rosenstone, *Crusade of the Left: The Lincoln Battalion in the Spanish Civil War* (New York: Pegasus, 1969).

5. Rampersad, *Life*, 339.

6. Ibid., 338.

7. Ibid., 339. As Rampersad writes, Hughes published almost a dozen articles in the *Afro-American* (351).

8. Cary Nelson and Jefferson Hendricks, *Edwin Rolfe: A Biographical Essay and Guide to the Edwin Rolfe Archive at the University of Illinois at Urbana-Champaign* (Urbana: University of Illinois Press, 1990), 30–31. See also Rolfe's letter of 11 August 1937, in Nelson and Hendricks, ed., *Madrid, 1937: Letters of the Abraham Lincoln Brigade from the Spanish Civil War* (New York: Routledge, 1996), 291.

9. Nelson and Hendricks, *Edwin Rolfe*, 31.

10. Langston Hughes, "Hughes Bombed in Spain," *Baltimore Afro-American*, 23 October 1937, 1.

11. Ibid., 3.

12. Ibid.

13. Ibid.

14. Ibid.

15. Raymond Williams, *Marxism and Literature* (New York: Oxford University Press, 1977), 166.

16. Hughes, "Madrid's Flowers Hoist Blooms to Meet Raining Fascist Bombs," *Baltimore Afro-American*, 27 November 1937, 1.

17. Ibid.

18. Ibid., 2.

19. The article suggests in miniature a booklet Hughes planned to publish, in which, as Rampersad writes, "he would include portraits of individual Blacks on both sides of the fighting." See Rampersad, *Life*, 351.

20. Hughes, "Hughes Finds Moors Being Used as Pawns by Fascists in Spain," *Baltimore Afro-American* (30 October 1937), 3.

21. William R. Scott, "Black Nationalism and the Italo-Ethiopian Conflict, 1934–1936," *Journal of Negro History* 63, no. 2 (1978): 129–30. Scott addresses the role of the black press in informing African Americans about the conflict and, in some cases, prefiguring left-wing newspapers' more direct participation in hostilities through their editorial urgings for volunteers to travel to the war and join in to defend the beleaguered nation (128). In the booklet he planned to publish on Spain, Hughes intended to include a chapter explicitly comparing Spain and Ethiopia, both victims of international fascism (Rampersad, *Life*, 351).

22. Hughes, "Hughes Finds Moors," 3.

23. Ibid., 1.

24. Ibid.

25. Hughes, "Laughter in Madrid," in *Good Morning Revolution: Uncollected Writings of Langston Hughes*, ed. Faith Berry (New York: Citadel, 1991), 119; originally published in *Nation*, January 1938.

26. Hughes, "Air Raid: Barcelona," *Esquire* (October 1938), 207.

27. Hughes, "Negroes in Spain," in *Good Morning Revolution: Uncollected Writings of Langston Hughes*, ed. Faith Berry, (New York: Citadel, 1991), 106; originally published in *Volunteer for Liberty*, September 1937.

28. Hughes, "A Letter from Spain Addressed to Alabama," in *The Collected Poems of Langston Hughes*, ed., Arnold Rampersad (New York: Vintage, 1994), 201; originally published in *Volunteer for Liberty*, November 1937.

29. In his autobiography, *I Wonder as I Wander*, Hughes recalls that when he read "A Letter from Spain" for a group of soldiers at the front, some "objected to the lack of correct grammar and the slightly broken English. They said that many of their Negro comrades in arms were well educated; furthermore, I might mistakenly be aiding in perpetuating a stereotype" (378). Hughes's response makes clear the rhetorical aim of the poems' form. He explicitly compares blacks from the American South to the North Africans and argues that "A Letter" demonstrates that "even the least privileged of Americans, the Southern Negroes, were represented in the International Brigades, fighting on the side of the Spanish peasants and workers to help them preserve a government that would give peasants and workers—as were most Negroes, too—a chance at schools and the learning of grammar." See Hughes, *I Wonder as I Wander* (1956; New York: Hill and Wang, 1964), 378.

30. Robin D. G. Kelley, "'This Ain't Ethiopia, But It'll Do,'" in *African-Americans in the Spanish Civil War*, ed. Danny Duncan Collum, (New York: G K. Hall, 1992), 18.

31. On the Black press and its relationship with the Left, see Patrick S. Washburn, *A Question of Sedition: The Federal Government's Investigation of the Black Press During World War II* (New York: Oxford University Press, 1986), especially chapter 2, "The Negro is Seeing Red: 1917–1941," 11–41. Works on individual editors of African-American newspapers also include information on the "black-red" nexus as it manifests itself in the black press. See, for example, Andrew Buni, *Robert L. Vann of the "Pittsburgh Courier"* (Pittsburgh: University of Pittsburgh Press, 1974) and Roi Ottley, *The Lonely Warrior: The Life and Times of Robert S. Abbott* (Chicago: Henry Regnery, 1955).

32. Dan Carter, *Scottsboro: A Tragedy of the American South* (Baton Rouge: Louisiana State University Press, 1979).

33. Lawrence Hogan, *A Black National News Service: The Associated Negro Press and Claude Barnett, 1919–1945* (Cranbury, N. J.: Associated University Presses, 1984), 120.

34. Rampersad, *Life*, 339.

35. Hogan, *Black National News Service*, 120.

36. *Norfolk Journal and Guide*, 4 December 1937, 1.

37. William Pickens, "What I Saw in Spain," *The Crisis* 45, no. 10 (October 1938), 22.

38. "Abe Lincoln Battalion Leader Killed in Spain," *Pittsburgh Courier*, 24 July 1937, 1.

39. On Donowa's departure, see "To Aid Spain," *Pittsburgh Courier*, 31 July 1937, "To Aid Spain," *Atlanta Daily World*, 23 July 1937, "Loyal Doctor Goes to Spain," *Amsterdam News*, 24 July 1937; on his wounding, see "Dr Arnold Donowa, Former Dean at Howard University, Shot in Spain," *Pittsburgh Courier*, 30 October 1937; Rolfe's article, "Ex-Howard Dean at Spanish Front," *Baltimore Afro-American*, 1 October 1937, is one of the few cases in which a white writer comments on events in Spain on the pages of an African-American newspaper. Rolfe also wrote on Donowa for the Communist Party's newspaper, the *Daily Worker*. See his "American Negro Surgeon at Spanish Front Appeals for Medical Supplies for Loyalists," *Daily Worker*, 23 September 1938, 4.

40. Richard Wright, "American Negroes in Key Posts of Spain's Loyalist Forces," *Daily Worker*, 20 September 1937, 2.
41. Ibid.
42. "Spanish Reds Offer Independence to Moors: 'We Fight for Our Liberty and Yours' Says Leaflet: Proclamation Issued in Arabic," *Chicago Defender*, 13 February 1937.
43. "Moors Refuse to Fight in Spanish War," *Atlanta Daily World*, 23 July 1938.
44. Hughes, "Too Much of Race," *Volunteer for Liberty*, August 1937, 3–4.
45. Ibid.

Part IV

World War II and Postwar America

Chapter 9   "Kin in Some Way"

C. K. DORESKI

The Chicago Defender Reads the Japanese Internment, 1942–1945

Racial discrimination in any form and in any degree has no justifiable part whatever in our democratic way of life. It is unattractive in any setting but it is utterly revolting among a free people who have embraced the principles set forth in the Constitution of the United States. All residents of this nation are kin in some way by blood or culture to a foreign land. Yet they are primarily and necessarily a part of the new and distinct civilization of the United States. They must accordingly be treated at all times as the heirs of the American experiment and as entitled to all the rights and freedoms guaranteed by the Constitution. . . . There is no higher title in America than that of "citizen."

    —JUSTICE FRANK MURPHY, dissenting opinion, *Korematsu v. United States* (18 December 1944; 323 U.S. 214)[1]

THROUGHOUT THE SECOND WORLD WAR, few newspapers captured the national character or the racialized strangeness of America's war on its citizens better than John Sengstacke's *Chicago Defender*, the preeminent African-American weekly. While white dailies, Pathé, Movietone, and March of Time newsreels, and civil defense films featured such patriotic and public home-front activities as Victory gardens, scrap metal drives, and civil defense drills, the *Defender* every week, in critique of the dailies, exhorted readers to the only civil action that would guarantee America's international success: defeat of foreign *and* domestic fascism.[2]

An instigator of black America's migration from the rural South to northern industrial cities, in the wake of the Great War, founding editor Robert Abbott had committed the *Defender* to the destruction of race prejudice and full enfranchisement for all American citizens. Though aggressively nativist—stressing black America's natal rights— the paper could be counted on to consider if not investigate domestic fascism on all fronts. And so readers familiar with the paper's early years should not be surprised by Sengstacke's interest in the government's wartime abridgements of civil rights whether at the federal, state, or local level.

The geopolitical realignment of the paper's wartime editorial pages reflected more than Sengstacke's national ambition or the paper's na-tional readership: it marked a radical departure from the racial and geographical binary oppositions—black and white, North and South— associated with Robert Abbott's founding "platform." As agent and ben-eficiary of black America's first great migration, the *Defender*'s corridor of influence had followed the tracks of the Illinois Central Railroad as its features, columns, and regional news linked the industrial North of the migrants to the rural South of their families. By 1942, a second war-time migration was under way, this time to the West and Northwest. Encouraged in part by the "evacuation" and "relocation" of more than 110,000 Japanese and Japanese Americans from "military exclusion zones," African Americans joined the migration west, making Califor-nia the "nation's new racial frontier."[3] Geographically or racially dis-tanced from the social and legal oppression of Japanese and Mexicans, *Defender* columnists pondered a new wartime calculus of cultural and political authority, derived from the coupling of the concepts of "mi-nority" and "alien," "migrant" and "immigrant."

The *Defender*'s sporadic narrative—usually developed through opin-ion columns or editorials rather than dispatches—of the evacuation, relocation, and internment of the Pacific Coast Japanese cultivated in its readers an unexpected and uneven solidarity with a "foreign" popu-lation. Typically the West Coast black weeklies read into the intern-ment of "aliens" an opportunity for African-American migrants to secure employment and homes in the West; even John Robert Badger, the *Defender*'s West Coast correspondent who was himself black, initially saw the incarceration of the "disloyal" as a chance to demonstrate the loyalty of America's native citizens. His reliance on unsubstantiated sources suggests the difficulties inherent in wartime reporting during periods of intense propaganda and censorship. Even the most aggressive investigative reporters, encountering silence "for the duration," relied upon the appearance of emotional truth in the policies and actions witnessed and reported upon. Under such circumstances, "informed" journalism bore more than the usual personal inflection as reporters carried their beliefs into the field. Yet it readily superimposed a collective negative identity upon minorities. Still, the familiarly racist rhetoric employed by General John L. DeWitt (commanding officer of the Western Defense Command who oversaw the evacuation) had a cumulative effect on black readers coast to coast. His capsulization of the "Jap Problem"—"A Jap's a Jap"—made headline news in the white dailies and even some of the West Coast black weeklies, startling readers into wartime readiness and racially self-conscious fear.[4] His rationale for this racial demonization would, in the end, produce suspicion and anger in the majority of African-American readers as well as among the staff of the *Defender*. As DeWitt justified the federally instigated and state supported evacuation as a wartime measure predicated upon racial realities: "In the war in which we are now engaged racial affinities are not severed by migration. The Japanese race is an enemy race and while many second and third generation Japanese born on United States soil, possessed of United States citizenship, have become 'Americanized,' the racial strains are undiluted."[5] For readers of the black press, such formulaic pronouncements recalled the racialized rhetoric of the South and intensified perceptions of the ever-contingent citizenship status for America's citizens of color. This understanding, especially when expressed through the politically maturing voices of the *Defender's* columnists, would over the course of the war render the Japanese "kin in some way" to many African Americans.[6]

The story of how the mediational structures within a regional black weekly nationalized and then globalized the civil death implicit in America's internment policy began a year before America's entry into the war, with Franklin Roosevelt's grandiose reiteration of American democratic aspirations. In January 1941, in his State of the Union address, President Roosevelt pledged an Allied victory contingent upon domestic sacrifice and a cohesive home front dedicated to the Atlantic

Charter and his "Four Freedoms."[7] "Since the beginning of our American history," the president stressed in his annual message, "we have been engaged in . . . a revolution which goes on steadily, quietly adjusting itself to changing conditions—without the concentration camp or the quick-lime in the ditch."[8] Wielding the power of the state, buttressed by the philosophical abstractions of the nation, Roosevelt sought to prepare the country for war by asking citizens to rededicate themselves to the nation's foundational ideals. Yet the very next year he would employ the authority of his office to deny "anomalous" citizens their constitutional rights and freedoms by empowering the military to create exclusionary zones "from which any and all persons may be excluded."[9] Though Executive Order #9066, signed 19 February 1942, was neither ethnically nor racially specific, in spirit if not letter it targeted all inhabitants of Japanese ancestry—alien residents (issei) as well as citizens (nisei)—on the West Coast. The order, though federal in origin, was the culmination of and response to an entrenched anti-Japanese sentiment led by such nativist organizations as the American Legion, the Native Sons of the Golden West, and the California Joint Immigration Committee. Weeks before the "evacuation" and "relocation" order had been signed, upon declaration of war, citizens of enemy nations were declared "enemy aliens," their assets frozen, travel restricted, and publication of foreign language newspapers either suspended or terminated.[10] Nisei soldiers not immediately relocated or discharged were reclassified 4–C, "unfit for service because of ancestry."[11]

On 20 December 1941, just weeks after the Japanese attack on Pearl Harbor, the *Defender*'s lead editorial presumed national authority to address the "moral force" of the black press "against such ultra violences as lynching, burning at stake, and judicial murder."[12] Champion of "national unity" and "working democracy"—reciprocal discourses in which democracy is an actuality not an ideal—Sengstacke contended that "opposition" was the "essence of loyalty and devotion to democracy—and a free press."[13] Weekly denunciations of lynching, poll taxes, and segregation in the military and the blood banks were soon joined by columns noting analogies between the South's "states' rights" subjugation of blacks and the West's federally sanctioned internment of the Japanese. While this second front on domestic fascism earned the paper a "no-pledge" rating from a Justice Department anxious for a contention-free home front, it intensified, what W.E.B. Du Bois would call by war's end, "the mounting pressure of popular demand for democratic methods"—a demand that increased circulation and secured the paper's national status.[14]

On 21 November 1942, the *Defender* announced that "FIVE NEW COLUMNISTS" would join staff regulars Lucius C. Harper, executive editor and columnist ("Dustin' Off the News"), Enoc P. Waters, Jr., city editor ("One Man's Journal"), and "Charley Cherokee" ("National Grapevine" from Washington, D.C.);[15] Walter White, secretary of the NAACP ("People, Politics, and Places" from New York); Langston Hughes ("Here to Yonder" from Harlem); Dr. U. G. Dailey, surgeon and professor at Northwestern University ("Until the Doctor Comes" from Chicago); S. I. Hayakawa, professor of semantics at the Illinois Institute of Technology ("Second Thoughts" from Chicago); and John Robert Badger, African-American correspondent on foreign affairs ("World View" from the West Coast).[16] Interspersed with Jay Jackson's serial comics and political and domestic cartoons, these columns regraphed race, nation, and ethnicity on a cross-cultural grid of citizenship and identity.

Ethnically, racially, and geographically diverse, these columnists registered the cultural and political instability of home-front democracy; united behind the paper's race platform, they were fighting partisans in the national struggle for civil rights. Langston Hughes and S. I. Hayakawa, born into jointed predications of racialized national identity, initiated their columns with routine inquiries into the political, social, and cultural authorities that relegate the subordinate populations of America. Each saw the "American" as a product of sedimentation, "Americanization" a mechanism by which the strata of race, ethnicity, and national origin conglomerate into the translational (and often transnational) structures of citizenship. In 1941, shortly before joining the *Defender*, Hughes had confounded the Selective Service by categorizing himself as "mixed blood white Negro Indian,"[17] and Hayakawa had challenged readers of *Language in Action* with the creative heterogeneity of his status as Japanese by race, Canadian by nationality, American in essence.[18] Hayakawa, however, unlike Hughes, would not always write with a full understanding of the implications of his own background.

Whether emigrant or immigrant, evacuee or internee, the subjects of these interlocking opinion pieces taxed the conceptual and expressive reserves of the columnists. Linkage between foreign and domestic fronts was absolute, for as Hughes noted in the "why and wherefore" of his column, "Things that happen away off yonder affect us here. . . . Hitler is about to freeze your salary or your work, although his activities at the moment are centered around Stalingrad. But it is not so far from here to yonder."[19] Hayakawa's first column established the political intensity of the logocentrism that would follow: maturity of expression corresponded to sophistication of ideas. When Hayakawa, anxious to move beyond the heated and corrupt journalism of the Hearst syndicate, asked his prospective editor whether he might challenge his readers, Metz Lochard responded: "What do you think we're hiring you for if not to say something?"[20]

In the waning weeks of 1942, as the long year of the "resettlement" initiated by Executive Order #9066 drew to a close, while John Robert Badger pondered black contributions to the Allied forces in North Africa,[21] Hayakawa and Hughes rejected the credo of racial superiority and consequent economic and social tyranny of the majority population. In a rare self-reference as minority, Hayakawa offered the earliest opinion on the "mighty" and "not-so-mighty" that resulted in the internment:[22] "When minorities, whether Negroes, or Jews, or Mexicans, or Pacific Coast Japanese-Americans, or anybody else, are discriminated against, they are the victims of the two-year-old mentalities in the majority culture. Haven't we, who are members of minorities, got troubles enough without making even more trouble for ourselves for acting like two-year-olds towards each other?"[23] Hayakawa returned often to the racialized ignorance of Americans in general—even black Americans. He noted in a column devoted to anti-Semitism among blacks: "When will people understand that racial prejudice is of one piece, and that in perpetuating one kind of prejudice they are perpetuating all other kinds at the same time?"[24]

Badger, the paper's "authoritative West Coast writer on foreign affairs," broke new ground in the *Defender*'s assessment of the "evacuation" and "relocation." He read "citizenship" as a collective and political identity subject to documented "loyalty," and his column anticipated Morton Grodzins's postwar discussion of the "making of Un-Americans."

Badger interrogates the government's war on its citizens, considers their Japanese culture and history, and finds them demonstrably "disloyal."[25] In a chance example of what Hayakawa termed the "two-valued orientation of propaganda," Badger exploits the authority of witness and the weight of testimony to sanction the government's evacuation and relocation.[26] Prompted by the nisei draft and a loyalty screen of internees,[27] "Tagore Addresses Japan" (6 March 1943), unwittingly assumes the posture of the War Relocation Authority (WRA) in its propagandistic assertions of disloyalty on the part of Japanese Americans. Seeing the induction of "loyal Japanese-Americans" as an "important stroke for democracy," Badger sympathizes: "It was unfortunate that the presence of pro-Fascist and traitorous elements among the Japanese-Americans rendered their evacuation from the Pacific Coast a military necessity. But a necessity it was, and few loyal Japanese-Americans will deny the wisdom of it." At once journalistic and jingoistic, Badger's column, as it unfolds in successive revelations, reveals his allegiance to the occupation mentality of the West Coast. He cannot resist the WRA's influence upon the promotional nature of his rhetorical excess: "Now that the evacuation has been achieved and our defensive power in the Pacific restored, whatever can be done to integrate these Japanese-Americans into the national community will improve the people's morale and rebuff the Fascist regime of Premier Hideki Tojo." Though Badger concedes that "loyal Japanese-Americans could answer Tojo now" and comprehends that Americans must "eventually" understand the consequence of their attitudes "toward colonial peoples, toward colored peoples in general, toward Japanese-Americans as well," he ignores or is not fully aware of the contexts fundamental to the organized federal campaign.

Paradoxically, because of the military-political origins of the evacuation and relocation, Badger, the West Coast reporter, was perhaps less skeptical than his geopolitically removed colleagues in Chicago, New York, or Washington, D.C. His credulity may be measured by his misprision of a document received third-hand that with each successive remove grows more enigmatic, less translatable. Badger claims Isamu Noguchi, the "proud, sensitive, extraordinarily intelligent, kind and courageous" sculptor, to be his confidant. He keys his evidence—Noguchi's decision to leave "some money, many connections" in New York City and "go with the other Japanese-Americans to the evacuation camps"[28] —to testimony of uncertain provenance and complex significance. Explaining the crucial timing, Badger reveals : "Before he left, Isamu gave me a copy of a letter written to his father [the poet Yoné Noguchi], who lived in Japan, by the great Indian poet, Rabindranath Tagore. . . . Isamu wanted me to use it as ammunition against Tojo's 'Asia for Asiatics' slogan." Sensing a scoop for "World View" readers, Badger heralds Tagore's charges of Japanese "atrocities" against the Chinese and "warmonger" crimes against humanity. Lacking information about cultural settings or relational chronology,[29] readers of Badger's essay must discriminate between "witness" (firsthand report) and "testimony" (the Tagore letter) thus discerning their applicability to the current war and the internment.

Throughout the spring and summer, the *Defender* headlined "race riots" at West Coast shipyards that would spread across the country to military installations and "defense zones." "Alien" sabotage and disloyalty—fears reserved for the now-incarcerated Japanese were displaced to the Mexican populations of Los Angeles—were the persistent subtexts of signed and unsigned opinion pieces.[30] And yet, even as West Coast "foreign" anxieties became news and opinion at the *Defender*, its columnists and editors redoubled efforts to clarify the language and articulation of racism. Such columns as Hayakawa's "Human Grade-Labelling" (17 April 1943)—in which he considers the "bitter end" of "'master race' theory"—or Hughes's "America After the War" (22 May 1943)—a time and place when "American citizens of Japanese parentage will be released from their concentration camps. . . . Mexicans, in the Southwest, will receive the same courtesy in public places . . . as do any other citizens. Color won't matter any more"—displayed (what Holocaust studies often call) the "split witnessing" of America's partitioned citizenship. From the multiple fronts and frontiers of a democracy at war, *Defender* correspondents with increasing frequency acknowledged the linkage between "words" and "offense," "bigotry" and "policy."

The relocation "out yonder" had impressed many citizens as reprehensible, but it took the zoot-suit riot in Los Angeles to convince midwestern readers that West Coast racial turmoil was too close to ignore.[31] For the week following 3 June 1943, "servicemen" (military enlisted personnel on leave, Los Angeles police officers, and neighborhood

Anglos) and "pachucos" (Mexican Americans) enacted an increasingly violent drama of loyalty and disloyalty. As the relocation had collapsed "race" and "national origin" into the suspect category of "racial origin," so the riot fused "alien" and "colored"[32]—supporting Chester Himes's immediate impression that "zoot riots are race riots."[33]

Within a week of the riots, Hughes resurveyed American race prejudice. "Key Chains with No Keys" (19 June 1943) revises the war, as conclusively as Du Bois would, into a contest of "color and democracy"; the zoot-suit rioting is merely the catalyst for this review:

> Mobs are strangely illogical—just as race prejudice is illogical. When the government started evacuating Japanese to concentration camps, they didn't evacuate just Japanese enemy-aliens, but American citizens of Japanese descent as well. Why the government left in peace the Italians and Germans—naturalized and unnaturalized—I will never know, since we are at war with Italy and Germany, too.
>
> From the saffron-skinned Japanese-American citizens of Los Angeles to brown-skinned Mexican-American citizens is only a step. Of course, the Mexican government is our ally—but unfortunately, the Mexicans are an Indian-brown people. From the brown Mexicans to the vari-colored Negroes is only a step, too. Of course, we Negroes are pure Americans, here several generations, but still the wrong color.

Like Badger's earlier column on the relocation, Hughes's column on the riot identifies insurrections on the home front with global dislocations and struggles. But where Badger accepted federal accusations of disloyalty on the part of the "foreign" Japanese, Hughes, particularly in the wake of the riot and in anticipation of the Supreme Court's decision of *Hirabayashi v. United States*,[34] perceived the illogic of the mob psychology in the actions of the WRA and the LAPD at national and local levels. The reiteration of "citizen" in counterpoint to modifiers of loyalty ("enemy-aliens" or "naturalized and unnaturalized") and of color ("saffron-skinned," "brown-skinned," "Indian-brown," "vari-colored Negroes") signifies the ways in which the war had become an increasingly global struggle for persons of color while emphasizing the bitter irony for blacks who are "pure Americans."

The civil implications of names and racialized identities increasingly dominate *Defender* columns as the "human grade-labelling" that Hayakawa had feared earlier in the year became the mode of choice for the majority of white dailies. For Hughes, it was a streetcar row between "two pure Americans" (one of whom takes exception to the other speaking in a "foreign tongue") that occasions further consideration of language, citizenship, and rights. In "Get Together, Minorities" (17 July 1943), written the month following the Detroit riot (20–21 June 1943), Hughes meditates upon the ways "riots against . . . Mexicans put in the 'pure American's' head the idea to start bawling a strange man out about his language in a street car." Dubious that his own "pure American, though colored" status would spare him Jim Crow treatment from the "foreign born and second-generation Americans," Hughes concedes a necessity for the duration of the war: "with the 'pure Americans' getting so tough about things, for our own protection, it would be good if the foreign-born, the Jews, the Mexicans, and the Negroes all formed some sort of protective unity—before we get our collective heads beat for not being 'pure American.'" Though excluded from this particular catalogue, the Japanese remain the unarticulated "minority vs. minority" population.[35]

Hayakawa discerns the juvenile discontent of the pachuco culture in the sartorial extremes of the zoot suit: "Their clothes are a strange but understandable expression of their discontent with the meaninglessness of slum life" (19 June 1943). He indicts city officials who relinquished juvenile mob control to the mob. More poignant perhaps is his reflection upon the semiotics of the suit itself, glamorized in the pages of all black weeklies: "The zoot suit is not to be regarded just as an extreme fashion or a crazy idea kids get. The zoot suit is a symbol of the youthful rebellion against slum life. It is the symbol of the dash and glory that these young people would like to have but cannot get. . . . That is why Italian slum children in New York, Mexican kids in Los Angeles, Negro youths in practically all large cities go in for zoot suits."[36] Even some relocation camps, in the wake of the riot, acknowledged the zoot suit as a signal of defiance. The week of 12 June 1943, nisei cartoonist Bennie Nobori, recently transferred from the Topaz Relocation Center in Utah (where he was known for the cartoon "Jänkee") to the Heart Mountain Relocation Center in Wyoming, inaugurated "Zöotsüo," a five-panel serial cartoon detailing the zoot-suit-clad title character's rebellious adventures at camp.

Toward the end of the second full year of the war, Hughes concluded that America's political and spiritual leadership in the postwar world depended on its treatment of citizens of color. Reflecting upon the year's national tide of civil insurrection, "The Snake Is in the House" (16 October 1943) maintains the dangers of a domestic fascism that is immediate and local, while potentially global in its effect: "The same American that for generations has mistreated the Negro, lynched him, Jim Crowed him physically, humiliated him spiritually, packed up all the West Coast Japanese citizens (I didn't say aliens—I said citizens) and put them into concentration camps. Lately Los Angeles has started in a big way on the Mexicans. Anti-Semitism is growing. The racist idea spreads." Challenging "Americans of good will . . . the well-meaning liberals, the good-hearted souls who wouldn't lynch anyone," Hughes obligated the majority to act as agents of justice for all citizens. Few federal initiatives captured Hughes's "racist idea" better than the Selective Service's loyal registration and draft campaign in the relocation centers.

The government's attempt to draft an all-nisei unit—what many within the camps (in several of the camp newspapers) derisively called a "Jap-Crow" unit—as well as identify and segregate the "disloyal" among the internees had dramatically increased social tensions within the camps, and generationally within families. The loyalty questionnaire—"Statement of United States Citizenship of Japanese Ancestry" (Selective Service Form 304A)—produced anxiety through its specificity of claim as well as its vagary of consequence. The key loyalty questions came at the end:

No. 27. Are you willing to serve in the armed forces of the United States on combat duty wherever ordered?

No. 28. Will you swear unqualified allegiance to the United States of America and faithfully defend the United States from any or all attack by foreign or domestic forces, and forswear any form of allegiance or obedience to the Japanese emperor, to any other foreign government, power or organization?[37]

For the issei, Japanese nationals, allegiance to the United States—the country that had refused them citizenship—required renunciation of loyalty to Japan, the country of their citizenship. For the nisei, as citizens of America *and* Japan, service in the military dictated more than fidelity to the nation that had betrayed them; it forced separation from family members who might well be repatriated for "disloyalty" to Japan. Tule Lake registered what the government perceived to be the highest concentration of dangerous aliens (42 percent answering "no" on the loyalty question), securing its future as a high-security segregation center. For the remainder of the war, "Tule Lake" encoded the "loyalty issue" for journalists, politicians, and internees alike.[38]

In "American Vansittartism" (20 November 1943),[39] Badger dismisses the "recent press furor over the disturbances among the disloyal Japanese-Americans at Tule Lake." His prior commitment to the federal policy of internment allowed him to read the transformation of Tule Lake as both a further vindication of government policy and a testimonial to the "loyalty and patriotism of the majority of Japanese-Americans, who helped U.S. authorities ferret out the Tojo agents and members of the Black Dragon society." Anxious to promote the relative sophistication of the black weeklies, Badger used the "furor" to condemn the Hearst syndicate dailies for "drag[ging] back on page one . . . lurid yellow 'dispatches'" as well as the "hullabaloo over the Tule Lake affair and the revival of hate-inspiring stories about the Japanese people." By spring, the release of internees to work or school in cities like Chicago further domesticated Badger's West Coast "aliens" into the neighbors and employees commended by Hughes in "At Long Last, Thanks" (19 March 1944). In unexpected roles, native black Americans experience the American-ness of the Japanese in their employ. Teasing the significations of "colored" and "folk," reversing the syntax of modifiers for emphasis ("*American*-Japanese"), the column introduces and reviews the new America resulting from the migrations, forced and elective, of the war: "At last, colored people have found in midwestern cities, folks who work for them courteously, efficiently, and willingly. Who are they? Well, in case you don't know, they are Japanese. In Chicago, Cleveland, and Detroit of late I have come across colored offices and homes having in their employ American-Japanese citizens who are proving most satisfactory . . . a good thing for the Japanese and the Negroes." Nationalizing the force of discrimination—"White America put the Japanese Americans, early in this war, in concentration camps"—

relieves Hughes of the need to particularize judgments regarding initial government policies. What interests him here is the potential analogy between regional hostility toward African Americans and Japanese Americans. Like Chicago's black migrants, the Japanese immigrants hope they have come to a land of opportunity. No longer the "disloyal" abstractions of Badger's "authoritative" columns, these citizens add to the cadre of color that Hughes imagines will build the postwar world:

> American-born Japanese are Americans, but that did not keep them from being locked up in concentration camps. American-born Negroes are Americans, too, but that does not keep them from being locked into the restricted-covenant ghettoes of our big cities, forced into Jim Crow cars. . . .
> What has happened lately to the American Japanese and what has happened all along to us, puts American Negroes and American Japanese in the same boat.[40]

Hughes's equation of citizenry relies upon a barely tested associational state of equilibrium among migrant populations—new and old—in Chicago, pointing (as his columns often would) to the unrealized potential of American democracy.

The cases of Fred T. Korematsu (*Korematsu v. United States*) and Mitsuye Endo (*Ex parte Endo*)—deliberated by the Supreme Court in October and decided in December—prompted a *Defender* editorial on "The Bill of Rights and Japanese-Americans" (22 April 1944) that was at once case particular and a summary of the entire relocation saga. Identifying the "interest" and "apprehension" of its readers, the editorial charges the "direct violation of the Bill of Rights" as it distinguishes between the cases—the Korematsu case questioning "whether or not the constitutional rights of Americans of Japanese descent have been violated," the Endo case examining (in the words of the *Washington Post* summary) whether the government may "'confine persons not suspected of any crime or intention to harm the United States'"—and concludes that:

> The entire program of "evacuation" and "relocation" to which Japanese-Americans have been subjected is the result of pure racialism, fanned to white heat by the Hearst press and California vigilantism . . . [and concurs with] The *Washington Post*'s

> suggestion that the relocation centers be changed from "places
> of detention" to "temporary shelters" to be used by evacuees
> "on a wholly voluntary basis."

Linkage to black America's fate follows Hughes's precedent as the editors, in a spectacular conflation of race and nationality, question the
potential significance of the court decisions: Would unfavorable decisions "mean that if the United States were at war with Liberia, all
Americans of Negro descent would also have to be detained in 'relocation centers?'"

More than two years into the relocation, as *Korematsu v. United
States* (323 U.S. 214 [1944]) and *Ex parte Endo* (323 U.S. 283 [1944])
were being argued before the Supreme Court, Hayakawa finally committed a column (rather than an aside) to the relocation.[41] "Japanese-
Americans in Wartime" (28 October 1944) begins as an interrupted but
essentially known serial that has gained currency in the courts: "You
all know the story by now of the Japanese-Americans during this war:
how they were uprooted from their homes, citizens and non-citizens
alike, how they were moved off the Pacific Coast into assembly centers farther inland, and later how relocation centers were put up for
them in desert regions of Arkansas, Arizona, Utah, Wyoming, and Colo-
rado." Yet his pretense of concern fades quickly into conjugate digres-
sions: "let us leave aside . . . the grave issue of the constitutionality . . .
let us leave aside too the value of this entire relocation to the Japanese
propagandists."[42] Acceding to the hegemony and authority of the
WRA's "civil servants," Hayakawa subordinates the internees into a
"shocked and bewildered populace, bitterly resentful of the doubts cast
upon their loyalty." Employing the rhetoric long familiar to readers—
black and white—of Chicago dailies covering earlier clashes between
Irish immigrants and black migrants, he ignores language's informative
and affective connotations—essential to his semantic theories expressed
in *Language in Action* as he familiarizes the "foreign" Japanese into the
residential Irish: "My own feeling is that it was a lucky thing that, if
they [WRA officials] had relocated anybody, they picked the Japanese.
If they had tried to relocate, for example, Irishmen I am sure there would
have been mass rioting. Japanese are, especially in matters pertaining
to government, surprisingly docile." Hayakawa notes that the blind paci-
fication of the Japanese into ungrateful objects subjugated by the fed-

eral authorities, within and without the centers themselves, failed to prevent "thousands of evacuees [from overcoming] their resentment and [looking] upon WRA as their best friend." Though correctly attributing external complications to those who play "upon race prejudice"— Martin Dies, chair of HUAC, and the Hearst dailies with their "pictures and sensational editorials"—he neglects to upbraid fellow *Defender* columnist Badger for his repeated assertions of disloyalty among the Japanese. Throughout his column Hayakawa denies the Japanese subject positions—that is, capable of deciding to pursue education or reemployment—and infantilizes them into objects manipulated by the good offices of the WRA and JACL.

Seemingly a more benign column, "Race-Consciousness in Relocation Camps" (11 November 1944) nonetheless continues to perpetuate virtuous stereotypes of the WRA staff—the "Caucasian" teachers, "good teachers . . . [who have] develop[ed] profound affection for their students"—as well as the internees—"the brightness of the children, the politeness and charm of the parents, the patient good nature of the older people." This catalogue of virtues fails to admit perspectives from the bereft, cynical, embittered, and broken victims of mass prejudice. Ebulliently, Hayakawa advances the WRA educators, strengthened by their "special task" (indoctrination?) to train students to deal with prejudice, as the hope for African-American schools because "they have had the experience of preparing their students for the contradictions within our democracy." This autoexemptive pretext, through which Hayakawa seems unable to imagine himself as evacuee or victim of prejudice, assumes the authority of the state and offers nothing to the embattled citizen. His disregard for his peculiar and particular peripheral status— noncitizen Japanese Canadian—underwrites his opinionated overview of the plights of Japanese Americans and African Americans.

Hayakawa cultivates this coextensive racialized drama in his review of Carey McWilliams's *Prejudice: Japanese-Americans, Symbol of Intolerance*, a consideration informed by Gunnar Myrdal's *An American Dilemma: The Negro Problem and American Democracy* (1944).[43] "Negroes and Japanese" (16 December 1944), noting the pervasive ignorance many "east of California" whites had about the relocation, examines the widespread awareness of many black Americans that the "Japanese-Americans were being driven out because of their 'race.'" These anecdotes from Japanese who have resettled in Chicago and "found their first friends in the outside world among Negroes" find little correspondence in the black weeklies on the West Coast. Even Badger's on-the-scene dispatches for the *Defender* insist that cultural traits be read as racial traits. Hayakawa, withdrawing from racial categories of authorship (writing *as* Japanese Canadian) and audience (writing *for* a black readership), concludes that "this is as it should be. Not enough Negroes and not enough Japanese-Americans realize the extent to which they are in the same boat." In a sketchy and misrepresentative overview of *Prejudice*, he telescopes a complex argument (that is at once sectional and national) into "international diplomacy in the Far East and in Europe constantly being upset by California racism." McWilliams explains in some detail the ways in which the anti-Japanese sentiment in California "represented an affirmative national, not sectional, vote."[44]

A less avuncular and more insightful Hayakawa reconsiders McWilliams's thesis the week following the Supreme Court's ruling in *Korematsu v. United States*.[45] "Anatomy of Racism" (23 December 1944) reviews the military's specious arguments of sabotage on the West Coast, emphasizing McWilliams's point that "the Japanese Government, very sensibly, did not employ Japanese-Americans for espionage . . . [because] the Japanese . . . often suspect them of being 'American spies.'" Of particular note to *Defender* readers is the generalizing force of Hayakawa's summary: "Perhaps the most impressive fact about the entire evacuation story is that almost one year after all the Japanese had been expelled so that California no longer had any 'Japanese problem,' the anti-Japanese agitation burst out with greater virulence than had ever been known before."

The intensity of anti-Japanese sentiment grew unabated on the "Jap-free" West Coast. Walter White, breaking his long silence on the issue, devoted his weekly column to an Associated Press dispatch from Oregon and its implications for national race relations. In "Anti-Japanese Prejudice" (13 January 1945), White relays the wire story of 2 December 1944: the Hood River American Legion Post erased the names of "16 Americans of Jap ancestry" and "would attempt to have excluded from the Hood River Valley all persons of Jap ancestry."[46] White reads the "news item" against a tide of testimony from China, India, and Burma—"and other Far East countries [that] were increasingly turning toward Russia because of distrust of Great Britain and the United States with their 'white uber alles' policies." Beyond the incalculable propagandistic value of such actions, White reckons the cost in morale: "What must be the state of mind of loyal American soldiers of Japanese ancestry mired deep in foxholes in Europe and the Pacific as they read that even the transitory glory of having their names appear on a wooden war memorial in a hick town shall be denied them. A town, incidentally, located in a valley whose richness was in large measure created by incredible industry and frugality of their own people." Though unexplored in the column, bigotry and provinciality effect the debasement of "home town"—shared by each name on the memorial—to the "hick town" of the provincial Legion.

In "'Most Sweeping and Complete Deprivations'" (10 February 1945) Hayakawa considers Justice Frank Murphy's dissenting opinion in *Korematsu v. United States*. The column highlights Justice Murphy's recognition of "obvious racial discrimination" against "the heirs of the American experiment [who are] entitled to all the rights and freedom guaranteed by the Constitution." Having skirted the relocation issue for years, Hayakawa now speaks as a partisan by chiding the black press for "commenting comparatively little on the outcome of the Endo and Korematsu cases."[47]

As Hughes had in the aftermath of the zoot-suit riot, Hayakawa revisits the dialectic of color and democracy in America. "Spanish-Speaking Americans" (14 April 1945), appearing two days after President Roosevelt's death, conjectures that the deepening prejudice against Mexican Americans is an extension of racialized prejudice throughout the nation. The awkward deference of Denver's "polite people"—who refer to Mexicans as "Spanish-speaking Americans"—reveals the perceptual dislocation evident in reading cultural and social status in America. Noting the "actual reason . . . for this awkward and inaccurate expression is the fact that prejudice against Mexicans has been so intense that the word 'Mexican' has come to sound more like a cussword than an ethnic designation." Behavior recalling that in Los Angeles—white gangs cruising the Latino sections of the city, "looking for people to beat up"—provokes the same disparity of treatment: "It is charged by Mexican youths . . . that when they are caught with weapons, they are 'given the works' by the police, but that when white youths

are caught, they are given a mild reprimand and sent home." Citing
the "desperately inadequate" recreational facilities for citizens of color—
"Mexicans, Negroes, and Japanese-Americans are excluded from many
commercially-operated places of amusement"—Hayakawa concludes
that "minorities must stand together and make a common cause with
the enlightened portion of the majority." Removed from the solidarity
of the minorities, he stands aloof as well from the thoughtful majority.

Two weeks after V–E Day (18 May 1945), with the world's attention drawn to the final act of the Pacific theater, Hayakawa reflected
upon the relocation experience and its broader, long-term significance
for America's citizens of color. "Back to the Pacific Coast" (2 June
1945)—occasioned by the gradual departure of Japanese-Americans
from internment camps "to their former homes" or, "having made satisfactory adjustments," to "Chicago, New York, Iowa, Ohio, Minnesota,
and other relatively civilized portions of the United States"—deliber-
ates upon the individual and societal impact of the federal policy of incarceration. Hayakawa retains the rhetorical passivity of his earlier
depictions of internees, describing a people "bogged down in indeci-
sion . . . rather old to be starting a new life in the unknown Middle-
west or East; the rest . . . too young." The cumulative effect of the
internment (with its attendant "institutional complex"), adverse judgments in the courts (in particular, the Hirabayashi and Korematsu decisions), and "terrorist attacks" on the property and produce of former
internees lead Hayakawa to conclude that "all minorities [are] in danger."

West Coast "leaders of the anti-evacuee bloc" believe the "Southern white man's 'ideas of white supremacy have solved the Negro
question' . . . and that 'deportation of Japanese-Americans to Japan is
a good idea because it would undoubtedly lead to like treatment for
other minorities within the United States.'" The stress that returning
Japanese-Americans add to the "housing problems of Negroes" is a consequence of the wartime history of southern migrants assuming tenancy
in Japanese neighborhoods vacated by the relocation. "Second
Thoughts" credits the Los Angeles weeklies and *Pacific Citizen* (official
publication of the Japanese American Citizens League) for standing "un-
compromisingly for the right (of evacuees) to return" without mention-
ing the complicity of the West Coast black press (in particular, the *Los
Angeles Sentinel*) in supporting (as Badger earlier had done) actions

against the "disloyal Japs" that created jobs and homes for the wartime migrants.

As the battle for Okinawa raged, the end of the war in sight,[48] the *Defender* read the terrorist activity against the Japanese returning to the West Coast against the race bias against black farm workers in Rockland County, New York. "The Plight of Japanese-Americans" (9 June 1945), reflecting upon racism as the sustaining antagonism of the country, forecasts that "racial strife is about to become rampant unless steps are taken to curb this trend . . . reflected in the antagonistic attitude toward Japanese-Americans on the West Coast." Though reiterating the federal position that the relocation was a military necessity, the editorial notes that the policy involved the "imposition of a terrible hardship" and dangerous precedent for citizens of color. Labor unions, American Legion posts, and agricultural business interests combined into a vigilantism that "use[d] racial difference as an instrument of exploitation." As the racialized demonization of Japan intensified in the remaining months of the war, the *Defender* feared that the "abominable acts committed by the Germans, including their unbelievable atrocities, will be forgotten"—as an ongoing war against America's citizens of color. As Simple would underscore the following month in Hughes's "This Snaggle-Tooth World" (28 July 1945): "I have been in this snaggle-tooth world a long time, and it look like to me white folks is mean as they ever was, if not meaner . . . it ain't right to Jim Crow me, neither is it right to Jim Crow the Japanese that live in America."

The *Defender*'s most curious reflections upon the compound identity politics of race and nation occur in Hayakawa's two columns, which straddle the bombings of Hiroshima and Nagasaki, on "how to deal with Japan when the fighting is over." "What to Do with Japan?" (4 August 1945) and "A Common Front Possible?" evince intimacy and ignorance predicated upon the authority (or lack thereof) of his Japanese name. Dismissing emperor worship as an "impossibly idiotic notion" and that of the state "equally idiotic," Hayakawa illustrates the centrality of the cultural and political beliefs embodied in the Constitution. Despite his war-long discussions of America's war against its citizens of African, Mexican, and Japanese descent, Hayakawa resorts to the hollow platform rhetoric of the imperial "we." Imagining Japan's difficulty in comprehending "the emotional significance of *our* more intellectualized symbols of political unity," he speculates that "if *we* in the United States were deprived by force of our Constitution, *we* might still reorganize our lives around other symbols" (emphasis added). Failing to examine the coextensive nature of foreign and domestic shortcomings of democracy, these columns pronounce upon without illuminating the citizenship crises for the Japanese, and for *Defender* readers as well. In a remarkable self-betrayal, Hayakawa counsels: "Let us, by all means, give democratic, equalitarian, and global-minded precepts to the Japanese. Let us encourage peasants and workers and intellectuals to emerge from their miserable condition and put an end to the raw deal they have been getting." Reasonable readers might question whether a country that had so compromised the "democratic" and "equalitarian" at home could possibly instruct postimperial Japan.

Three days after V–J Day (15 August 1945), the *Defender* devoted its primary editorial page to issues of race and the "atom bomb." "Splitting the Atom of Race Hate" (18 August 1945), its lead editorial, globalizes the critical mass of race and hatred that was at once the cause and enduring legacy of the war. The "frightful terror and devastation" unleashed by this multibillion dollar malignant "investment" prompts the war's conclusion but encourages a plea: "Truly in all the earth today, man has no more dangerous enemy than hate—hate of other men, whether it be for their race, their religion or their nationality. It should not stagger the imagination to picture thousands of social scientists and other experts financed by the same two billion dollars that went into the atomic bomb at work in America to isolate and destroy the venom of race hate."

By the end of the war, even Hughes's Simple was weary of interracialism, race relations, and human relations: the empty rhetoric of liberalism. "Simple and the Atom Bomb" (18 August 1945) introduces the sudden and stark lesson of America's nuclear experiment, as surely a product of hyper-rationalism as the Holocaust: "'The trouble with [human relations],' said Simple, 'is that we will have no human relationships left when we get through dropping that new atomical bomb on each other. The way it kills people for miles around, all my relations and—me, too—is liable to be wiped out in no time.'"[49] Clearly Simple comprehends Du Bois's insistent formulation of "color and democracy" in the aftermath of Hiroshima and Nagasaki: "And how come we did not try them ['atomical bombs'] out on Germany? . . . [because] they just did not want to use them on white folks. Germans is white. So they wait until the war is all over in Europe to try them out on colored folks. Japs is colored." Imagining a better use for the billions spent on the bombs, Simple reconfigures a postwar New Deal in which "crackers" are educated so that Americans of color can vote in every state.

Simple acknowledged Harlem's part in the nation's success. "V–J Night in Harlem" (25 August 1945), with equal measures of joy and cynicism, reports that "the way Harlem celebrated V–J night when the news came that the war was finally over, indicated that Harlem had long since accepted the war as its own." Unlike Hayakawa and Badger, Hughes never condescends to his readers, even in celebrating the end of the war. Simple reminds his readers that the race struggle is far from over, and the political future, at home and abroad, remains uncertain: "fascism really hasn't been beaten in the world yet, only defeated in its boldest military form. . . . Death has beaten death, force has beaten force." Simple's words foreshadow the cold war, in which America would even more deeply compromise its sociopolitical ideals, and a civil rights struggle empowered, in part, by a new awareness of the pervasive oppression of "colored folks" here to yonder.

These differing perspectives within the black press reveal as much about the individual temperament and politics of the columnists as they do about the genuine diversity of opinion in minority America. They also point to common ground: concern for the rights of minorities and an attempt to wrestle with the complexities of citizenship in a diverse nation.[50] Examining the oppression of Japanese Americans empowered the black press by diverting it from issues of parochial concern to those of national significance. *Defender* writers initially saw themselves, consistent with the black press attitude toward immigrants in the first four decades of the century, as more American than their subjects. This gave the columnists a powerful position. For black press columnists to protest Jim Crow laws in the South exposed their own marginalized citizenship. Their association with the oppressed group made their protests seems partisan. But in writing about the internment of Japanese Americans they (even Hayakawa, a Canadian) were empowered by a sense of being more fully American, more safely enclosed in the civil fabric, than those of whom they spoke. Such empowerment could be broadening and often led to a stronger understanding of the sociopolitical kinship among all minority groups, even those stigmatized as alien. This in turn generated a larger concern with citizenship issues that makes the writings of these columnists, and many others of the war years, essential to any serious consideration of the place of minority populations in American democracy.

Notes

1. *Justice Delayed: The Record of the Japanese American Internment Cases,* ed. Peter Irons (Middletown, Conn.: Wesleyan University Press, 1989), 95–96.
2. By 1943, "Negro news" was available in segregated theaters carrying the white-financed American Negro News-Reel.
3. Carey McWilliams, *Brothers Under the Skin,* rev. ed. (Boston: Little, Brown, 1951), 7–8.
4. See Charley Cherokee [Alfred E. Smith; see n. 15], "National Grapevine," *Chicago Defender,* 22 May 1943: "The boys hate to see where old Gen. John DeWitt says 'a Jap's a Jap.' They remember back home how everybody always say 'a nigger's a nigger.' But they say old Walter White knows what he's talking about when he says: 'Unless the race problem is solved, there'll be just an interval between wars.'"
5. U.S. Army, Western Defense Command, *Final Report: Japanese Evacuation from the West Coast, 1941* (Washington, D.C.: Government Printing Office, 1943), 34.
6. Many Japanese Americans were alert to the racism of the South; some used it as a reference when describing the relocation experience (in particular, the nisei draft). See, for example, Editorial, *Poston Chronicle,* 7 February 1943 (WRA Record Group): "Loyal American citizens of Japanese lineage once again are being subjected to a salvo of vicious, indiscriminate propaganda, obnoxiously smacking of Axis ideology. Rep. Rankin (Dem.) Mississippi, recently took the House floor to denounce our Secretary of War Henry L. Stimson for his plan to organize a Nisei Combat unit. . . . Rep. Rankin . . . maintains that the 'japs' should be put into labor battalions where each and every one of them could be watched at all times.'"

   Even the introduction to the WRA Record Group microfilm of the camp newspapers employs the language of "evacuation" and "removal" familiar from federal documents concerning the national policy toward Native Americans: "Though the Relocation Centers were the permanent homes of the Japanese for the greater part of the War, they should be distinguished from the ASSEMBLY CENTERS, which were operated by the Army as stopping places for the Japanese between their evacuation from their homes and their removal to the Relocation Centers."
7. For the precise aims of Roosevelt's speech and the Atlantic Charter, see Henry Steele Commager, ed., *Documents of American History,* 7th ed. (New York: Appleton-Century-Crofts, 1963), 446–49, 451.
8. The *Defender,* like the *Pittsburgh Courier* with its "Double V" campaign, envisioned a global democracy that, while falling short of W.E.B. Du Bois's global projection of "color and democracy," anticipated that end-of-war linkage. See Du Bois, *Color and Democracy: Colonies and Peace* (1945; reprint, Millwood, N.Y.: Kraus-Thomson Organization, 1975), preface.

9. For the specifics of Executive Order #9066, the Relocation Order, see Commager, *Documents of American History*, 464–65.

10. Many Japanese English-language community newspapers—such as *Rafu Shimpo* (July 1914–March 1942; January 1946 resumed), *Kashu Mainichi* (5 November 1931–March 1942; January 1946 resumed)—were suspended during the war. *Pacific Citizen*, the official publication of the Japanese American Citizens League (JACL), published as a monthly until 4 June 1942, when it became a weekly based in Salt Lake City.

11. U.S. Department of the Interior, War Relocation Authority, in collaboration with the War Department, *Nisei in Uniform* (Washington, D.C.: Government Printing Office, 1944), n.p.

12. Sengstacke, president of the Robert S. Abbott Publishing Company and general manager of the *Defender*, and Lochard, Parisian-educated editor of its international section, were loyal to the precept of a constitutionally guaranteed free press. They sought citizenship from, what Frederick Douglass had called nearly a century before, "the great principles of political freedom and of natural justice." See "What to the Slave is the Fourth of July?" in *The Frederick Douglass Papers: Series I*, ed., John W. Blassingame (New Haven: Yale University Press, 1982), 2:367; see also Patrick S. Washburn, *A Question of Sedition: The Federal Government's Investigation of the Black Press during World War II* (New York: Oxford University Press, 1986).

13. Editorial, "Freedom of Negro Press," *Chicago Defender*, 21 December 1941.

14. Du Bois, *Color and Democracy*, 84.

15. Identity of "Charley Cherokee" was a mystery to *Defender* readers. Sengstacke seemed to have a stake in preserving his columnist's anonymity. Prominent ads for the column bore his "name" above a space-filling question mark. Hayakawa twice remarks in his column on the mystery of his neighboring columnist's identity. And yet Alfred E. Smith, the "Cherokee" of the columns, was a prominent member of President Roosevelt's "Black Cabinet" (African Americans in senior federal positions who advised the president on race-related issues), an administrator and adviser in the Federal Works Progress Administration, and founder of the Capitol Press Club in 1940 (in response to the exclusionary practices of the National Press Club). See Series 2, Non-Governmental Professional Activities, Boxes 5–8, University of Arkansas, Fayetteville: Alfred E. Smith Papers.

16. Titles of the columns—"Here to Yonder," "Second Thoughts," "World View"—are consistent throughout the war. In-text citation identifies weekly contributions by subject, first running head, and date; pagination varies edition to edition, therefore, it is not noted.

17. Hughes to Selective Service, 28 September 1942; quoted in Arnold Rampersad, *The Life of Langston Hughes: I Dream a World, 1941–1967* (New York: Oxford University Press, 1988), 2:53.

18. See "Classifications," chap. 10, in *Language in Action* (New York: Harcourt, Brace and Co., 1941), 153; "Classification," chap. 13, in *Language in Thought and Action*, rev. ed. (New York: Harcourt, Brace, and World, 1949), 211.

   In matters of "race" and "nationality," the way in which classifications work is especially apparent. For example, the present writer is by "race" a "Japanese," by "nationality" a "Canadian," but, as his friends say, "essentially" an "American," since he thinks, talks, behaves, and dresses much like other Americans. Because he is "Japanese," he is excluded by law from becoming a citizen of the United States; because he is "Canadian," he has certain rights in all parts of the British Empire [Commonwealth]; because he is "American," he gets along with his friends and teaches in an American institution of higher learning without any noticeable special difficulties. Are these classifications "real"? Of course they are, and *the effect that each of them has* upon what he may do and what he may not do constitutes their "reality" [Note: In the revised text, the closing sentence is italicized from "the effect" to "their 'reality'"].

19. Hughes, "Why and Wherefore," *Chicago Defender*, 21 November 1942.

20. For Hayakawa's recollection of his early association with Lochard, see S. Hayakawa and Margedant Peters Hayakawa, *From Semantics to the U.S. Senate, Etc., Etc.* (Berkeley: University of California Press, 1994), 113. Semantic alertness failed to guard Hayakawa from his ever-surfacing personal and racial elitism. See, in particular, his memory of his first meeting with the French-speaking Dr. Metz Lochard: "He was the editor. He was a reasonably well-educated man. He sort of fancied himself an Intellectual. I was glad to join in with him and treat him as one. It was He who hired me to go on the *Chicago Defender*. Later on, I discovered that Nobody else on the *Defender* staff had any particular enthusiasm for me."

Few studies capture the war-accentuated tensions between America's "unity of ideals and diversity of culture" better than Gunnar Myrdal's *An American Dilemma: The Negro Problem and Modern Democracy* (New York: Harper & Brothers, 1944), chap. 1.

21. See John Robert Badger, "A Stroke of Irony" (21 November 1942) and "Four Freedoms and Africa" (28 November 1942). Here he contemplates the magnitude of "integrating" Africa with black Allied forces and "mobilizing" the native populations into antifascists. In a particularly poignant postcolonial vision, Badger imagines "Negroes . . . [becoming] . . . articulate spokesm[e]n on behalf of a New Deal for Africa" and concludes that "the Allied conquest of North Africa has thus offered to Negro America a new lever for contributing its progressive influence to the achievement of victory and peace" (28 November 1942).

22. Hayakawa may have been responding to Harry Paxton Howard, "Americans in Concentration Camps," *The Crisis* (September 1942), 201–202, 222; this article was featured in a *Defender* display ad.

23. Hayakawa, "A Relative World," *Chicago Defender*, 12 December 1942.

24. Hayakawa, "Sauce for the Goose," *Chicago Defender*, 13 February 1943.

25. Grodzin—a University of California at Berkeley graduate assistant to Dorothy Thomas's Japanese American Evacuation and Resettlement Study and author of *Americans Betrayed: Politics and the Japanese Evacuation* (Chicago: University of Chicago Press, 1949)—revisited the "pathology" of loyalty and disloyalty in *The Loyal and Disloyal: Social Boundaries of Patriotism and Treason* (Chicago: University of Chicago Press, 1956); see, in particular, chap. 7.

26. Hayakawa, *Language in Action*; see, in particular, chap. 11, "The Two-Valued Orientation," for his discussion of the semantics of propaganda.

27. In a year that would be best known for national civil insurrection—riots in Los Angeles, Chicago, Detroit, and Harlem as well as at Manzanar and Tule Lake—1943 is recalled by many Japanese Americans as the time of the "loyalty question" and the nisei draft. For the details of issei and nisei reactions to the "loyalty" test, see Michi Nishiura Weglyn, *Years of Infamy: The Untold Story of America's Concentration Camps* (1976; reprint, Seattle: University of Washington Press, 1996), chap. 8; Audrie Girdner and Anne Loftis, *The Great Be-*

trayal: The Evacuation of the Japanese-Americans during World War II (London: Macmillan Co., 1968), chap. 10; Donald E. Collins, *Native American Aliens: Disloyalty and Renunciation of Citizenship by Japanese Americans during World War II* (Westport, Conn.: Greenwood Press, 1985); Roger Daniels, *Concentration Camps: North American, Japanese in the United States and Canada during World War II*, rev. ed. (Malabar, Fla.: Krieger Publishing, 1993), esp. chap. 6.

28. Badger's intimacy with Isamu Noguchi is questionable. If they were close associates, Badger should have noted that Noguchi's father, the poet Yoné Noguchi, was interned at Poston and was the primary reason that Isamu "voluntarily" joined the internees there. For further consideration of Yoné and Isamu Noguchi at Poston, see Girdner and Loftis, *The Great Betrayal*, 174, 225, 249, 250, 263, 463, 465; Bruce Altshuler, *Noguchi* (New York: Abbeville Press, 1994), 28, 38–39, 55, 65, 114.

29. Badger's failure to situate this letter in time suggests that he is ignorant of its dating and that of Yoné Noguchi's migration to the United States.

30. In "The Race War Bug-Bear" (13 March 1943), Badger moves from the propagandistic to the reflective as he considers recent conjecture—within communities of color at home and abroad—on the coming "race war." Reviewing black weeklies on the West Coast (in particular, in Los Angeles), he concludes: "Though race itself does not determine historical change, racial ideology as a political instrument certainly does, as the Nazification of the German youth will bear witness. Yet, it seems strange and utterly absurd that Negro-Americans, who have suffered as much as any people from the effects of racial ideology as a political instrument, should believe and disseminate views which tend to renew and perpetuate this instrument." The racial ideology at work in his castigation of the West Coast Japanese is forgotten here.

31. The zoot-suit riot integrated diverse public opinion on "foreigners," sartorial styles, military service, and (as William Allan Neilson apprehended) "racial minorities within our borders." For background on Anglo attitudes toward Mexicans, see William Allan Neilson, "'Minorities' in Our Midst," *Survey Graphic*, February 1939, 98–103; Carey McWilliams, *North from Mexico*, rev. ed. (New York: Praeger, 1990). For cultural details of pachuco culture and the zoot-suit (and its variance from African-American expressive culture), see Octavio Paz, *The Labyrinth of Solitude: Life and Thought in Mexico*, trans. Lysander Kemp (1950; reprint, New York: Grove Press, 1961), chap. 1. For accounts of the riot itself, "Zoot Suits and Service Stripes: Race Tension Behind the Riots," *Newsweek*, 21 June 1943, 35–36, 39, 40; "Zoot-Suit Riots, 125 Hurt," *Life* 21 June 1943, 30–31.

32. Months before the riot, reflecting upon the actions of the WRA, the American Civil Liberties Union (ACLU) had noted that "no such wholesale invasion of the liberties of American citizens on the basis of racial origin has ever before been undertaken, in war or peace; and it is to be explained only by the sectional fears and prejudices arising out of the extraordinary circumstances of the war." See *The Bill of Rights in War* (New York: ACLU, 1942), 4. Reflecting upon the significance for African Americans, the ACLU notes: "Cast upon the larger world stage of exploitation of the darker races in the colonies of democracies, their cause in the United States is taking on a new significance in the conduct and aims of the war" (8).

33. Chester B. Himes, "Zoot Riots are Race Riots," *The Crisis*, July 1943, 200–201, 222.

34. See Peter Irons, *Justice at War* (New York: Oxford University Press, 1983); for excerpts from the legal opinions themselves, see Irons, *Justice Delayed*.

35. In "Implications of a Name" (14 August 1943), written in the wake of the Harlem riot (1–2 August), Hayakawa disclaims assumptions about his personal "racial" identity: "I am Japanese in name only, having been born and brought up in Canada and educated in Canada and the U.S., so that I am unable to speak the Japanese language properly." Cultural dislocation has taught him that: "Every man who demands that he be treated as an individual, on his own merits, should begin by treating others likewise. It is no more intelligent to assume that all 'Jews' are rich or that all 'Japanese' know jiu-jitsu than it is to assume that all 'Negroes' steal chicken."

36. Riot issues missing from this microfilm reel; citations from transcript in Hayakawa and Hayakawa, *From Semantics to the U.S. Senate*, 142, 143.

37. Weglyn, *Years of Infamy*, 136.

38. See Dorothy S. Thomas and Richard Nishimoto, *The Spoilage: Japanese-American Evacuation and Resettlement During World War II* (Berkeley: University of California Press, 1946); see Weglyn, *Years of Infamy*, 310 n.16.

39. Badger notes that Vansittart was: "one of Britain's multi-millionaires and bluebloods [who] has been waging a campaign for military occupation of Germany, partition of the German state, and the infliction of severe penalties on the German people for the crimes of the Hitler regime. Vansittart doesn't draw a distinction between the Nazis and their dupes and the rest of the German people."

40. After six column-inches on solidarity between victimized populations, Hughes isolates the Japanese for a didactic purpose: "from the efficient Japanese-Americans we can learn to be more efficient in relation to ourselves."

41. Though Hayakawa made passing reference to the plight of Japanese on the West Coast, he had not previously responded to Badger's early charges of "disloyalty" or the WRA's policies.

42. Hayakawa's promotion of the WRA effectively marginalizes his citations of injustice—the Supreme Court "seems to be in no great rush" to consider the cases, West Coast policies were in response to the "government's yielding to . . . racist hysteria."

43. See Gunnar Myrdal, *An American Dilemma: The Negro Problem and American Democracy* (New York: Harper & Brothers Publisher, 1944), esp. introduction (which claims that Americans see the "Negro problem" as a "moral lag in the development of the nation") and chap. 29, "Social Segregation and Discrimination" (which notes that "Negroes . . . are kept as aliens permanently. . . . Only Orientals and possibly Mexicans among all separate ethnic groups have as much segregation as Negroes" [620]).

44. See Carey McWilliams, *Prejudice, Japanese-Americans: Symbol of Racial Intolerance* (Boston: Little, Brown and Company, 1944), 67.

45. On 18 December 1944, the Supreme Court—in spite of increasing uneasiness regarding the continued internment of Japanese Americans—upheld Fred Korematsu's conviction. For details of this and related internment cases, see Irons, *Justice at War*; Irons, *Justice Delayed*.

46. For consideration of the anti-Japanese activities of nativist organizations in California, see Donald E. Collins, *Native American Aliens: Disloyalty and the Renunciation of Citizenship by Japanese Americans during World War II* (Westport, Conn.: Greenwood Press, 1985).

47. Remarkably, some readers accepted Hayakawa's self-congratulatory perspective on the relocation. See, for example, "What the People Say: Lauds Hayakawa Column on Nisei" (24 February 1945) in which a reader writes: "This week I

have found more real substance in S. I. Hayakawa's column than ever before in his citation of the Endo and Korematsu cases. I agree with him that the Defender and other weeklies would do well to bring more emphasis to its treatment of news involving other racial minorities, Nisei, Mexicans, Chinese, Filipinos, and others. Many of our problems have a common basis and are of special interest to Negroes for that reason."

48. The home-front demonization of Japan, the remaining Axis enemy, intensified with the horrific toll of the battles for Iwo Jima (19 February through late March) and Okinawa (11 May through 22 June), deepening the anti-Japanese sentiment on the home front and further complicating the return of the Japanese to the Pacific Coast.

49. The jubilance and nonspecificity of most stories—even on the front page of the *Defender* (see "Atom Bomb? Shucks, That's Little Stuff to Civil War Vet," *Chicago Defender*, 18 August 1945, 1)—makes Simple's "in no time" terrifyingly prescient. For as the joint American Japanese study commission of Hiroshima would observe a few months later: "'Accompanying the flash of light was an instantaneous flash of heat. . . . Its duration was probably less than one-tenth of a second and its intensity was sufficient to cause nearby flammable objects . . . to burst into flame'" (Quoted in Richard Rhodes, *The Making of the Atomic Bomb* [New York: Simon and Schuster, 1986], 714).

50. For consideration of the theoretical implications of this managed diversity for Asian Americans, see Lisa Lowe, *Immigrant Acts: On Asian American Cultural Politics* (Durham, N.C.: Duke University Press, 1996), esp. chaps. 2, 5.

Chapter 10

On Sale at Your Favorite Newsstand:

Negro Digest/Black World and the 1960s

IT IS NEITHER SURPRISING nor inappropriate that most considerations of *Negro Digest* either steer clear of socioeconomic concerns and emphasize the magazine's role in refining a "Black aesthetic," or consider it an instance of heroic individual intellectual activism, or do both.[1] Without question, Hoyt Fuller, its editor, demonstrated remarkable skill, courage, and ambition in transforming his "inheritance," the somewhat staid "Digest," and in doing so did indeed become a primary architect of the Black Arts Movement. Julius Thompson says that Fuller "attract[ed] local, regional, national, and international writers, artists, and cultural activists" to the *Digest* (renamed *Black World* in 1970), and yet he remained "faithful to the need for a diversity of Black voices to reflect on the printed page the complexities of Black life in America and abroad." Walter Daniel called the *Digest* "the principal journal of the growing coalescence between political and artistic activism." And Clovis E. Semmes called Fuller "a major architect" of the mid–1960s and 1970s movement. "There can be no definitive analysis of the formation and substance of Afrocentric methods and discourse, Black literary criticism, Black aesthetics, and the like without examining the content of *Negro Digest/Black World*," she declared.[2]

Despite a somewhat "populist" relaunch, Johnson Publications (and John H. Johnson in particular) was ambivalent at best about the magazine's return. As Donald Joyce points it, "the second run of *Negro Digest/Black World* did not enjoy the commercial success of the first." The magazine's paid circulation was reported to have topped 100,000 in 1949, but monthly average circulation reached its peak at only 54,174, in 1971.[3]

Fuller was extremely innovative in carving out an interesting "middle space" for the magazine to exist as long as it did. Not quite a literary or "little" magazine, but not a glossy consumer mag, Fuller still dared to build a genuinely democratic cultural vehicle that proved both tractable and resilient in generating cultural conversations of significant quality. As an outlet for African-American literary production and a shaper of taste, it remains unsurpassed. But critics have been hard pressed to explain the publication's modest commercial accomplishment driven by the Johnson Publication's logic of capital while they also consider it a "revolutionary magazine."

My goal here is not so much to discard the consensus view as to refine it. What has never been fully articulated is a complete picture of the relationship between the magazine's origins, its 1960s audience, Fuller's personal vision, and a perceived collective shift in consciousness. *Negro Digest/Black World*'s accomplishment is more than significant; indeed, it is arguably one of the most accomplished cultural magazines in twentieth century America, but there is a kind of intellectual procrastination in engaging the most troubling issues that the *Digest*'s story raises: What are the limits of magazine journalism in constructing new racial and cultural formations? Is a mass journal of "critical thought" a contradiction in terms? Was the "second run" of *Negro Digest* as distinct a progression or evolution as some celebrants would have us believe? Most important, how are we to tell the story of the magazine's demise, and, closely related, how should scholars "feel" about the marriage of (black) capitalism and black cultural activism? Given that many of these questions have been elided and perhaps even avoided, I want to further argue that part of the historical importance of the *Negro Digest/Black World* was the way in which these questions were "performed" each and every day of the magazine's existence. Indeed, these performances—the magazine's experimental character—makes it a crucial piece of the post-World War II American cultural puzzle.

David Lionel Smith's seminal essay, "The Black Arts Movement and Its Critics" looked to instigate a pointed and extended evaluation of African-American cultural production in the 1960s.[4] He describes the ways in which the contemporary African-American literary scene is indebted to black arts' efforts. Although he argues that a lingering sense of embarrassment (especially as regards racial and gender chauvinism that is perceived endemic within movement writings) hampers efforts to sustain conversation about the movement's accomplishments and limitations, it might also be argued that our collective hesitance has more to do with the recognition that issues central to its demise remain firmly part of our intellectual landscape. We ignore (or ritually celebrate) the accomplishment of a Hoyt Fuller because we recognize the unresolved contradictions of our own scholarly existence. If the academy has come to dominate a certain portion of the black literary marketplace and replace many of the midwifing and gatekeeping tasks previously held by civil rights organizations *and* black entrepreneurs, old tales are being retold. The struggle to articulate and promote specifically black aesthetic accomplishment remains—perhaps more complexly than ever—entangled with class aspiration, both black and white.

The intellectual, cultural, and political achievement of Hoyt Fuller and *Negro Digest/Black World* is so substantial that there is little danger of its erasure by a full examination of its limitations. Much more dangerous would be to blindly ignore imperfections, blindspots, and the resiliency of hegemonic cultural formations. Insofar as most responses to the Black Arts Movement, both positive and negative, continue to be relentlessly polemical, one gets the sense that there is something very fundamental at stake about our current scholarly self-understanding, something, as David Smith suggests, that "cannot stand unaltered."[5]

Most accounts of *Negro Digest*'s second run provide only cursory treatment of its first appearance. This critical choice reinforces an understanding of the black aesthetic movement that emphasizes originality and novelty over a perspective on twentieth-century African-American literary history in which there is continuous enthusiasm for the black vernacular. This choice also makes difficult a satisfactory reading of the status and meaning of *Negro Digest/Black World* by distancing it from its genitive role in the formation of Johnson Publications and its ideology. A return to that advent moment allows for treatment of the magazine's relationship to uplift ideology and the imposing and inescapable presence of John H. Johnson.

Early on, Johnson championed a black middle class rooted in the mainstream of American consumerism. Johnson perceived potentially lucrative opportunities in packaging a product sensitively aimed at the social, cultural, and psychological particularities of the black consumer. While this might never emerge as a fully articulated "nationalism," he maintained some in-group consciousness and certainly stoked black pride. Johnson, however, would have to negotiate with white bankers, printers, advertisers, and distributors. Almost immediately, Johnson recognized that the long-term success of his magazine publishing ventures would depend upon the courting of national advertisers. Their interest and investment was contingent upon the continued growth of black spending power, itself directly related to civil rights protections in employment, education, and commerce.

What emerges from this complexity is the necessity of pragmatic ideological shifting. Johnson's new magazine would not be apolitical. An absence of any agitation would neither concretely improve the economic prospects of the black middle class nor acknowledge that class's unique history and contemporary political situation. To be completely involved in the task of agitation, however, would be to scare off advertisers interested in stability and growth potential, and, moreover, to demolish the necessary relationship between a relentless optimism and the emergence of modern consumerism. In retrospect, Johnson's great accomplishment is his significant insight into the psychology of American capitalism. His magazines would simultaneously offer—first with *Negro Digest*, but most spectacularly with *Ebony, Jet,* and *Tan*—the articulation of black consumer desire frustrated by Jim Crow *and* the aura of black success.

How did "pragmatic ideological shifting" specifically manifest itself in the first appearance of *Negro Digest*? Certainly Johnson's first choice of an editor indicates his willingness to be flexible. Johnson began the *Digest* by inviting the white communist Ben Burns to be the de facto managing editor. Johnson was self-critical enough to recognize that he needed Burns's editorial and writing skills, even though Burns's politics and race made him a potential problem. (It was not until some years later, however, that Burns's presence and contribution was acknowledged on the magazine's masthead.) The adoption of the format of *Reader's Digest* was, of course, the most audacious act of claiming a broad swath of the publishing mainstream. By reprinting articles, rather than seeking out new articles, *Negro Digest* was able to distance itself from an obvious political stance, while at the same time drawing upon the aura of respectability and quality of the original publishing outlets. While *Reader's Digest* was politically conservative and staunchly anticommunist in editorial policy, *Negro Digest* more readily replicated its "formal commitment"—right down to copying specific design elements including cover typescript—to the largest readership possible, rather than mimic tone and editorial tact.

Although *Negro Digest* was surely in the political mainstream, it also recognized the value of controversy. Part of this was the magazine's success in capturing many recognizable names, sometimes breaking the "digest" format, when a particularly compelling author might be included. (The first run of the *Digest* included either original contributions or reprints by Langston Hughes, Carl Sandburg, Paul Robeson, Ruth Benedict, W.E.B. Du Bois, Fannie Hurst, Norman Thomas, George Seldes, Walter White, Lewis Martin, Roi Ottley, and George Schuyler, among many, many other prominent Americans. It is also worth noting that, by 1946, Johnson was listing Arna Bontemps, Sterling Brown, Arthur Davis, Langston Hughes, Zora Neale Hurston, Alain Locke, Saunders Redding among others as "advisory editors.") Neither was the magazine totally distant from the more sensationalist style of many of the newsweeklies and oftentimes was riddled with hints of vaguely anachronistic "tales of miscegenation." At its very best—and arguably at its most clever and malleable—the magazine's feature "If I Was a Negro . . ." somehow combined concrete social analysis with titillation and contention. Eleanor Roosevelt, Orsen Welles, and Marshall Field were among those that Johnson (or perhaps Burns) managed to convince to contribute to this ingenious commentary. For a token fee (usually fifteen dollars), the magazine convinced very public figures to contribute reflection on the subject of "what they would do if they were Black," despite the inevitability of vigorous rebuttal and, more often than not, knowing skepticism.

Although Johnson insisted that *Negro Digest*'s political perspective was strictly nonpartisan, this is, of course, obfuscation. Despite attempts to demonstrate an almost absurd "neutrality"—Burns went so far as to reprint a "letter to the editor" from New York's *PM* magazine in which lynching was justified as a means of keeping "social order" in response to the *Digest's* own commissioned antilynching piece—the magazine's ideological commitment was, by necessity, to the expansion and stability of the black middle class. There is some truth to the insistence of some commentators that the magazine's distancing of its style and tone from that of the newsweeklies—the *Chicago Defender* and the *Pittsburgh Courier*, in particular—was a large part of its success, such choices should not be framed as disinterest. Indeed, stylistic distancing itself should be at least partially framed as an attempt to emphasize a particular set of class values, an attempt to make clear the difference in sensibility between a potentially assimilable black middle class and the more raucous black masses.

Burns described mid–1940s efforts to generate subscriptions as "patriotism mixed with commercialism."[6] Many, if not most, of the early *Negro Digest's* efforts at capturing readers spoke directly to the war effort, either encouraging readers to purchase subscriptions for black G.I.'s or insisting upon the crucial necessity of remaining informed. ("Part of army morale is keeping up with the world—reading. That's where *Negro Digest* fills the bill"— *Negro Digest*, August 1944). Johnson recognized the concrete possibilities presented by a captive audience of overseas black servicemen and the ways in which to communicate black loyalty in the war effort might mobilize traditional black middle class commitment to American ideals and desire to belong. Johnson liked to brag that *Negro Digest* was the only Negro publication that the U.S. government sent overseas to military installations.

Negro Digest was, of course, not the only magazine attempting to capture black middle-class readership.[7] Competitors, mostly regional or local, came and went. The difficulty for them was that Johnson had gotten it right and got there first. Timing was everything. Johnson was able to take advantage of both the increased incomes of black families working in war-related industries and the important market of black G.I.'s themselves. Given the ways that the *Digest's* flexibility was appropriate for a community betwixt and between unfettered ambition and accomplishment worth celebrating in the context of Jim Crow, newcomers found that they could only duplicate the formula. In a finite market, where the benefits of duplication were not obvious, this meant that Johnson and his significant marketing expertise (and, somewhat later, his firm management control) could largely carry the day.

By the mid–1940s, only a few years after the *Digest's* launch, Johnson was an understandably confident entrepreneur. *Negro Digest's* circulation was steady, if not on an upward trek. Given this relatively rare security, perhaps Johnson's boldest move ever was to step away from the *Digest* to focus his energies on two new periodicals, *Ebony* and *Jet*. If *Negro Digest* sought to inscribe a specific class-based difference, *Ebony*, in particular, would instead opt to mobilize and maximize class desire, to satisfy aspiration toward, and admiration of, officially designated signs of American "success," fantasy activity open to both those who have made it and those still struggling. By displaying or "covering" prominence in entertainment or athletics, acts of conspicuous consumption, achievement in business, the attainment of substitute aristocracy, Johnson made possible the first truly black mass circulation magazine. Not surprisingly, after only six months of publishing *Ebony*, Johnson decided to seek out national advertisers. The process was slow, but, as always, he was able to cultivate lasting relationships with white corporate executives by emphasizing that there was money to made.[8]

It would be cynical, of course, to downplay the importance of Johnson's survival or his advocacy of the collective buying power of African Americans. Although more often than not appealing to the self-interest of advertisers, rather than, say, the moral suasion of the civil rights revolution, it remains reasonable to suggest that Johnson's first publishing venture may have contributed positively to forming a sense of collectivity that assisted later challenges to the status quo. Without question, *Negro Digest's* emphasis on the positive—and certainly that was the outlook of *Ebony* to come—challenged the increasing pathologization of black life. The difficulty was, and is, that a relentless optimism without political cognizance inevitably becomes its own pathology. (Indeed, *Ebony's* circulation dip in the mid- to late 1950s caused Johnson to step back and reconsider the formula that had served him so well for the previous fifteen years; he knew that he could not remain out of touch with the new spirit of the age.) Before moving on to discuss Johnson's subtle ideological shift and the role played by the second run of *Negro Digest*, it is important to meditate upon the point at which "pragmatic ideological shifting" ceases to be in the distinct service of "growth" and when it begins to serve something more like "preservation." Communications pioneers like Johnson played an invaluable role in establishing the basic conditions of community action and self-consciousness. At some point, however, in the process of becoming a national corporation or "family fortune," Johnson loses an obvious relationship between community well-being and the growth of that capitalist entity.

Negro Digest made its return in June 1961. The decade of its absence had been dramatic. Labor and social historians have effectively challenged an understanding of the modern Civil Rights Movement as somehow emerging *sui generis* in the mid–1950s, but there were significant changes in the tone, appeal, and visibility of civil rights efforts in the 1950s. A youthful cadre of thinkers and activists emerged who were eager to challenge the kinds of speech boundaries that *Ebony* and *Jet* merely manipulated.

Johnson described the return of the magazine in the folksy, personal, and accommodating voice that he had used so effectively on previous occasions to generate funds, contributors, advertisers, and subscribers. "Scores of loyal readers have dutifully written to inquire when the magazine would reappear and an astonishingly large number have steadily mailed in their subscription checks," he wrote, "just as if the magazine were being delivered to them every month!" And he continued that "the publisher finds both flattering and irresistible" calls for the *Digest*'s revival.[9]

In addition to this "popular demand," Johnson suggested, there were two other compelling reasons for the magazine's return: (1) "recent events"—by which he meant civil rights agitation in the United States and decolonization in Africa—and their coverage by international media; and (2) his instinct that the "talented young Negro writer does not always find a ready outlet for his creative efforts." Johnson is nothing if not prescient here. Indeed, *Negro Digest* would comprehensively address these two important concerns. The magazine remains to this day an important historical record of civil rights activity, Pan-Africanist thought and reflection, and is perhaps now only surpassed by *Callaloo* in its commitment to publishing a diversity of creative black voices.

But it may be a mistake to accept uncritically Johnson's self-effacing remarks. Albert Kreiling's important essay "The Commercialization of the Black Press and the Rise of Race News in Chicago" is largely dismissive of the 1960s as any kind of revolutionary moment. In his evaluation of the emergence of mass market periodicals for black audiences, he insists upon a certain inevitability to demographic shifts and the final triumph of consumer magazines over the black weekly newspaper. From his perspective, Johnson's renaming of Negro Digest as Black World was straightfoward evidence of the way in which he had tried to "add the militants as a market."[10] But this understanding of the importance of Negro Digest/Black World is somewhat counterintuitive; it does not explain Johnson's resistance to adding advertising to the magazine nor does it explain the magazine's slow and somewhat contentious evolution. Although Kreiling's perspective on the final triumph of black consumerism has as evidence the collapse of any significant role for black newsweeklies in American politics and furthermore Black World's own demise, Kreiling is too dismissive of the ways in which there were— however temporary—significant questions to be debated and, in some cases, reader's lives changed forever by Negro Digest/Black World's creative mix of opinion, debate, exposition and literary expression. I am seeking to argue that the import and significance of Negro Digest must be approached—not only in terms of its own distinction—but as at least partially about the creation of an image of the company as a whole. Part of the legacy of Negro Digest is that it had some role to play in the preservation of the audience for Ebony and Jet.

To get at the real significance of the second run of Negro Digest must mean to move back and forth inventively between socioeconomic imperative and both the possibility and reality of cultural transformation. To ignore John H. Johnson's efforts to maintain the hegemony of Johnson Publications is to naively pursue a view of the past in which African-American intellectual activity is safely apart from questions of ambition, the impact of capital, and strategic political and cultural decisions in which loss and gain are complex measures. With varying degrees of success, for instance, Robert Weems and William Van Deburg have each documented the ways in which the "new Black consciousness" was easily commodified and marketed.[11] (The ease of which further complicates Johnson's resistance to advertising in the Digest.) Their efforts signal the possible historical gains to be made from contextualizing the activity of post World War II African-American creative intellectuals in terms of the large and ever-present framework of American consumer capitalism.

If Ben Burns was a somewhat surprising choice to take up the management and editorial direction of the first run of *Negro Digest*, Johnson's decision to make Hoyt Fuller editor is equally puzzling and prescient. Fuller was no doubt among the most experienced black journalists of the day with stints at the *Detroit Tribune*, the *Michigan Chronicle*, the Amsterdam *Haagse Post* and Johnson's own *Ebony*. What complicates the decision is that Fuller left *Ebony* disillusioned at its politics. Robert L. Harris, Jr., writes that having observed the monumental events of 1954 and 1955—the *Brown v. Board of Education* decision, the Montgomery Bus boycott, and the lynching of Emmett Till—Fuller resigned from *Ebony* because "it was not relevant enough to the Black struggle for freedom and equality."[12] Fuller could not have arrived with the expectation that he would be unfettered to shape a magazine that would be at any significant distance from the parent company's ideological conviction. Yet there were still few enough options for an ambitious and educated African-American man of his generation that it would have been hard to turn down the opportunity. And Johnson offered a national magazine with significant distribution resources, dedicated solely to African-American cultural concerns, located in what was arguably the most resourceful black community in the United States, with the likelihood that Johnson's magazines would be faced with the necessity of some kind of evolution.

The magazine, reappearing in June 1961 with the volume and issue numbering that left off in 1951, foreshadowed the topics that would dominate it for some time. Reprints from *Down Beat*, *Atlantic Monthly*, *True*, *Commonweal*, *Ebony*, and others ranged from the substantive ("The American Theatre Needs Desegregating Too") to the frivolous ("Sarah Vaughn Tells Why—Plain Girls Can Make It Too"). In other words, it relied upon the tried and true combination of the politically noteworthy and the slightly sensational. The best material, such as an excerpt from C. Eric Lincoln's *The Black Muslims in America*, addressed both modes. Most important, however, was the presence of Fuller the writer himself, both in an article ("An Apertive in the Plaza") and the first appearance of his "Perspectives" column. If Fuller brought respect for the earlier *Digest*'s formulae, then his own writing (and intellect) created a distance much greater than the ten-year span in which the journal was silent, in terms of both political and intellectual distinctiveness. Almost immediately, he marked the magazine with his cosmopolitanism, his international and specifically Pan-African concerns, and his sharp wit.

Of course, an investigation into a "revolutionary" magazine requires us to contextualize the idea of Hoyt Fuller fighting and working in splendid isolation as a "heroic individual." Indeed, Fuller had only a few assistants, but they were incredibly able. During the magazine's first half dozen years under Fuller's leadership, Doris Saunders acted as a buffer between the upper reaches of the Johnson Publications' bureaucracy and Fuller's ambition. Carole Parkes assumed a different role as assistant managing editor in the magazine's later years, but the labor and intellectual work of both these women kept things afloat when Fuller absented himself to pursue his own literary and scholarly interests. (Between them, Saunders and Parkes contributed close to twenty articles to the *Digest*.) Furthermore, in-house designers and marketers, such as Herb Temple, created the sharp and often witty two-color newsprint covers.[13]

By 1964, Fuller and his team had created a significant expanse between the *Digest* and Johnson Publications' implicit and explicit ideology.[14] First, he weaned the magazine from the digest format itself. The magazine featured famous (and soon to be famous) African-American writers, artists, and intellectuals not to conspicuously display their qualifications and "success" but rather to utilize and evaluate their diagnoses of American cultural ills. As Fuller's network of writers and commentators grew—and as the civil rights era metamorphosed into the age of Black Power—the magazine became a resilient, flexible, and relentlessly relevant instrument of criticism. In 1965 alone, for instance, at merely the cusp of what I would call *Negro Digest*'s golden age, the magazine received contributions from Arna Bontemps, Gwendolyn Brooks, Henry Dumas, Mari Evans, Ronald Fair, Julia Fields, John Hope Franklin, E. Franklin Frazier, Sam Greenlee, Nathan Hare, Robert Hayden, Langston Hughes, Leroi Jones, Etheridge Knight, David Llorens, Audre Lorde, Clarence Major, Julian Mayfield, Louise Meriwether, Lewis Nkosi, Dudley Randall, Conrad Kent Rivers, Leopold Senghor, Wole Soyinka,

Wyatt T. Walker, John A. Williams, and, of course, Fuller himself. It is hard to imagine any American magazine that had more ready access to such a diverse and capable group of contributors.

Whether conscious or not, part of Fuller's genius was the decision to focus significant energy on reporting on the activities of a relatively new cultural phenomena, the writers' or artists' conference.[15] Most often held at colleges and universities and newly formed black arts organizations between 1963 through the mid-1970s, these conferences interrogated, not only old questions about "right representation," but new urgent questions of "right action," too. The high velocity emergence of a new black consciousness meant that the events were volatile high-stakes affairs and, most important, made for good copy. The *Digest's* coverage conveyed the excitement of these public performances and communicated to its audience that a very significant cultural transformation was taking place. Whether reporting on the First World Festival of Negro Arts in Dakar, Senegal, or the seminal Fisk University Black Writers' Conferences, Fuller and his correspondents provided "play-by-play" to a decade of evolution and revolution. Fuller also employed W.E.B. Du Bois's strategy at *The Crisis* in the 1920s to direct cultural debate with forums and surveys. Fuller's "Survey: Black Writers' Views on Literary Lions and Values" (January 1968) and its predecessor's "Negro Rights and the American Future" (October 1966) and "The Meaning and Measure of Black Power" (November 1966) offer an enormous range of opinion and serve as crucial historical measures of the commitment and experience of African-American writers in the 1960s.

Despite Fuller's considerable success, the question remains: Were his significant intellectual abilities best used in the daily struggle of magazine production?[16] Fuller had stunningly good editorial instincts (perhaps only matched by those of Jessie Fauset as the literary editor of *The Crisis* in the first half of the 1920s), and his ability to (ironically) utilize gate-keeping to create a sense of inclusiveness, movement, and evolution within the black creative and intellectual community of the 1960s' should certainly be recognized as one of the most determined and ethical cultural mediations in twentieth-century American culture. But, as I discuss, Fuller himself had reservations about whether this was the absolute best use of his time and energies and, for that matter, whether the *Digest* was really a long-term proposition. If part of the legacy of the 1960s was a fundamental reconsideration of the character of American democracy, especially its economic and political dimension, in what ways was a cultural magazine part of the Johnson Publications empire limited in its ability to participate in such study and challenge?

Many commentators have described *Negro Digest/Black World* as "a revolutionary magazine," but no one has pursued its inherent doubleness. "Revolutionary" suggests that the magazine played a tangible role in the radical challenges to the social and political order. Carolyn Gerald, in speaking of not only *Negro Digest* but also the whole exciting wave of late 1960s black cultural literary magazines, suggested that the "revolutionary Black journal" appeared "when Black people began to forsake civil rights and integration, and began to seek out a sense of self." Moreover, she insisted, the journals were "the literary enactment of the crisis of the Sixties: the Break With The West."[17] "Enactment" strikes me as being an especially tricky word here, but her testimony suggests the ways in which *Negro Digest* might come to have a powerful symbolic role to play, to model as such, the possibilities of an alternative political and cultural order.

What was the essence of what I call the *Digest's* experimental character, and how might it be conceived of as revolutionary? Four elements shape a heuristic device: (1) *Negro Digest* pushed at the limits of and often redefined contestatory cultural journalism by focusing on transformative cultural performances, either reported or initiated by the magazine. (2) Furthermore, it vigorously explored the limits of the pursuit of democratization through publishing, by opening up its pages to not only those individuals who had already attained some status but also young writers and thinkers, many of whom would have been otherwise distant from any cultural apparatus.[18] (3) It intelligently pursued consideration of the possibilities and limits of cultural nationalism. (4) And, finally, least self-consciously, it represented an inquiry into the nature and ends of corporate support for the arts and culture. This complex "experiment," as I have coined it, is certainly deserving of the designation *revolutionary* at least as pertains to *Negro Digest's* distinction from similar ventures. *Revolutionary* as pertains to political effectiveness, however, remains a more open question. *Negro Digest* can be called a revolutionary magazine as a unique marriage of form and content fundamentally in the context of a consumer society.

Negro Digest was limited in critiquing a model of black liberation invested in the acts of buying and selling. Significant distance was generated between the magazine's obvious bourgeois commitments early in the 1960s, and the later version heavily invested in pushing the idea of American cultural democracy. At best, however, it articulated a critique of redemptive capitalism only by analogy. By 1970, the magazine's long-term exploration of Pan Africanism centered around a vigorous critique of neocolonialism.[19] Was Johnson Publication's reliance upon the patronage of white/multinational advertisers itself a neocolonial situation? To push this question might seem dangerously trite—merely an academic paradox or, indeed, so "unnatural" as not to warrant extended consideration. But if there is some significant distinction to be drawn between John H. Johnson's insistence in 1968 that he did not "want to destroy the system," but rather "wanted to get into it," and other measures of the 1960s, any scholarly evaluation should investigate this complication.

The change of name of the magazine in May 1970 is one of the great "transformations" of the 1960s (perhaps on a par with the transformation of Cassius Clay into Muhammad Ali). Happening at the beginning of a new decade, the change offered an important culmination to much that black cultural activists had worked so hard to achieve. Fuller no doubt experienced more than a little joy in the transformation. The magazine's *prestige* had never been higher. Yet he was also clearly exhausted from a running battle with John H. Johnson over the magazine's support. By 1967, Fuller was exasperated with the magazine's backing and insisted that, if allowed to solicit advertising and have some authority over distribution, he could easily double its circulation. From 1967 through the magazine's demise, Fuller fought very regular battles with Johnson over everything from the quality of paper used to produce the *Digest* to his own salary and the size of his staff. After seemingly eliciting no response to a detailed request for support that he wrote in July 1968, Fuller wrote a resignation letter on 6 August 1968: "I know you have ambiguous feelings about *Negro Digest*, and these feelings probably explain why the magazine gets no support. I would like to say again that *Negro Digest* has been an extremely important influence in the

community. I don't believe you have any idea of the magazine's importance to both the white and Black intellectual communities. I think
you will discover the magazine's importance when it is too late."[20]
Johnson must have made some compromise, but Fuller was soon back
to writing urgent notes about salary and support for the magazine.

Fuller's correspondence with David Llorens reveals that Fuller may
have felt that he made a Faustian bargain in returning to the *Digest*. In
November 1965, Llorens wrote Fuller that some Johnson Publications
staff "are extremely worried about the future of Digest. They don't do a
very good job of hiding it upon meeting me."[21] From Majorca, Fuller
replied:

> I know that *Negro Digest* is the only money-loser in the JPC
> magazine stable. I also thought you knew that. I had gone to
> some lengths to explain to you the special conditions underly-
> ing *Negro Digest's* existence, and I hoped you understood the
> very precariousness of the magazine itself. . . . As to Mr.
> Johnson's own feelings, well, I have no idea. Nor am I too much
> concerned about it. He is not particularly disposed toward me,
> of course, and he is not passionate about *Negro Digest* and its
> orientation. He has his own reasons for keeping the magazine—
> and for preventing it from becoming solvent (accepting ads;
> giving it a shot in the arm; pushing it)—and I gave up trying to
> discover what these reasons really are.[22]

In subsequent letters, Llorens struggled to make sense of the *Digest's*
circulation figures. John H. Johnson regularly stated publicly that its
circulation was "around 100,000." Fuller confessed to Llorens that, while
he sometimes personally stated 60,000, the truth was that circulation
had "stablized around 30,000."[23] By initially reporting high numbers,
Johnson was foregrounding an inevitable "circulation decline" as a rationale for closure.[24] Yet *Negro Digest's* "special conditions"—fragile existence without growth—preserved Johnson Publications' credentials as
the major communications organization to the black community most
broadly conceived.

Johnson's late capitalist management practices brought the final demise of *Negro Digest/Black World*.[25] Protection of the Johnson Publications "brand name" and, of course, profit were always the determining
factors in the administration of the magazine. As such, we might want

to reconsider, for example, Amiri Baraka's own "shift" to Marxist-Leninism, however overdetermined and lacking in subtlety—and, for that matter, much of the substance of Harold Cruse's critique in *Crisis of the Negro Intellectual*[26]—as growing recognition of the type of questions that might need to be asked of black cultural production in the 1960s and could never be asked in this "context." No matter how substantive the achievement of *Negro Digest/Black World*, it seems important to vigorously consider the ways the "new" magazine remained wedded to an ideology and set of business practices that first took shape in the early 1940s. An important line of further inquiry into the achievement of *Negro Digest/Black World* (and that of other black cultural institutions of the decade themselves "attached" to capital too) must be not only to sort out what questions were successfully pursued and debated but also to imagine those questions that could not even get on the table.

Despite the ways in which John Johnson—and, for that matter, even some commentators on the political and cultural Left—insisted that *Ebony* (and Johnson Publications generally) had shifted *toward* "militancy,"[27] such shifts must be seen as relative and always at least partially a process of masking. Was Fuller's ambition—indeed, the ambition of a whole generation of African-American creative intellectuals who saw the *Digest* as a kind of home—manipulated by John H. Johnson? It certainly seems likely, although, no activist or intellectual, including myself, can fully escape such compromise. Neither, however, should this inevitability be seen as an inherent cynicism toward the enthusiastic use of the language of revolution and transcendence by Fuller's most committed supporters. Thus, we need a full accounting of the work of those who labored so hard to make American cultural democracy a reality.

One unusual location for some of the *Digest*'s most pointed criticism was the back cover. They were incredibly witty, often caustic, a clever combination of eye-catching graphic and prose, both celebratory and confrontational. Perhaps the distinction of these interventions peaked in May 1969. The back cover featured a neatly dressed African-American man with the requisite middle-class status symbols of suit and tie, umbrella, brief case, fedora, and slightly aloof look toward the reader. "Sorry to discomfort you, Chauncey Warringham Hildreth III, Esq.," read the caption. The accompanying text detailed real disruptions that *Negro Digest* had sought to record. "We know how distasteful it is for you to be reminded that most Americans that resemble you are second-class citizens. We know you are the exception; after all, your parents were professional people who brought you up in a stable middle-class neighborhood." After a further catalogue of "demonstrations and freedom songs and sit-ins and boycotts," the "advertisement" concluded with a hard-hitting conclusion.

> We believe that a truly free America is an America of
> unsurpassable strength. It is even possible that your children
> will be the immediate beneficiaries, since they have a better
> education than most and are best qualified to accept the jobs
> which civil rights pressures are opening up. So have patience,
> Mr. Chauncey Warringham Hildreth III; the battle you are
> watching with such great aloofness, sir, is really your own.

As all these back covers concluded so did this one: "Knowledge is the Key to a Better Tomorrow. Read Negro Digest. On Sale at Your Favorite Newsstand."

There is plenty of irony here (both direct and implied). Literally, the text puts forth with contemptuous irony, an articulation of a specific hostility to skeptics of Black Power, those blacks who were protective of achieved or inherited class status. A slightly hidden but richer irony existed in the choice of the graphic. John H. Johnson had been featured eighteen months earlier in *Fortune Magazine* under the title "How John Johnson Made It."[28] The accompanying photo featured Johnson in suit and tie, overcoat, and fedora, with gaze directed toward the reader in a fashion almost identical to that of the mythic Chauncey Hildreth III, Esq. Fuller took a not-so-subtle shot at the "ambivalent" Johnson. Even acknowledging this as a readerly text, however, it is hard to imagine that the advertisement sought to "convince"; instead, its character is almost ceremonial. Its relevant and reasonable hostility is straightforward enough, but it was mostly a joke to be shared with the already converted. Despite its urgency and critical edge, *Negro Digest* remains consumerist in its orientation, whether through weary recourse to the discourse of nation or through its always necessary conclusion: "On Sale at Your Favorite Newsstand."

Notes

1. For a strong assessment of heroic individual activism, see Jerry Gafio Watts, *Heroism and the Black Intellectual: Ralph Ellison, Politics, and Afro-American Intellectual Life* (Chapel Hill: University of North Carolina Press, 1994).
2. Clovis E. Semmes, *Roots of Afrocentric Thought: A Reference Guide to Negro Digest/Black World, 1961–1976* (Westport, Conn.: Greenwood, 1998), xii-xiii; Walter C. Daniel, *Black Journals of the United States* (Westport, Conn.: Greenwood, 1982), 264; and Julius Thompson, "A Literary and Critical Analysis of the Role of Hoyt W. Fuller (1927–1981) *Negro Digest* and *Black World* Magazine During the Black Arts Movement, 1960–1976," in *African American Sociology: A Social Study of the Pan-African Diaspora*, ed. James Conyers and Alva Barnett (Chicago: Nelson-Hall, 1999), 240.
3. Donald Franklin Joyce, "Magazines of Afro-American Thought on the Market: Can They Survive?," *American Libraries*, December 1976, 682.
4. David Lionel Smith, "The Black Arts Movement and Its Critics," in *American Literary History* 3, no. 1 (1991): 93–110.
5. Smith, "Black Arts Movement," 102.
6. Ben Burns, *Nitty Gritty: A White Editor in Black Journalism* (Jackson: University of Mississippi Press, 1996), 32.
7. See Patricia Ann Friday Shaw, *"Negro Digest," "Pulse," and "Headlines and Pictures": African-Amerian Periodicals as Informants, Morale Builders and Articulators of Protest During World War II* (Ph.D. diss., University of Maryland, College Park, 1994).
8. The August 1947 issue of *Negro Digest* included a condensation "Business Can Learn to Its Profit that Uncle Remus is Dead: 14 Million Negro Customers," 57, that more or less served as a public announcement of Johnson's eventual pursuit of (and faith in) American consumer capitalism.
9. *Negro Digest*, June 1961, 3.
10. Albert Kreiling, "The Commercialization of the Black Press and the Rise of Race News in Chicago," in, *Ruthless Criticism: New Perspectives in U.S. Communication History*, ed. William S. Solomon and Robert W. McChesney (Minneapolis: University of Minnesota Press, 1993), 176–203 at 197.
11. Robert Weems, "The Revolution Will Be Marketed: American Corporations and Black Consumers During the 1960s," *Radical History Review* 59 (1994):94–107, and William Van DeBerg, *New Day in Babylon: The Black Power Movement and American Culture, 1965–1975* (Chicago: University of Chicago Press, 1992).
12. Robert Harris, "Introduction," in *Homage to Hoyt Fuller*, ed. Dudley Randall (Detroit, Mich.: Broadside Press, 1984), 12. For Fuller also see: *Nommo: A Literary Legacy of Black Chicago (1967–1987)*, ed. Carole Parkes (Chicago: OBAhouse, 1987); Pacifica Tape Library #BB 0896, "An Organ for Protest" [Audio Recording of Panel Discussion at the 1964 Negro Writers Conference: Hoyt Fuller, Bettye Hughes, Louise Merriwether] (Los Angeles: Pacifica Radio, n.d.); and Hoyt Fuller Papers, Robert Woodruff Library, Atlanta University. See *Negro Digest Series*, Folder 19, *Hoyt Fuller Collection*; especially informal memos to Fuller from other staff writers and Fuller's resignation letter of 12 February 1957, which seems to confirm this through its insistent denial of a problem.
13. Many commentators (including myself) point out the key years of 1965 and 1966, when the magazine began to advocate for the consideration of a black

aesthetic, without noting Fuller's absence to take a Whitney Fellowship and the able stewardship of David Llorens.

14. Fuller did continue to run articles on bourgeois comforts like "Financing and Insuring a Car"(December 1965) and "Save Money on Insurance" (October 1966).

15. See my forthcoming *Mercy, Mercy Me: African American Culture and the American Sixties* (Oxford) for more on the status and meaning of black writers' conferences in the 1960s.

16. Fuller did write a powerful travelogue and turned down numerous opportunities to establish Black Studies programs. See his *A Journey to Africa* (Chicago: Third World, 1971).

17. Quoted in Abby Arthur Johnson and Ronald Mayberry Johnson, *Propaganda and Aesthetics* (Amherst: University of Massachussetts Press, 1979), 165, originally published in *Negro Digest* (November 1969). *Propaganda and Aesthetics* remains the strongest reading of black literary magazines available; it evidences, perhaps, the way in which "cultural institutional history" has been overlooked in the past twenty years or so of African-American Studies work.

18. Certainly the annual poetry portfolios were the most striking evidence of this gesture. They included work of incredible thematic and stylistic diversity and often included the previously unpublished right next to the most celebrated poets of the day.

19. See, for example, Hussein Mohammed Adam, "Frantz Fanon: His Understanding," *Black World*, December 1971; Alioune Diop, "Three Objectives of a Cultural Policy," *Black World*, December 1973; and Walter Moore's "Nigeria and the Black Future," *Black World*, May 1970, among many others.

20. Hoyt Fuller Collection, *Negro Digest* Series, Folder 20.

21. Hoyt Fuller Collection, Box 16, Folder 14.

22. Ibid.

23. Fuller to Llorens, 8 December 1965.

24. In his autobiography, *Succeeding Against the Odds*, Johnson says that "when the Freedom Movement ebbed, the circulation of *Black World* dropped from 100,000 to 15,000" (289).

25. On Johnson's management style, see Eliza G. C. Collins and Wanda A. Lankenner, "Failure is a Word I Don't Accept," *Harvard Business Review* 54 (March/April 1976):79–88.

26. Harold Cruse, *Crisis of the Negro Intellectual* (New York: Morrow, 1967).

27. See, for instance, Walter Goodman, "*Ebony*: Biggest Negro Magazine," *Dissent* 15 (September/October 1968): 403–409. Also relevant is Paul M. Hirsch, "An Analysis of *Ebony*: The Magazine and Its Readers," *Journalism Quarterly* 45 (Summer 1968):261–92.

28. James A. Reichly, "How Johnson Made It," *Fortune*, January 1968, 152–53, 178–79.

Chapter 11	"Photographs Taken in Everyday Life"
MAREN STANGE	Ebony's *Photojournalistic Discourse*

IN ITS INAUGURAL ISSUE of November 1945, the monthly magazine *Ebony* famously editorialized that it would "try to mirror the happier side of Negro life—the positive, everyday achievements from Harlem to Hollywood. But when we talk about race as the No. 1 problem of America, we'll talk turkey."[1] Like *Life* nine years earlier, *Ebony* was an instant success; its initial printing of twenty-five thousand sold out in hours, and another twenty-five thousand copies were immediately prepared. After six months, publisher John H. Johnson announced that the magazine would accept advertising;[2] eventually he secured accounts unprecedented for black journalism. Between 1949 and 1952 the magazine virtually doubled its size;[3] by the 1970s *Ebony's* circulation had grown to two million, and it was estimated to reach six million readers by 1980 and nine million per issue by 1992.[4]

A heavily illustrated "consumer" magazine with feature stories in photo-essay format as well as other modes of photojournalistic display, *Ebony*, though monthly, was consciously modeled on the weekly *Life*, by 1945 the primary vehicle for conveying the news visually to a mass American (and, increasingly, international) audience, and it is hard to avoid comparisons. As inaugural executive editor Ben Burns noted, "I had copies of *Life* constantly in front of me to emulate, and I did so religiously" in assembling early issues.[5] There were, however, significant

variations. One was *Ebony*'s "Speaking of People" department, positioned to correspond to *Life*'s "Speaking of Pictures." In contrast to the
Life section, which called attention to the photographic medium itself,
Ebony's department offered several pages of black-and-white photographs
showing people casually posed, clearly in their homes or workplaces,
crowded four or five to a page almost like family-album snapshots. Those
featured in early issues included a television news cameraman, a woman
bank manager, a couple who each held Ph.D.'s, and an aquarium proprietor—all readily recognizable members of the middle class.

    Ebony's editorial foregrounding of depicted people rather than de-
picting medium is one indication of how sharply different were the
magazines' uses of photography, and how relatively complex was *Ebony*'s
goal of mirroring "positive, everyday achievements" in the segregated
society of pre–civil rights United States. *Ebony* editors deployed photography that would not only uphold familiar codes of journalistic objectivity but also detach images of blacks from their pervasive association
with equally familiar cultural representations as spectacular and/or degraded Others and victims, to be shown only "in a superficial or a caricatured way or as a problem," in photographer Roy DeCarava's words.[6]
In the language of semiotic analysis, *Ebony*'s visual intervention sought
to dismantle and construct anew the coded system of signs that signifies what Henry Louis Gates, Jr., has called the "Public Negro."[7] *Ebony*'s
images would detach, or disarticulate, racialized icons—that is, the recognizable black face and body—from the familiar markers of degradation, spectacle, and victimization to which they had always been linked
if represented at all; the pictures would, instead, reproduce iconic blackness articulated to equally naturalized and sanctioned symbols of class
respectability, achievement, and American national identity. As had
earlier re-formers of popular visual discourse, *Ebony* relied on the presumed "transparency" of photography's indexical representation of its
"real life" referents—the medium's "special status with regard to the
real"—to uphold its discursive interventions.[8]

    Ebony's photographs showed, overwhelmingly, people, falling for the
most part into four stylistic categories: informal snapshot-like portraits,
journalistic character studies, formal portraiture or glamour shots, and,
least common, classic documentary reportage. In part because it was
monthly, the magazine rarely carried the kind of dramatized spot news

coverage found in newspapers or weekly magazines. Too, its contestatory stance toward hegemonic racial and social "truths" constrained possibilities for "universal," autonomous, or aesthetically "original" images. Although *Ebony*'s photographs displayed recognizable journalistic conventions, they were generally not expressive. They eschewed techniques—such as dramatic lighting and camera angles, severe cropping, or soft focus—that were readily found in mainstream mass-circulation magazines as well as more aesthetically ambitious photography, and which invited viewers to emotional response. The magazine rarely deployed the photographic medium's full range of stylistic and expressive possibility.

To some extent, financial considerations enforced this diminution; photographs in early issues consisted primarily of inexpensive stock photo agency packages and publicity pictures.[9] In addition, although African Americans had been active as professional and artistic photographers since the medium's invention, "in the late 1940s not a single Negro worked as a staff photographer at *Life*, *Look*, or any other nationally circulated magazine or metropolitan newspaper," so Burns turned as well to white freelancers.[10] The magazine hired its first full-time staff photographer, Griffith Davis, only in 1948.[11] Despite the achievements of freelance contributors including Gordon Parks, Wayne Miller, and Marion Palfi, not until Pulitzer Prize–winning Moneta Sleet joined *Ebony* in 1955, finding his compelling theme in the heroism of the Civil Rights Movement, did the magazine's images regularly display distinctive stylistic consistency. Herbert Nipson, joining the staff in 1949, undertook much photo-editing with Burns as comanaging editor and eventually became executive editor.[12]

Thus it is unsurprising that discussion has generally bypassed the photography that attracted *Ebony*'s mass readership in order to focus on story content and textual expressions of editorial ideology. Rather than using *Ebony*'s photography to explore elements of what bell hooks calls African-Americans' "historical relationship to the visual,"[13] most commentators note the magazine's abundance of "latter-day Horatio Alger stories," analyze its advertising, or focus on its coverage of the 1960s Civil Rights Movement.[14] Historian Jacqueline Jones, noting that in the early 1950s *Ebony* had more black readers than any other black or white periodical, argues that *Ebony* "served as a militant advocate of

black civil rights" in the immediate postwar period; but she mentions
Ebony's photography only to find it "at first glance . . . contradictory"
in regard to women's issues and offers no further analysis of it apart from
the magazine's story content.[15]

Ebony and other "race publications" of the time responded to the
demographic shifts that the war accelerated, above all the formation of
a larger and more dominant northern "black bourgeoisie."[16] This was,
in Johnson's perspicacious vision, a "new Black consumer class" with a
"keen yearning to see itself in the glossy pages of a national magazine—
living, loving, dreaming, achieving."[17] Better education, fewer racial
barriers, and higher incomes in wartime defense work and, later, newly
accessible white-collar jobs (as well as unionized industrial work) enabled a larger proportion of northern city dwellers to enjoy relative af-
fluence and status in a wider range of occupations. During the 1940s,
the proportion of northern dwelling African-American men in clerical
and related work more than doubled, and that of women clerical workers
quadrupled.[18] By 1950, African Americans in white-collar work made
up more than one-fifth of the northern population, but only one-sixth
of the (still more numerous) southern population. As even E. Franklin
Frazier's blisteringly negative assessment acknowledges, the black press
succeeded when it responded to the "mental stimulation" and "awak-
ened imagination" of city dwellers, for all of whom, irrespective of educational and class level, "the northern metropolis opened a new world
of ideas and adventure."[19]

Ebony appealed to such urban readers because it could "draw a larger
circle" than had earlier black magazines, argues former *Jet* editor William Berry. Acknowledging city dwellers outside the small black elite
whom previous black magazines had specifically addressed, regular *Ebony*
features might spotlight "the boxer, the banker, the haberdasher, the
farmer, the debutante, the policy king, the faith healer, the educator . . .
so long as he worked hard" claims Berry.[20] Too, *Ebony* presented working wives and mothers in a "positive, and frequently positively heroic,
light" in the postwar years. *Ebony* editors—including Northwestern-
trained Era Bell Thompson after 1947—believed women to be a significant, perhaps majority, proportion of their readership, suggests
Jacqueline Jones, citing numerous features, profiles, and editorial de-

partments that "stressed the intelligence and diverse accomplishments of black women."[21]

Nevertheless, *Ebony* had to please advertisers as well as readers. Costing twenty-five (later thirty) cents and featuring covers in color by 1946, the magazine's beginnings were notably "mild [and] moderate," claims journalism historian Roland E. Wolseley.[22] Former editor Burns (a white leftist who probably wrote most early editorials) calls *Ebony*'s rejection of the racial militancy characterizing the black press during World War II "daring," even as he disparages Johnson's concern to placate the white media and particularly advertising agencies. *Ebony* emphasized "searching for black achievements to crow about" rather than witnessing racial injustice, insists Burns; it found a "sure-fire formula that it continued to follow for decades: first, only, biggest."[23]

In its first years, the magazine (perhaps purposely) established no consistent format and, highly sensitive to readers' opinions and preferences, was "unique" among national, large-circulation magazines in its "public attention to reader response," writes Paul Hirsch.[24] It ran a lengthy "Letters and Pictures to the Editor" section and "Backstage" column on its own production processes and personnel. It carried only a few invariable features, and masthead content categories often changed, regularly including entertainment and sports, as well as a changing selection from topics such as foreign affairs, religion, race, pets, medicine, business, sex, the military, education, and (in the 1940s) overseas. At the back of the book were "Date with a Dish," on cooking, and "Negro Homes of America," often featuring entertainers' or politicians' houses, and a "fashion" story that seems frequently to have required scantily clad models.

Along with advertising, the magazine soon incorporated (even more) "sexy articles, cheesecake pictures, and other come-ons," averaging 150 pages in 1952 and boosting circulation to a half-million until the recession of 1954.[25] Wayne Miller photographed a "tea [marijuana] party" in September 1948 (46–51) (Figure 1); his January 1948 cover story "Babies By Special Delivery" showed the birth of a baby in a South Side home (9–15) (Figure 2); Miller's feature piece on nightclub performers who were female impersonators ran in March of that year (61–65). Typical (and typically inexpensive) feature stories were "The

Figure 1. Wayne F. Miller, *Marijuana Smoker. Copyright Wayne F. Miller.*

Abortion Menace," in January 1951, which used staged pictures of anx-
ious-appearing young women interspersed with wire-service photos of
doctors convicted of performing illegal abortions (21–26), and, in February, "Is Dope Killing Our Musicians?" by Cab Calloway, featuring publicity shots of well-known performers recently convicted of drug-related
offenses (22–28). To counter sagging circulation in the mid–1950s,
Johnson offered a "new *Ebony*" devoid of "objectionable sensational-
ism" and stories "unsuitable for circulation to young people" as one

Figure 2. Wayne F. Miller, *Newborn Baby. Copyright Wayne F. Miller.*

prominently featured letter to the editor noted; the change worked, again increasing home circulation and advertising revenue.[26]

Many feature photo-essays in these years used the kind of small, snapshot-like black-and-white images carried in "Speaking of People." A November 1950 story on the perenially popular topic of interracial marriage, for example, included pictures of nearly twenty families; a two-page central spread offered ten photographs of smiling couples, many with children, strung along the top and bottom of the pages.[27] Decisions on picture size were probably economically determined: smaller pictures made more advertising space available, and essays were simpler and quicker to lay out. Also, such layouts lent the weight of numbers to their topics, and the small size minimized possible picture flaws. But such considerations should not preclude a critical reading of the ways these essays work formally to construct (or deconstruct) representational codes. Thus, for instance, the spread of snapshot-like portraits described above can be seen to refer to the "walls of images in southern black homes." There, suggests bell hooks, snapshots and sometimes studio portraits—informal self-representation that "did not resemble or please white folks' ideas about us"—constituted private, familial, sites of opposition. Hooks suggests that black life in general under segregation included a "passionate engagement" with all "informal photographic processes" because African Americans realized the power of spontaneously made snapshots to "expose" and "rebel against" sanctioned representational conventions whose Eurocentric aesthetic inevitably incorporated stereotypical "colonizing fantasies."[28] Thus, perhaps more by luck than intention, Ebony's small images and crowded layouts may have helped to draw its "wider circle" of readers especially because these graphic features connected the magazine's representation of current African-American life to older, valued family practices.

In contrast to the image-crowded layouts of feature photo-essays, Ebony's two-page "photo-editorials" consisted of a two-(rather than three-) column page of text opposite a newsworthy full-page photograph. In May 1946, the text titled "The Negro Veteran Tests America" faced a carefully framed, utterly static picture of two card-playing convalescing soldiers, one black and one white, photographed by Gordon Parks for the federal government's Office of War Information (OWI) (40–41). In March 1946, photographer Gordon Coster's full-page closeup character study of an interracial trio of CIO packinghouse unionists "splendidly symbolized . . . racial unity" for an editorial titled "Labor's Love Gained" (44–45). Like these, most large-scale pictures that appeared with feature stories were conventionally posed and framed and depicted noncontroversial people or subjects in the clear, well-lit style that historian Tina Olsin Lent has called the "mass-appeal aesthetic" found throughout mainstream pictorials.[29] These half- or full-page images showed celebrities (whose portraits might have been free), notable political figures, or "first, only, biggest."[30]

Unremarkable as they may now appear, Ebony's tactics of visual representation directly challenged harshly enforced codes. "The large number and variety of inherently racist images in American culture attest to a particularly American preoccupation with marginalizing black Americans by flooding the culture with an-Other Negro, a Negro who conformed to the deepest social fears and fantasies of the larger society," writes Henry Louis Gates, Jr. To escape such dehumanizing stereotype was to dig "out from under the codified racist debris of centuries of representations of blackness as absence, as nothingness, as deformity and depravity."[31] It was not only the "tens of thousands" of negative caricatures appearing as cartoons, postcards, salt and pepper shakers, tea cosies, children's games, and dolls, but also the exclusion of African Americans from all white-controlled purportedly objective mass media visual content that executed that "preoccupation."[32] Until the early 1950s, the *New Orleans Times-Picayune* had a "rule that blacks were not to appear in photographs it published, not even as part of a background," writes journalism historian Ira Harkey.[33] Jessie Jackson has recalled the "night of whiteness" imposed by a hometown paper with "never a picture of a Black wedding" nor "a story about a local Black businessman" nor "a decent obituary."[34] In his memoirs Gates remembers being "starved for images of ourselves," "search[ing]" television and "devour[ing]" *Ebony* and *Jet* to find them.[35] Deborah Willis likens her first encounter with Roy DeCarava's complexly beautiful Harlem photographs to "a veil [being] lifted."[36]

Life, from 1940 until at least 1960 the "worldwide leading picture magazine," practiced this "whiteout," as Johnson called it, assiduously.[37] Tracing the magazine's presentation of black Americans in "scenes of everyday life" through 1972, Mary Alice Sentman found such material "markedly absent," and she found coverage of "black America" generally only a "minute portion" of the magazine's content.[38] Similarly, historian Wendy Kozol's study of the centrality of the family to *Life*'s "representation of current events" found that images showing "representatives of 'America'" in the years 1945 to 1960 were "always [of] white families" who were always middle class. "Other kinds of families [and individuals] appear in the magazine as representatives of social issues or political problems," she writes, "but never as representatives of 'America.'"[39] Photo historian Bill Gaskins notes that only twenty-three covers in *Life*'s history as a weekly featured blacks,[40] and historian James Guimond shows that, in the many pictures and photo-essays celebrating progress, prosperity, and "the American way of life" in *Life*, in *Look*, or in 1940s and 1950s United States Information Agency pamphlets, "virtually everyone" is white, middle class, and a member of a small nuclear family.[41] *Life*'s special issues on topics such as "America's Assets," "This Pleasant Land," or "U.S. Growth," likewise represented a white nation. An essay on "Great American Churches," for instance, showed only white congregations and ministers, and one on the General Motors Corporation showed only white employees. No persons of color appeared in *Life*'s 1946 tenth-anniversary special issue, and in a 1950 special issue on "American Life and Times, 1900–1950" blacks appeared only in one historical picture in a nostalgia essay.[42]

Even as blacks and other persons of color were excluded from media constructions of a national, consensual discourse of progress, prosperity, and respectability, their images were used for other purposes. In its early years, *Life* did not hesitate to recycle familiar comic stereotypes, featuring "the watermelon theme" in two first-year issues and writing unabashedly of "mammies" and "pickaninnies."[43] And like other mass media, *Life* relied not only on "a dramatization of the pleasant," as Henry Luce called it, but also on sensational reporting to boost readership.[44] In *Life*'s heyday, when "about half the population of the United States read at least one issue . . . in every three-month period,"[45] there was virtually a "protocol" that allotted the representation of pleasant and/or typically American experience to middle-class white subjects and presented "outsiders"—foreigners and people of color—as designated victims "whose sufferings and corpses can be photographed and packaged as 'sensations,'" suggests Guimond. In war reporting, dead white Americans were generally shown "lying quietly," with faces obscured, but viewers could see the faces and other close-up details of black, Asian, and foreign victims.[46] Contemporary artist Pat Ward Williams's well-known piece "Can you be BLACK and look at this?" reproduces a photograph of a lynched black man chained to a tree, which appeared "uncredited" in an early *Life* issue, her accompanying text questioning possibilities of adequate or appropriate response.[47]

Discussing such images, Elizabeth Alexander reminds that "Black bodies in pain for public consumption have been an American spectacle for centuries."[48] In an essay addressing the recent proliferation of "post-mortem" images of murdered young black men, Deborah McDowell argues that "U.S. culture apprehends Black Americans, especially Black American men, largely through . . . photographic technology," that "their bodies have historically made good spectacle, have become seared in the nation's optical unconscious," and that the long history of viewing "black death [as] good spectacle" is implicit and "haunting" in even the most current, ostensibly respectable photojournalism.[49]

When *Life* did attempt a serious social coverage, the visual markers of difference and "deviance" were carefully coded and verbally emphasized. A 1938 *Life* photo-essay, "Negroes: The U.S. Also Has a Minority Problem," introduces its subject as "a minority more sharply set off than any of the world's other minorities."[50] Ten years later, Gordon Parks's first photo-essay for *Life*, "Harlem Gang Leader," about seventeen-year-old Red Jackson, was slightly more subtle.[51] The publication of the story, which Parks himself proposed to editor Wilson Hicks and which ran as a feature photographic essay, led to a staff position.[52]

As Parks clearly understood, he could expect the magazine to present Red as a social problem of some complexity, but not as a complex human being. The central, climactic image in the narrative of gang life shows "a night brawl" in which "Red's gang battles another suspected of killing their buddy" (102–103). This blurred, decentered composition, which occupies more than a full page, catches silhouetted figures in agitated motion to convey an overall impression of violent confrontation rather than the magazine's usual clear display of content. The next largest image—a full page—shows Red and another boy peering into the coffin of a gang member who had been "found dying on a Harlem sidewalk"; they were, according to the caption, scrutinizing the wounds visible around the corpse's mouth for signs that he had been murdered by a rival gang rather than dying of natural causes as the police claimed (100). Several smaller pictures elaborate the theme of violence (98–99, 101). From the essay's opening two-page spread, which collages an artily silhouetted profile of Red by a shattered window over a panorama of "the crowded tenements and the cluttered, dreary streets of Harlem, the U.S.'s biggest Negro community" (96–97), Parks's photography seems chosen for emotional connotation rather than clear visual content.

Within the bounds of such popular discourse, endlessly recycling "codified racist debris," *Ebony* and other black pictorials intervened by seeking to picture African Americans as "everyday, ordinary human Americans."[53] It is in this context that bell hooks valorizes even the most mundane photographic documents and foregrounds photography's power as "the central instrument" to "disprove representations of us created by white folks." "The degrading images of blackness that emerged from racist white imaginations and circulated widely in the dominant culture . . . could be countered by 'true-to-life' images," she insists. Though hooks leaves the meaning of "true to life" uninterrogated, her essay's comments on black families' "obsession with images of self-representation" help clarify her emphasis on "photographs taken in everyday life," that "announced our visual complexity."[54] Three *Ebony* feature stories represent key ambiguities and tensions inherent in the magazine's visual project, revealing the necessarily uneven and sometimes disjunct steps in its process of simultaneous dis- and re-articulation.

An early foray into sensational reportage was the May 1946 lead, "America's Year of Decision," with "exclusive bloody photographs of a Tennessee race riot" obtained, claims Ben Burns, free of charge as a "rejected photo package" from *Life* magazine's only black editor, Earl Brown. After comparing 1946 to 1919, "the worst year of racial violence in all U.S. history," the article pinpointed events in Columbia, Tennessee, as an "ominous omen of tomorrow" and featured pictures of white-perpetrated violence credited to Roger Atkins.[55] The half-page lead image of two white men with rifles is captioned "Stalking Negro Prey," and a following full-page shot of a prone body shows a "wounded Negro . . . bleeding in a Columbia street." Black women and men are shown with hands raised being searched and then "lined up and jailed in a sweeping [police] roundup." As we have seen, images of equivalent violence perpetrated by (and upon) people of color would have been unexceptional in *Life* and other mainstream media; but, according to Burns, the complaints of several *Ebony* advertisers about the negative portrayal of whites in this essay provoked Johnson's "ironclad rule" prohibiting any coverage of "race riots" in future issues.[56]

Though Johnson's unwavering eye on the bottom line does suggest that pleasing white advertisers was a primary motivation—and this issue was *Ebony*'s first to carry advertising—these images depart significantly from *Ebony*'s own carefully constructed visual parameters delimiting black achievement and respectability. Images of white violence against black bodies continue a process in which "black people have paradoxically had to witness their own murder and defilement in order to survive and then to pass along the epic tale of violation,"[57] proposes Elizabeth Alexander; Robyn Weigman points out that whether alternative or mainstream, newspaper stories documenting "the scenes of violence [and] . . . graphic detail of the practices of torture," especially lynching, served to reiterate African Americans' "secondary social position throughout the twentieth century." Weigman argues that all such stories "defined and policed" African Americans as "innately, if no longer legally, inferior," and they "extended the function of lynching as a mode of surveillance."[58] On these views, the Columbia images uphold narratives of subjugation and inferiority that *Ebony* aimed to disrupt.

"Reporter with a Camera" featured Gordon Parks in July 1946— just prior to his joining *Life*—as a classic "first and only" success story, incorporating several of his accomplished photographs (24–29). Parks had begun his professional career in Chicago and contributed to early *Ebony* issues;[59] after a period of documentary apprenticeship at the Farm Security Administration (FSA) Photography Project in Washington, he was then working on the Standard Oil of New Jersey (SONJ) project, headed by former FSA director Roy Stryker, and would join the staff of *Life* in 1948.[60] Emphasizing Parks's "high-paying [SONJ] contract" and glamorous work life, the essay includes some anecdotes about his early life later mentioned in his several autobiographies. A range of high-quality photographs by Parks and his SONJ colleagues were available (presumably free of charge), allowing *Ebony* editors to craft a visually effective piece. Like a classic *Life* photo-essay, it flows visually as well as textually; smaller shots organize narrative to advance the explication of Parks's life-story, and several full and half-page pictures punctuate it. Column-sized images show Parks "baggage-burdened" on assignment, in the "chaotic haven" of the SONJ darkroom, and on "dawn patrol" at his writing desk (25). The larger pictures are examples of his documentary work anchored to the life-story theme with tidbits of information about where and how Parks got the shot. These evocative images—a New England farmhouse, a grease-besmirched workman, a row of six "sardonic Canadian 'tough guys'" (Figure 3)—show how skillfully Parks had mastered the photojournalistic repertoire even before

Figure 3. Gordon Parks, *Canadian Tough Guys. Standard Oil (New Jersey), Special Collections: Photographic Archives, University of Louisville.*

joining *Life* (24, 26, 27). However, only one of the documentary images used by *Ebony* shows people of color.

A final essay page is devoted to Parks's home life in "the unique interracial community" of Parkway Gardens, New York, where Cecil Layne posed Parks with his family on the toboggan and in his spacious living room (29). The essay's "first and only" narrative line successfully contains two kinds of images: Parks's own photographs made on assignment to far-flung (but white-inhabited) places which testify to the persuasive powers of documentary photography, and photographs of Parks and his family, whose sober conventionality articulates these attractive figures to readily discernible markers of glamour, comfort, and success.

In 1951, Richard Wright's essay "The Shame of Chicago" broke *Ebony* precedent to give photographer Wayne Miller a byline accompanying the author's, and it used exclusively the evocative South Side pictures Miller had made during a 1946–1947 Guggenheim Fellowship awarded to photograph "The Way of Life of the Northern Negro." Like the Parks story, the six-page Wright piece combined documentary images with celebrity glamour. Burns had been Wright's colleague on the

Daily Worker in the 1930s, and the first issue of *Ebony* featured Wright.[61] The new essay was commissioned in fall 1950, just after Wright had returned to Chicago to film scenes for a movie version of his best-selling 1940 novel *Native Son*, set on Chicago's South Side. Finally published in December 1951, the essay coincided with the film's Hollywood premiere.[62]

Wright's skillfully organized text interwove general impressions with accounts of the filmmaking project. Overall, the city offered a "single impression of industrial dominance that spelt a kind of queer and unique poetry," making Chicago "powerfully and impressively ugly." Visiting "old neighborhoods that held . . . a thousand tangled memories," he commented on the sometimes bizarre proximity of newly flourishing businesses and civic neglect, so that owners of cars that were "gleaming and new" parked on "piles of garbage." His surprise to find none of the "condemned, empty buildings . . . [that he] had written about in *Native Son*" is explained by the increased immigration of the war years that caused "those empty and condemned buildings . . . to be used again!" Frustration over hotel reservations for the film crew reveals that "Chicago was still Chicago [where] the old racial lines and attitudes still ruled"; as do Wright's accounts of placating a South Side precinct caption and bribing corrupt police in order to complete the location filming.

Returning in conclusion to housing, "the crux of it," Wright pressed home points that must have given Johnson pause. "The racial situation here is an intentionally fabricated one and the whites want to keep it that way," insisted an anonymous member of the Human Relations Commission. Urban anthropologist Louis Wirth explained that "the slums of Chicago's South Side are subsidized in the sense that they are kept like that. It's deliberate." Wright links such comments to "the shameful Cicero riot" of the previous summer, the largest and most violent of numerous recent incidents of white harassment and intimidation of black families hoping to live in white neighborhoods. In light of the tinderbox situation Cicero represented, a rebutting photo-editorial's claims for "many Negro families living next door to whites, in some of the finest homes in city," for "undeniably tremendous gains scored by Negroes . . . in the past decade," ring hollow. The editorial's temporizing proclamations—Wright's reporting was at once "trenchant . . . honest,

Figure 4. Wayne F. Miller, *Chicago Tenements, Rear View. Copyright Wayne F. Miller.*

sincere and distinguished" and "warped, often-naive and incomplete"—
sound fabricated and forced (100).

Wright was an accomplished amateur photographer who may have
known Miller's South Side work.[63] Miller's striking opening spread
shows the once-abandoned and now reoccupied tenements from the
back; despite hanging laundry and other signs of life, no people are visible (24–25) (Figure 4). The rickety wooden back porches create a
gridded wall that blocks out the sky, allegorizing the barricades long
imposed by "unwritten restrictive codes enforced by terror and violence," as the editorial affirms (100). Just as the article title superimposed against this image recalls Lincoln Steffens's Progressive-era
muckraking journalism, the photograph rehearses tenement studies familiar from early social documentary; "An Old Rear Tenement in
Roosevelt Street" from the Jacob Riis Collection at the Museum of the
City of New York, for instance, constructs a similar view from the 1880s.
Other Miller pictures show the dirt, disorder, and ugliness that Wright
found, and they detail makeshift living arrangements—a sled piled high
with coal sits in the snow by spindly wooden tenement stairways (26)
(Figure 5). Prices in a store window show "the high cost of living" (26),
and churches "spring up everywhere in basement flats and store fronts"

Figure 5. Wayne F. Miller, *Chicago Tenements in Winter. Copyright Wayne F. Miller.*

because "spiritualism flourishes among [the] insecure" (27). In the only closeups of people, an unidentified mother "pleads for her son with juvenile officers" in a courtroom (30), and a newborn receiving oxygen at segregated Provident Hospital faces a "life span . . . much shorter than white Chicagoans" (28).

Miller had gained a remarkable entre throughout the South Side; his Chicago work includes packinghouse picket lines and railroad workers, midwives and newsdealers, baseball players and nightclub entertainers.[64] Many of these images might have effectively complemented Wright's essay; however, the statically composed, scantily-peopled photographs that were selected appear subtly dated, as if relics of a bygone era, despite their actual currency. Their stylistic references to classic documentary traditions, exemplified by the Riis Collection parallel, distance implicitly the wretched conditions they show, just as the editorial associates Wright's text with "the throes of depression" (100). The essay included neither any images of Wright—who played the lead in the film—nor the authorities he quotes. Such an unusual, for *Ebony*, eschewal of the chance to exploit celebrity glamour indicates the importance of undermining Wright's authority and mediating the impact of his essay.

As we have seen, *Ebony* had access from the start to highly skilled journalistic and documentary photography, which it sometimes featured. Nevertheless, the display of creative talent, photographic expressivity, or socially critical reportage was not necessarily a high priority in these years. More important was the magazine's transformative work on extant and familiar iconic signs of blackness. The scope of this work was constrained both aesthetically and politically, inevitably to be found both insufficient and enabling. To appreciate it is to understand and value anew the terms, boundaries, and possibilities of our present discourses.

Notes

1. "Backstage," *Ebony*, November 1945, 1; this is volume 1, number 1. I thank Regina Neal and Barbara Radin for acquainting me early on with this material.
2. Information on *Ebony*'s early years can be found in Roland E. Wolseley, *The Black Press, U.S.A.*, 2d ed. (Ames: Iowa State University Press, 1990), 142. Ben Burns, *Nitty Gritty: A White Editor in Black Journalism* (Jackson: University Press of Mississippi, 1996) recounts his experiences as editor at the *Chicago Defender* and then editor-in-chief at *Ebony* until 1955.
3. Paul M. Hirsch, "An Analysis of *Ebony*: The Magazine and Its Readers," *Journalism Quarterly* 45, 2 (Summer 1968): 264.
4. Hirsch, "An Analysis," 269; Wolseley, *Black Press*, 142; "From *Negro Digest* to *Ebony, Jet*, and *EM*," *Ebony*, November 1992, 54.
5. Burns, *Nitty Gritty*, 85.
6. DeCarava is quoted in my "'Illusion Complete within Itself': Roy DeCarava's Photography," in *A Modern Mosaic*, ed. Towsend J. Ludington (Chapel Hill: University of North Carolina Press, 2000), 279–305.
7. Henry Louis Gates, Jr., "The Face and Voice of Blackness," in *Facing History:*

The Black Image in American Art, 1710–1940, ed. Guy C. McElroy and Christopher C. French (Washington, D.C.: Bedford Arts, Publishers in association with the Corcoran Gallery of Art, 1990), xxv.

8. Photography's relation to "the real" is in Rosalind Krauss, "Tracing Nadar," *October* 5 (Summer 1978): 5; her essay discusses photography's indexical status at length. "Articulation" is defined as "any form of semiotic organization which engenders distinct combinable units," in Robert Stam, Robert Burgoyne, and Sandy Flitterman-Lewis, *New Vocabularies in Film Semiotics* (New York: Routledge, 1992), 32. Defining "to articulate" as meaning both "to express" and "to join together," John Storey usefully summarizes articulation as a key concept in neo-Gramscian perspectives on culture, suggesting (after Chantal Mouffe and Stuart Hall) that popular culture, as a "contested landscape" of cultural negotiation, is in constant processes of disarticulation and re-articulation by contending social groups, in his *Introductory Guide to Cultural Theory and Popular Culture* (Athens: University of Georgia Press, 1993), 13–14. I contend here that this process of negotiation and struggle to specify the meanings of representational codes by controlling the articulation of their elements was a central task at this moment of *Ebony*'s visual intervention. For discussion of the relation of photography to social reform, see my *Symbols of Ideal Life: Social Documentary Photography in America, 1890–1950* (New York: Cambridge University Press, 1989).

9. Burns, *Nitty Gritty*, 86.

10. Ibid., 98; Deborah Willis, *Black Photographers, 1840–1940: An Illustrated Bio-Bibliography* (New York: Garland, 1985), and Willis, *An Illustrated Bio-bibliography of Black Photographers, 1940–1988* (New York: Garland, 1989), and Willis, *Reflections in Black: A History of Black Photographers 1840 to the Present* (New York: W. W. Norton, 2000), detail the history of African-American photographers.

11. Burns, *Nitty Gritty*, 98.

12. Wolseley, *Black Press*, 246.

13. Bell hooks, "In Our Glory: Photography and Black Life," in *Picturing Us: African American Identity in Photography*, ed. Deborah Willis (New York: New Press, 1994), 52.

14. Irwin D. Rinder, "A Sociological Look into the Negro Pictorial," *Phylon* 20, 2 (1959): 74; see Laurel Frances Hollowaty, "Achievement, Equality of Opportunity and Equality of Access: Ideology and Aesthetics in Advertisements in *Life* and *Ebony*, 1945–1975," (Ph.D. diss., University of California at Irvine, 1984); Leslie Sargent, Wiley Carr, and Elizabeth McDonald, "Significant Coverage of Integration by Minority Group Magazines," *Journal of Human Relations* 13, 4 (1965): 484–91, compares "racial integration pictures" in *Ebony* and *Life* magazines; see Valerie Stephanie Saddler, "A Content Analysis of *Ebony*'s and *Life*'s 1955–1965 Reporting on Black Civil Rights Movement Issues" (Ph.D. diss., Ohio University, 1984).

15. Jacqueline Jones, *Labor of Love, Labor of Sorrow: Black Women, Work and the Family, from Slavery to the Present* (New York: Basic Books, 1985), 269–70.

16. Johnson founded Johnson Publishing Company in 1942; his inaugural *Negro Digest* continued later as *Black World* until 1976, and his weekly newsmagazine *Jet* (1951) proved another enduring success. Competitors have included New York City's monthly *Our World*, "The Picture Magazine for the Negro Family," published by John P. Davis from 1946 to 1955, and, in the 1950s, George Levitan's large-format *Sepia* and later his short-lived *Hep, Jive, Soul Confessions*

and *Bronze Thrills*, which never really challenged Johnson. Burns, *Nitty Gritty*, 39.

17. Rinder notes as well a race pride and a passionate group identification; see his "Sociological Look," 169; the "new Black consumer class" is in William Earl Berry, "The Popular Press as Symbolic Interactionism: A Social and Cultural Analysis of *Ebony* 1945–1975" (Ph.D. diss., University of Illinois, 1979), 71; Johnson's quote is in "Introduction," *Ebony*, November 1990, 26.

18. E. Franklin Frazier, *Black Bourgeoisie* (Glencoe, Ill.: Free Press, 1957), 48–49,47,49.

19. Ibid., 176, 178.

20. Berry, "Popular Press," 70.

21. Jones, *Labor of Love*, 269, 270.

22. Wolseley counters Jones's view of *Ebony*'s "aggressively integrationist" stance and mix of "optimism and rage" in the 1940s. Wolseley, *Black Press*, 142; Jones, *Labor of Love*, 270.

23. Burns, *Nitty Gritty*, 88, 94.

24. Hirsch, "Analysis of *Ebony*," 263.

25. Wolseley, *Black Press*, 142, Hirsch, "Analysis of *Ebony*," 264.

26. Letters to the Editor, *Ebony*, September 1955, 10; Wolseley, *Black Press*, 142.

27. "The Case Against Mixed Marriage," *Ebony*, November 1950, 52–53.

28. Hooks, "In Our Glory," 50–51.

29. Tina Olsin Lent, "Situating *The Americans*: Robert Frank and the Transformation of American Photography" (Ph.D. diss. University of Rochester, 1993), 48.

30. See, for instance, "Ball Playing Councilwoman," *Ebony*, November 1950, 48, and "Mr. Death," *Ebony*, January 1951, 29.

31. Gates, "Face and Voice of Blackness," xxix.

32. Ibid., xxix,xliv.

33. Ira Harkey, quoted in Carolyn Martindale, *The White Press and Black America* (Westport, Conn.: Greenwood Press, 1986), 55.

34. Jesse L. Jackson, "Growing Up with *Ebony*," *Ebony*, November 1995, 50J.

35. Henry Louis Gates, Jr., *Colored People, A Memoir* (New York: Vintage Books, 1995) 19, 23.

36. Willis, "Introduction: Picturing Us," in *Picturing Us*, 4.

37. Rudolph Janssens and Gertjan Kalff, "Time Incorporated Stink Club: The Influence of *Life* on the Founding of Magnum Photos," in *American Photographs in Europe*, ed. David E. Nye and Mick Gidley (Amsterdam: VU University Press, 1994), 223; "From *Negro Digest*," 52.

38. Mary Alice Sentman, "Black and White: Disparity in Coverage by *Life* Magazine from 1937 to 1972," *Journalism Quarterly*, 60 (Autumn 1983): 508.

39. Wendy Kozol, *LIFE's America: Family and Nation in Postwar Photojournalism* (Philadelphia: Temple University Press, 1994), 13.

40. Bill Gaskins, "The World According to *Life*: Racial Stereotyping and American Identity," *Afterimage* 21 (Summer 1993): 16.

41. James Guimond, *American Photography and the American Dream* (Chapel Hill: University of North Carolina Press, 1991), 170–71.

42. Ibid., 172–73.

43. Sentman, "Black and White," 504, 506–507; Gaskins, "The World According to *Life*," 16.

44. Guimond, *American Photography*, 157.

45. Janssens and Kalff, "Time Incorporated Stink Club," 223.

46. Guimond, *American Photography*, 157, 158.
47. Williams writes that she found the image in *The Best of Life* (New York: Time-Life Books, 1973).
48. Elizabeth Alexander, "'Can You Be BLACK and Look at This?': Reading the Rodney King Video(s)," in *Black Male: Representations of Masculinity in Contemporary American Art*, ed. Thelma Golden (New York: Whitney Museum of American Art, 1994), 92.
49. Deborah E. McDowell, "Viewing the Remains: A Polemic on Death, Spectacle, and the [Black] Family," in *The Familial Gaze*, ed. Marianne Hirsch (Hanover: University Press of New England, 1999), 154.
50. Gaskins, "The World According to *Life*," 15.
51. "Harlem Gang Leader," Photographs for *Life* by Gordon Parks, *Life*, 1 November 1948, 96–106; page numbers henceforth are given in parenthesis in the text.
52. Gordon Parks, *To Smile in Autumn, A Memoir* (New York: W.W. Norton & Company, 1979), 45.
53. *Ebony*, December 1945, 23.
54. Hooks, "In Our Glory," 51.
55. Burns, *Nitty Gritty*, 95. Burns names the photographer as Edward Clark, apparently incorrectly.
56. Ibid., 95–96.
57. Alexander, "Can You Be BLACK," 105.
58. Robyn Weigman, *American Anatomies: Theorizing Race and Gender* (Durham, N.C.: Duke University Press, 1997), 91.
59. Burns, *Nitty Gritty*, 98.
60. See Parks, *To Smile in Autumn* and *A Choice of Weapons*.
61. "Black Boy in Brooklyn," *Ebony*, November 1945, 19–22.
62. Michel Fabre, *The Unfinished Quest of Richard Wright*, trans. Isabel Barzun (New York: William Morrow & Co.,1973), 350.
63. See my "'Not What We Seem': Image and Text in *12 Million Black Voices*," in *Iconographies of Power*, ed. Ulla Haselstein, Berndt Ostendorf, and Peter Schneck (Heidelberg: C. Winter Press, 2001) for Wright's Chicago photographic work.
64. Miller worked closely with Edward Steichen on the 1955 *Family of Man* exhibition and book, contributing several pictures. His Chicago work can be seen in *Ebony* and in Wayne F. Miller, *Chicago's South Side, 1946–1948* (Berkeley: University of California Press, 2000).

Chapter 12

RODGER STREITMATTER

Black Panther Newspaper

A Militant Voice, a Salient Vision

W HEN THE AVERAGE WHITE American hears the words "Black Panthers," the image that instantly comes to mind is of a band of clench-jawed, gun-toting black thugs dressed in leather jackets and military berets marching defiantly through the streets of America's urban centers, spreading fear and hatred in their path. In the minds of only a very few people do the words "Black Panthers" evoke the image of a cluster of highly dedicated, forward-thinking young journalists bending over their typewriters into the wee hours of the morning in order to craft and articulate a political ideology to guide America's poor and powerless into the new millennium.

Despite the ubiquity of the first image, the second one is fully valid as well. The same militant activists who led the Black Panther Party into legendary status as one of the most fear-inducing organizations in America also produced a weekly newspaper that committed a remarkably far-reaching vision onto newsprint. In fact, it can be argued that the powerful, poignant, and often graceful prose that appeared in the newspaper may be the activists' most enduring legacy.

This essay examines the history and editorial content of the *Black Panther* newspaper, with an emphasis on the publication's initial four years, from 1967 to 1971, when the party was at its peak. The bulk of the study discusses the three major themes that dominated the pages of that journalistic endeavor—police brutality, self-defense, and economic oppression. By summarizing and quoting from the articles and essays that legendary Black Panthers—such as Huey P. Newton, Bobby Seale, Eldridge Cleaver, and David Hilliard—wrote for their weekly newspaper, this study documents that these leaders were not only militant racial activists and social revolutionaries but also accomplished and far-sighted journalists and political strategists.

Illuminating the history and content of the *Black Panther* is important because, even though scholars have committed considerable time and energy to telling the story of the cadre of marauding political insurgents in the Black Panther Party, journalism historians have paid scant attention to studying or analyzing the content or significance of the group's weekly news organ. The standard history of American journalism devotes only two sentences to the newspaper (ironically, those two sentences communicate inaccurate information about both the year and the city in which the *Panther* was founded).[1] Other histories of American journalism make no mention of the *Panther* whatsoever.[2] The standard history of the African-American press combines its description of the *Panther* with that of the Nation of Islam's *Muhammad Speaks*, devoting a total of only two paragraphs to the two publications.[3] The standard history of the American dissident press limits its description of the *Panther* to two sentences.[4]

Despite the meager attention that journalism historians have accorded the *Black Panther*, it merits scholarly examination for several reasons. First, the newspaper's circulation surpassed that of any commercial African-American newspaper being published at the time; whether that figure was two hundred thousand (as some sources say) or one hundred thousand (as others say), the *Panther* definitely attracted more readers than any other black newspaper of the era.[5] Second, the *Panther* was global in its reach; copies were read by African Americans living in urban centers throughout the United States, as well as leaders of several African liberation movements, staffs of many foreign embassies, and people living in Cuba, Europe, Asia, and Africa.[6] Third, the period of publication that is the focus of this study, the late 1960s and early 1970s, was an era of unparalleled turmoil and change in America, particularly in black America. Fourth, the *Panther* offers a rare example of a publishing endeavor that was truly grassroots in nature; it provided a venue in which members of an oppressed minority group spoke with a strong and vibrant voice. Finally, as the findings of this study document, the most important reason for studying the *Black Panther* is its enduring impact on the consciousness of black America well beyond the date that it ceased publication.

Huey P. Newton and Bobby Seale founded the Black Panther Party in Oakland, California, in fall 1966 because, as Newton wrote, "We want freedom. We want power to determine the destiny of our Black Community."[7] The two young men—Newton was twenty-four, Seale twenty-nine—belonged to African-American families that had migrated west during World War II in search of jobs in the naval shipyards and munitions factories that had burgeoned on the West Coast during the country's wartime defense buildup. The families successfully escaped the rigid segregation of the South; however, they soon experienced California-style discrimination in employment, housing, and education—forces that thrust both families into poverty. Newton and Seale spent their childhoods in Oakland and met while studying at Merritt College. They joined forces to add classes in black history to the curriculum and hire black professors to the faculty. Encouraged by each other's enthusiasm, the young men then sought to improve life in Oakland's ghettos by knocking on doors and asking their neighbors what programs they needed or wanted. Newton and Seale translated those answers into the programs at the center of the Black Panther Party—classes in black history and the political process, free breakfasts for school children, and free health clinics for the poor.

But the community-based activity that caught the public's attention involved armed patrol cars. Newton, Seale, and the other young African-American men they recruited into the party would climb into their cars—a gun in one hand, a law book in the other—and trail police cruisers around Oakland slums. Whenever police stopped black suspects, the armed Panthers made sure the officers did not violate the constitutional rights of the men and women they detained. The police were outraged that armed black men were monitoring them, even though it was fully legal at that time for Californians to carry unconcealed guns; the African-American community was impressed that the young men were committing their time and energy to protecting the rights of black citizens. Most important, harassment and brutality that the Oakland police previously had directed against black men and women soon declined.

The white power structure, however, was less concerned about the ill treatment of black citizens than about armed black men cruising the streets of Oakland—a sight that most white people found absolutely terrifying. In early 1967, East Bay legislator Don Mulford proposed a bill crafted to disarm the Panthers by making it illegal to carry a loaded gun in public. When twenty Panthers stormed into a chamber of the California Assembly brandishing loaded rifles, pistols, and shotguns to protest the proposed bill, newspapers across the country captured the moment in photos—and the Black Panthers were instantly known nationwide.[8] Although the bill was later passed, the party was soon boasting a membership of ten thousand and a community of supporters many times that number.[9]

The catalyst for creating a Panther newspaper was a police incident. According to the police report, in the early morning of 1 April 1967, when a Richmond, California, white deputy sheriff tried to arrest Denzil Dowell on suspicion of stealing a car, the twenty-two-year-old black man fled. The deputy then shot and killed Dowell. The death was ruled justifiable homicide; Dowell's family charged that the deputy had known and threatened to kill the young black man long before the incident. When the mainstream media failed to give the case the attention that Newton and Seale believed that it deserved, they started their own newspaper.

The premier issue of the *Black Panther* appeared on 25 April 1967. That issue and the next consisted of two mimeographed sheets that were stapled together and distributed to some three thousand residents of Oakland's black neighborhoods. By the third issue, the weekly paper arrived on tabloid-size newsprint and sold for twenty-five cents a copy. In the next few years, the paper expanded to twenty-four pages, and the initial circulation increased manyfold. The paper was distributed nationwide via the network of local Black Panther Party chapters that erupted in thirty cities and extended to supporters around the world as well.

The *Panther*'s editorial content was dominated by opinionated and often strident essays that insisted that African Americans would secure freedom through nothing short of a social and political revolution. References to the United States being a fascist nation were frequent, and numerous essays contained shrill demands for change. "People are not going for all the bullshit America preaches," one stated. "The inconsistencies are becoming clearer and oppressed peoples of the U.S. are forming a proletarian internationalistic force that will rise and crush the pig power structure. ALL POWER TO THE PEOPLE!!"[10] In another essay, Newton asserted, "The only way that we're going to be free is to wipe out once and for all the oppressive structure of America."[11]

Although news stories were less prominent than essays, they were by no means an insignificant element in the editorial mix. The establishment press opted not to cover many events in America's black communities, and the *Panther* often provided the only source for information. When African-American high school students in High Point, North Carolina, were suspended because they had asked that Black Studies be added to the curriculum, the story appeared in the *Panther*; the mainstream North Carolina press did not report the incident.[12] Likewise, when a Los Angeles landlord objected to his black tenants operating a day care center in the house they rented from him, that too became a story in the *Panther*. The incident turned bizarre, the *Panther* reported, when police chose not to inform the tenants that the landlord was displeased, but to herd the teachers and children onto the lawn and hold them at gunpoint; the Los Angeles mainstream press did not cover the story.[13]

These and other news articles were written by blacks who were not members of the Black Panther Party but who took their grievances to the party newspaper. By printing the stories, the *Panther* gave poor and politically dispossessed African Americans a venue for community news that they had never had before. Bobby Seale argued that giving common people a voice was one of the *Panther*'s most significant benefits because the stories "come from the hard core of the black community, the grass roots."[14]

Artwork was integral to the editorial mix. Images of pistols, shotguns, machine guns, hand grenades, and clenched black fists dotted every issue, and photographs of the handsome Newton—tall and unsmiling in black leather jacket and beret, with a pump shotgun and bandolier of shotgun shells strapped across his chest—often filled an entire page. Among the other compelling graphics were cartoons, created by Emory Douglas, that featured pigs dressed in police uniforms.

Some of the cartoons depicted the police as inept and foolish—one showed a cluster of pigs/policemen firing pistols into the air while dancing and swigging alcohol;[15] another had a pig sleeping in the driver's seat of his police car as black men and women surrounded the vehicle and aimed their weapons at the hapless officer's head.[16] Other of the images were not humorous but sinister: one showed an angry black man preparing to thrust a huge knife into a crying pig/policeman's head;[17] another showed a black man holding a shotgun that he had just used to kill the pig/policeman that was lying lifeless at his feet.[18]

Absent from the mix was the mainstay of mainstream publications: advertisements. The party's vehement opposition to capitalism ensured that the newspaper would not promote major businesses—not that they would have supported the *Panther*'s revolutionary rhetoric anyway—and very few of the small, black-owned enterprises that the party would have supported ideologically could have afforded to buy ads. So the newspaper depended on circulation revenue to pay printing costs. Sales grew so rapidly in the late 1960s that the newspaper was soon supporting the party's other activities. The Panthers who wrote, edited, and distributed the paper received no payment for those activities.

Eldridge Cleaver, the party's minister of information, served as the first editor of the paper, but Newton, the party's minister of defense, emerged as the strongest and most articulate voice. Other frequent bylines belonged to Seale, chairman of the party, and David Hilliard, the chief of staff who handled the party's day-to-day operations. Although men dominated the leadership positions in the party, women assumed a larger role in the newspaper. Women handled most production details, such as typing stories and laying out the pages, and many essays carried female bylines, including that of Angela Davis.

The *Black Panther* eschewed the strict language boundaries observed by conventional American journalism. The paper has been credited with originating the term *pig* as a derogatory term for "policeman,"[19] and the slogan "Off the Pigs!" was sprinkled liberally throughout the paper. Expletives such as *shit, fuck,* and *motherfucker* appeared frequently as well. Seale wrote, "The language of the ghetto is a language of its own and as the party—whose members for the most part come from the ghetto— seeks to talk to the people, it must speak the people's language."[20]

The prominent role that police brutality played in the editorial content of the *Black Panther* was evidenced by how the Denzil Dowell incident dominated the premier issue. A large photo of Dowell ran under a hand-lettered headline that read "WHY WAS DENZIL DOWELL KILLED?" Sharing page one was a boxed statement that announced a community meeting about the Dowell incident and ended by saying "EVERY BLACK BROTHER AND SISTER MUST UNITE FOR REAL POLITICAL ACTION." The rest of the issue was filled with a list of unanswered questions related to the killing and an essay raging against police brutality writ large.[21]

The essay provided a preview of the powerful prose style that would become a hallmark of the militant journalistic voice. "In the past, Black People have been at the mercy of cops who feel that their badges are a license to shoot, maim, and outright murder any Black man, woman, or child who crosses their gun-sights," the essay said. "But there are now strong Black men and women on the scene who are willing to step out front and do what is necessary to bring peace, security, and justice to a people who have been denied all of these for four hundred years. The Black Panther PARTY *moves*. The PARTY takes action."[22]

Later essays specified exactly what kind of action the party believed was necessary to stop police brutality. In one essay, Newton argued that sending police officers who were not products of the ghetto to patrol those neighborhoods was comparable to the "occupying army" of American soldiers fighting in Vietnam. "When historically men are recruited from the oppressor race to patrol the communities of the oppressed people, an intolerable contradiction exists. THE RACIST DOG POLICEMEN MUST WITHDRAW IMMEDIATELY FROM OUR COMMUNITIES, CEASE THEIR WANTON MURDER AND BRUTALITY AND TORTURE OF BLACK PEOPLE, OR FACE THE WRATH OF THE ARMED PEOPLE."[23] In another strident essay, Newton articulated precisely how that wrath would be manifested. First arguing that the mass demonstrations used in the Civil Rights Movement were less effective than "guerrilla methods," Newton then endorsed the murder of racist police officers. "When the masses hear that a gestapo policeman has been executed while sipping coffee at a counter and the revolutionary executioners fled without being traced," he wrote, "the masses will see the validity of this type of approach."[24]

Editorial attention to police brutality extended beyond angry essays. Residents of black neighborhoods across the country contributed a constant stream of news stories reporting instances of police mistreatment in Chicago and Detroit, Boston and Philadelphia, New Haven and Winston-Salem.[25] And many stories were illustrated by drawings that featured pigs dressed in police uniforms as they beat, tortured, and humiliated African Americans. The *Panther* defined a pig as "a low natured beast that has no regard for law, justice, or the rights of the people,"[26] and Eldridge Cleaver wrote of the paper's ubiquitous symbol of police brutality: "A dead pig is desirable, but a paralyzed pig is preferable to a mobile pig."[27]

As illustrated by Newton's and Cleaver's open advocacy of killing racist police officers, the *Black Panther* did not embrace the nonviolent credo that had been central to the Civil Rights Movement. While the movement's Rev. Martin Luther King, Jr., unequivocally opposed violence, Newton and Seale opted for Malcolm X's emphasis on black power and securing freedom "by any means necessary." Like Malcolm X, Newton and Seale believed that the nonviolent tactics used in the Civil Rights Movement in the rural South would be ineffective in the urban North. The Panther leaders often quoted Malcolm X's famous statement: "We should be peaceful and law-abiding, but the time has come to fight back in self-defense whenever and wherever the Black man is being unjustly and unlawfully attacked. If the government thinks I am wrong for saying this, then let the government start doing its job."[28]

The central role that self-defense would play in the Black Panther Party—and, subsequently, in the *Black Panther* newspaper—was immediately evident when Newton and Seale selected a name for their organization. They chose the panther as their namesake because, Seale said, "It is not in the panther's nature to attack anyone first, but when he is attacked and backed into a corner, he will respond viciously and wipe out the aggressor."[29] A drawing of a fearless panther, with its claws extended and teeth bared, appeared on the top of page one each week, and additional drawings of the fierce animal appeared on inside pages as well.

The various leaders reinforced the importance of self-defense in their essays. Newton wrote that black America had to be prepared to defend itself: "Black people can develop Self-Defense Power by arming themselves from house to house, block to block, community to community, throughout the nation."[30] David Hilliard wrote that self-defense sometimes extended to killing the enemy, including police officers: "We only advocate killing those that kill us. And if we designate our enemy as pigs, then I think that it would be justified to kill."[31] And Cleaver wrote:

> We seek no bloodshed. But Black people, this day, this time, say HALT IN THE NAME OF HUMANITY! YOU SHALL MAKE NO MORE WAR ON UNARMED PEOPLE. YOU WILL NOT KILL ANOTHER BLACK PERSON AND WALK THE STREETS OF THE BLACK COMMUNITY TO GLOAT ABOUT IT AND SNEER AT THE DEFENSELESS RELATIVES OF YOUR VICTIMS. FROM NOW ON, WHEN YOU MURDER A BLACK PERSON IN THIS BABYLON OF BABYLONS, YOU MAY AS WELL GIVE IT UP BECAUSE WE WILL GET YOUR ASS AND GOD CAN'T HIDE YOU.[32]

The most vehement endorsements of self-defense published in the *Panther* were tantamount to calls for violence. In a 1969 essay, "If You Want Peace You Got to Fight for It," for example, David Hilliard singled out President Nixon as the man ultimately responsible for the oppression of black America. Hilliard's tone grew angrier and angrier as the essay progressed, and his final words sounded like those of a warrior intent upon attacking his enemy: "We will kill Richard Nixon. We will kill any motherfucker that stands in the way of our freedom. We ain't here for no goddamned peace, because we know that we can't have no peace because this country was built on war. And if you want peace you got to fight for it. ALL POWER TO THE PEOPLE."[33]

Although the *Black Panther*'s essays raging against police brutality and promoting self-defense received the most attention in their day, essays on those topics were, in reality, outnumbered by editorial statements that focused on economic oppression as the root problem facing African Americans. Virtually every issue of the paper included at least one lengthy treatise focusing on economics, often extolling the virtues of a Marxist approach to the redistribution of wealth.

The specific economic theme that appeared most often in the pages of the revolutionary newspaper was Newton's demand that white America provide financial reparation to black America for the debt created by the institution of slavery. The cofounder of the party argued that the heinous practice of human bondage had relegated blacks to their current subservient social and political status and therefore the government should right that wrong by sending large quantities of tax revenue into the nation's poor black neighborhoods. "The racist government has robbed us and now we are demanding the overdue debt," Newton repeatedly stated. "Forty acres and two mules was promised 100 years ago as restitution for slave labor and mass murder of Black people. We will accept the payment in currency which will be distributed to our many communities. We feel that this is a modest demand that we make." [34]

Other writers echoed Newton's demand. "WE WANT LAND, BREAD, HOUSING, EDUCATION, CLOTHING, JUSTICE, AND PEACE," Seale began one of his manifestos. "The exploited, laboring masses and poor, oppressed peoples throughout the world want and need these demands for basic human survival." [35] Seale labeled the economic oppression meted out by white America "domestic imperialism" and argued that its victims included not only African Americans but also Chicanos and Native Americans. "Domestic imperialism at home is in fact fascism," he wrote. "What in essence is it? I think Black people if we go over the concrete experiences that we've had in America and what's going on now against us we can understand exactly what it is— to be corralled in wretched ghettoes and look up one day and see numerous policemen occupying our community, and brutalizing us, killing our brothers." [36]

Many essays about economic repression were written by women. Connie Matthews focused on how the technological advances of an industrialized nation threatened black Americans. "Most of you will become redundant," she told *Panther* readers. "You in the middle, who think you have something, who have those bills and those $20,000 houses, you are the ones who are going to find out that the mortgage or interest or whatever it is that you are going to have to pay back is about twice what you thought originally." Matthews assured her readers that the Black Panthers would support economically oppressed African Americans—up to a point. "We will stay until everyone of us is killed or imprisoned by the racist pigs, but then someone will have to take over. So don't let us all die in vain. POWER TO THE PEOPLE." [37]

FBI documents show that Director J. Edgar Hoover conducted an illegal program to obliterate the Black Panther Party. In a memo recently obtained through the Freedom of Information Act, Hoover directed his agents, in August 1967, to "expose, disrupt, misdirect, discredit, or otherwise neutralize the activities of Black nationalists, hate-type organizations and groupings, their leadership, spokesmen, membership, and supporters."[38] In response to Hoover's order, agents planted informants inside the party in an effort to destroy the organization from within. By 1970, the FBI had succeeded in having more than seven hundred Panthers arrested, often on fabricated evidence, and thereby had forced the party to spend five million dollars and much of its energy not agitating for revolution but defending its beleaguered leaders.[39]

A mind-numbing series of arrests, trials, convictions, imprisonments, mistrials, overturned convictions, escapes to foreign countries, and violent deaths took a devastating toll on the party. In October 1967, Newton's arrest on a charge of killing an Oakland police officer led to the *Panther*'s most ardent voice being jailed and tried; "Free Huey!" became a pervasive plea in the paper. In September 1968, Newton was convicted of manslaughter, but then he was released in August 1970 after the conviction was overturned. In April 1968, party treasurer Bobby Hutton was shot to death as he attempted to surrender to Oakland police; Cleaver and Hilliard were among the seven Panthers arrested on murder charges in connection with Hutton's death. Cleaver, who already had spent time in prison and feared being jailed again, fled to Cuba and then Algeria. In May 1969, Seale was charged with killing party member Alex Rackley (Seale suspected Rackley of working for the FBI); Seale spent two years in prison until a mistrial was declared. Also in 1969, Seale was sentenced to four years in prison for contempt of court because he had disrupted his trial on charges of conspiracy to incite a riot during the 1968 Democratic National Convention in Chicago; Seale and other defendants became known as the "Chicago Eight." Meanwhile, Hilliard was indicted for threatening President Nixon during a rally in Chicago—a threat he repeated in the *Panther*. In 1974, police charged Newton with killing a prostitute, which prompted the Panther leader to flee to Cuba for three years. When Newton returned to the United States, he withstood three costly trials before charges were finally dropped.[40]

By 1971, the FBI's strategy was succeeding, and the Black Panther Party had been reduced to a shell of its earlier self. And as the party diminished in strength, so did its journalistic voice. The editorship changed hands many times,[41] and essays crafted by such prominent leaders as Newton and Cleaver appeared only rarely. During the 1970s, the *Panther's* editorial content included little of the editorial fire that had defined its early years. The weekly became a biweekly (in the late 1970s) and then a monthly (in 1980), before the newspaper ceased publication in October 1980.[42]

The *Black Panther* charted a unique journalistic course. By committing the angry messages of legendary black revolutionaries into print, the newspaper performed a singular service for the Black Panther Party during its heyday in the tumultuous period of the late 1960s and early 1970s. Each week, this dissident journalistic voice discussed topics that the mainstream American press shunned: urban police were brutal; African Americans needed to defend themselves even to the point of taking up arms to commit violent acts; and economic oppression was the root cause of the suffering that remained a continuing reality in the lives of Americans of African descent. The audience that the newspaper reached was substantial; at least one hundred thousand copies, and possibly twice that many, were distributed not only across the United States but also internationally.

Dwarfing the role that the *Black Panther* played during its years of widespread publication, however, is the impact that the paper's editorial content has had since that time. Many of the themes raised in the pages of that revolutionary journalistic voice some thirty years ago did not disappear when the *Black Panther* ceased publication. Indeed, the issues that dominated the *Panther's* editorial content either never died or temporarily became latent, but they resurfaced and are now playing prominent roles in the sociopolitical movement that continues to work toward racial equality in this country today.

The most conspicuous example is the pig as a symbol of the American police officer. The *Panther* was the first publication to use this disparaging reference, in written form through editorials and graphic form through the cartoons that depicted pigs wearing police uniforms (one of the newspaper's signature elements). The symbol was immediately embraced as part of the radical vocabulary of the American underground, and today, some three decades later, it has become a universally recognized symbol.

Another salient issue discussed in the *Panther* was Huey P. Newton's proposal that the U.S. government should make restitution to African Americans for the sins of slavery by committing large quantities of tax money to black communities. Although such proposed compensation was scoffed at by the vast majority of Americans in the late 1960s and is still far from becoming a reality, that same proposal remains a subject of debate in the halls of the U.S. Congress into the twenty-first century.[43]

The subjects of various other *Panther* essays are also very much alive today. The massive public response to the videotaped beating of Rodney King in 1991, the subsequent acquittal of the Los Angeles police officers who inflicted the beating, and the massive riots that the acquittal sparked are vivid reminders that police brutality remains an important racial issue in this country; the economic disparity between black Americans and white Americans—the median black family income is less than 60 percent of the median white family income—provides dramatic evidence that economic oppression remains another major problem.[44]

One reason that the concepts that were communicated in the pages of the *Black Panther* did not fade with the passage of time is that, when the newsprint on which the paper was printed began to yellow, the original essays and artwork were preserved in other forms. The Black Panther Party took on legendary proportions as the first nationwide black political phenomenon—as distinguished from religion-based phenomena such as the Civil Rights Movement—that unequivocally and steadfastly refused to back down, even when attacked by the FBI.[45] So the revolutionary essays and artwork that had appeared in the *Panther* began to be reprinted in book form. During the 1970s, three books reproduced hundreds of essays and cartoons from the newspaper,[46] and by 1990 more than thirty additional books, including some distributed by such major publishing houses as Random House and Simon and Schuster, had reproduced lengthy excerpts from the newspaper.[47] The hunger for the ideology that the *Black Panther* had espoused still did not abate. In the current decade, a dozen more books have been added to the holdings of American libraries and book stores,[48] and several of the earlier books have been reprinted.[49]

The fact that radical ideas that originated in a dissident newspaper three decades ago are more widely accepted today—and, in fact, have outlived many of the revolutionary youths who originated them— is consistent with previous research on alternative presses. In Lauren Kessler's standard in the field, *The Dissident Press: Alternative Journalism in American History*, she observes that "radical, unpopular, even ridiculed notions" initially discussed only in dissident presses have, throughout American history, repeatedly "filtered into the mainstream marketplace" to become "accepted political doctrine." Kessler wrote that this phenomenon had occurred with the women's suffrage press, utopian press, African-American press, populist press, antiwar press, and counterculture press.[50]

As shown by the findings of this study of the *Black Panther* newspaper, scholars of alternative journalism now have another example to add to the list of dissident presses that have not only provided a venue for radical ideas but also have ultimately played a critical role in helping those ideas find their way into the mainstream of American thought.

Notes

1. Michael Emery and Edwin Emery, *The Press and America: An Interpretive History of the Mass Media*, 8th ed. (Boston: Allyn and Bacon, 1996), 432. Emery and Emery state that the *Black Panther* was founded in 1966 in San Francisco; it was founded in 1967 in Oakland.
2. Margaret A. Blanchard, ed., *History of the Mass Media in the United States: An Encyclopedia* (Chicago: Fitzroy Dearborn, 1998); Wm. David Sloan and James D. Startt, *The Media in America: A History*, 3d ed. (Northport, Ala.: Vision, 1996); Jean Folkerts and Dwight L. Teeter, Jr., *Voices of a Nation: A History of Mass Media in the United States*, 3d ed. (Boston: Allyn and Bacon, 1998).
3. Roland E. Wolseley, *The Black Press, U.S.A.*, 2d ed. (Ames: Iowa State University Press, 1990), 90–91.
4. Lauren Kessler, *The Dissident Press: Alternative Journalism in American History* (Beverly Hills, Calif.: Sage, 1984), 45.
5. On the circulation of the *Panther* being two hundred thousand, see Kessler, *Dissident Press*, 45. On the circulation being one hundred thousand, see Clint C. Wilson II, *Black Journalists in Paradox: Historical Perspectives and Current Dilemmas* (New York: Greenwood, 1991), 85; Wolseley, *Black Press*, 90. On the *Panther* having a larger circulation than any commercial black newspaper of the time, see Wilson, *Black Journalists in Paradox*, 85; Wolseley, *Black Press*, 90.
6. JoNina M. Abron, "'Raising the Consciousness of the People': The Black Panther Intercommunal News Service, 1967–1980," in *Voices from the Underground: Insider Histories of the Vietnam Era Underground Press*, ed. Ken Wachsberger (Tempe, Ariz.: Mica Press, 1993), 352–53.
7. Huey P. Newton, "What We Want; What We Believe," *Black Panther*, 20 July

1967, 3. This statement was the first of the ten points published in numerous editions of the newspaper.

8. "Armed Negroes Enter California Assembly in Gun Bill Protest," *New York Times*, 3 May 1967, 24.

9. Abron, "Black Panther," 356.

10. John Coleman, "Chicago 8," *Black Panther*, 15 November 1969, 2.

11. Huey P. Newton, "To the R.N.A. [Republic of New Africa]," *Black Panther*, 6 December 1969, 10.

12. Dora Gray and George Dewitt, "Fascism at Central High School," *Black Panther*, 17 October 1970, 3. No coverage of the incident appeared in the *Greensboro News and Record*, the regional paper for the High Point area, during the month of October 1970.

13. "Pigs Attack Child Care Center," *Black Panther*, 14 November 1970, 4. No coverage of the incident appeared in the *Los Angeles Times* during the two weeks following 4 November 1970, the date the incident occurred.

14. Bobby Seale, *Seize the Time: The Story of the Black Panther Party and Huey P. Newton* (New York: Random House, 1970), 181.

15. Untitled cartoon, *Black Panther*, 28 September 1968, 4.

16. "In Defense of Self-Defense," *Black Panther*, 18 May 1968, 21.

17. Untitled cartoon, *Black Panther*, 15 January 1969, 11.

18. Untitled cartoon, *Black Panther*, 12 October 1968, 14.

19. On the *Black Panther* originating the term "pig" for "police officer," see Abron, "Black Panther," 351; "Guns and Butter," *Newsweek*, 5 May 1969, 40; Martin Rywell, ed., *Afro-American Encyclopedia* (North Miami, Fla.: Educational Book Publishers, 1974) 1: 304.

20. Quoted in Philip S. Foner, ed., *The Black Panthers Speak* (New York: Lippincott, 1970), 82.

21. "WHY WAS DENZIL DOWELL KILLED?" *Black Panther*, 25 April 1967, 1.

22. "ARMED BLACK BROTHERS IN RICHMOND COMMUNITY," *Black Panther*, 25 April 1967, 3–4.

23. Huey P. Newton, "Functional Definition of Politics," *Black Panther*, 4 January 1969, 5.

24. Huey P. Newton, "The Correct Handling of a Revolution," *Black Panther*, 18 May 1968, 8.

25. *Black Panther*, "On the Murder of Ronald Redrick," 21 November 1970, 8; Norman, "Out with the Old Fascist in with the New," 14 November 1970, 5; Semaj, "Pigs Let Injured Brother Lie in the Street for 36 Minutes," 21 November 1970, 13; Lynn Smith, "Avenge Raymond Brooks," 14 December 1970, 3; "Reese Drug Store New Haven, Conn. Site of Fascist Brutality Against the People," 19 December 1970, 3; Malik, "Pig Responsible for Death of 15 Year Old Brother," 17 October 1970, 2.

26. "What is a Pig?" *Black Panther*, 14 September 1968, 3.

27. Eldridge Cleaver, "Eldridge on Weathermen," *Black Panther*, 22 November 1969, 5.

28. Foner, *Black Panthers Speak*, xvi.

29. Rywell, *Afro-American Encyclopedia*, 302.

30. Newton, "Functional Definition," 5.

31. David Hilliard, "Interview with CBS News," *Black Panther*, 10 January 1970, 3.

32. Eldridge Cleaver, "On Violence," *Black Panther*, 23 March 1968, 3.

33. David Hilliard, "If You Want Peace You Got to Fight for It," *Black Panther*, 22 November 1969, 11.

34. Newton, "What We Want," 3.

35. Bobby Seale, "The Ten-Point Platform and Program of the Black Panther Party," *Black Panther*, 18 October 1969, 2.

36. Bobby Seale, "Black Soldiers as Revolutionaries to Overthrow the Ruling Class," *Black Panther*, 3 January 1970, 6.

37. Connie Matthews, "On the Vietnam Moratorium," *Black Panther*, 25 October 1969, 11.

38. Memo from J. Edgar Hoover to all field offices, 25 August 1967, U.S. Department of Justice, FBI Headquarters, Washington, D.C.

39. Abron, "Black Panther," 347.

40. Newton was shot to death in August 1989, and two years later Tyrone Robinson was convicted of the murder. Robinson was a member of the Black Guerrilla Family, a group organized to protect black prisoners from white racist prisoners. Many members of the Black Guerrilla Family blamed the Panthers for the death of their founder, George Jackson, but many Panthers believed that the FBI had instigated the rumor that the Panthers had killed Jackson.

41. Eight different Panthers edited the paper after Cleaver fled the country in late 1968. They were Raymond Lewis, Frank Jones, Elbert Howard (all in 1969), Elaine Brown (1970), Ericka Huggins (1971), David Du Bois (stepson of W.E.B. Du Bois, 1972–1976), Michael Fultz (1976–1978), and JoNina Abron (1978–80).

42. Abron, "Black Panther," 357.

43. Rep. John Conyers, Jr. (D-Mich.), dean of the Congressional Black Caucus, has repeatedly sponsored legislation to establish a committee to study reparations, and the NAACP has passed several resolutions in support of reparations, including one at the organization's national convention in July 1997.

44. The median black family income is $26,522, and the median white family income is $44,756; see U.S. Bureau of the Census, Current Population Reports, P60–197, *Money Income in the United States: 1996* (U.S. Government Printing Office: Washington, D.C., 1997), 14–15.

45. Rywell, *Afro-American Encyclopedia*, 303.

46. Foner, *Black Panthers Speak*; G. Louis Heath, *The Black Panther Leaders Speak* (Metuchen, N.J.: Scarecrow, 1976); G. Louis Heath, ed., *"Off the Pigs!": The History and Literature of the Black Panther Party* (Metuchen, N.J.: Scarecrow, 1976).

47. For example, David Armstrong, *A Trumpet to Arms: Alternative Media in America* (Los Angeles: J. P. Tarcher, 1981); Gilbert Moore, *A Special Rage* (New York: Harper & Row, 1971); Huey P. Newton, *To Die for the People: The Writings of Huey P. Newton* (New York: Random House, 1972); and Robert Scheer, ed., *Eldridge Cleaver: Post-Prison Writings and Speeches* (New York: Random House, 1970).

48. For example, Jim Haskins, *Power to the People: The Rise and Fall of the Black Panther Party* (New York: Simon & Schuster Books for Young Readers, 1997); Hugh Pearson, *The Shadow of the Panther: Huey Newton and the Price of Black Panther Power in America* (Reading, Mass.: Addison-Wesley, 1994); and Huey P. Newton, *War Against the Panthers: A Study of Repression in America* (New York: Writers and Readers, 1996).

49. For example, Moore, *A Special Rage* was reprinted by Carroll & Graf in 1993, and Newton, *To Die for the People* was reprinted by Writers and Readers in 1995.

50. For the quotation, see Kessler, *Dissident Press*, 16. On ideas filtering into the mainstream from the suffrage press, see 85–86; utopian press, 56, 58; black press, 25, 35; populist press, 120; antiwar press, 149; counterculture press, 152–53.

Chapter 13

The Black Press in the Age of Digital Reproduction

ANNA EVERETT

Two Exemplars

A significant development for African Americans and new technology has been the establishment of both local and national "Drum" lists. These Drum lists, which are essentially e-mail mailing lists, allow one African American to communicate with many others....The result is a digital cascade of information which is not unlike the sounds of call and response delivered by the drums our forefathers used in Africa.

—R. Cadet (*Conduit* 1995)

I see a long road ahead....A luta continua *means the struggle continues.*

—Talibah L. Chikwendu (*Afro-Americ@*: 1998)

AFRICAN AMERICANS' long-standing quest for racial equity and due process in the United States is marked by a series of epochal migrations. During slavery it was the clandestine migrations following the North Star to Canada and American cities above the Mason-Dixon line. Following the postwar Reconstruction era, African Americans migrated in large numbers to nonsouthern states in search of escape from the South's unrelenting and pervasive racial persecution. For most African Americans fleeing southern degradation and repression, northern destinations represented real-world equivalents to the scriptural promised land. More recently, however, the cumulative effects of economic stagnation in the urban Northeast, attacks on civil rights, and increasing interethnic con flict above the Mason-Dixon line in the wake of the racially polarizing Reagan-Bush 1980s have contributed to a notable reverse black migration southward. This return signals a sort of black acquiescence to the intractability of America's politics of privileged whiteness that erases any doubt that, indeed, the struggle continues.

Throughout these migrations the black press has sustained African Americans, but not without setbacks and struggles of its own. Today, in some intellectual circles it seems fashionable to assign blame for the diminution of the black press's significance and other socioeconomic setbacks in the black community to integration, particularly in this post–Civil Rights era.[1] It is important to note, however, that black suspicion of integration is not an exclusively contemporary conceit. As far back as 1949, Thomas W. Young, then president of the Negro Newspaper Publishers Association (NNPA), presciently connected integration with the "prospective death of Black newspapers."[2] According to *A History of the Black Press*, by Armistead S. Pride and Clint C. Wilson II, Young believed that "once the [mainstream white press] routinely reported the Negro's personal and group news, crusaded against injustices and inequalities, and chronicled the achievements of the race, the foundations for Negro organs 'would cease to be,'"[3]

By contrast, *Louisville Defender* city editor Fletcher Martin, a contemporary of Young, "saw no occasion for all Black publishers to close up shop following some long-awaited gains in civil rights, education and living conditions. 'The Negro press won't die.'"[4] Instead, Pride and Wilson report that most black publishers were inclined toward Carl Murphy's view that extinction or "self-liquidation" was not even on the agenda. Murphy, then the publisher of his family's historic *Afro-American* chain of newspapers, expressed this counterview in his 1954 presidential address to the NNPA, wherein he proclaimed, "We have the facility to change with the times."[5] Nevertheless, as Pride and Wilson put it, "Negro newspapers went out of business at an alarming rate throughout the 1960s, 1970s, and 1980s."[6]

What Young and Murphy's dialectic attests to is the tremendous calculated risk that the black press took on behalf of its constituency in its often successful negotiations that pushed for a more inclusive democratic reality in U.S. civil society. The enormous cost was the "liquidation" and/or erosion of influence and viability of the very black presses that agitated for the conditions most responsible for their own demise. At the same time, it is difficult not to regard the black press's new guard as the proverbial Phoenix arisen from the ashes of the same black press old guard that it eulogizes. By 1989, one of the legatees of the historic black press, *Black Enterprise* magazine, tallied the cost of the changed order of black journalism: "The end of the civil rights era and the advent of integration appear to have spawned a generation of young black adults who are unimpressed with black papers that don't display the spit and polish of mainstream newspapers."[7]

With integration's apparent devastation of the historic black press, and the remaining presses' refusal to be forced into oblivion by mainstream and new digital media technologies, replete with high-tech "spit and polish," it is remarkable that today's black press is yet again at the forefront of a bold new migration. Only this time the migration is to the digital promised land of cyberspace. It is fitting, indeed, that Carl Murphy's own enduring *Afro-American* newspaper organization fulfilled his prophecy of adapting to the times by becoming one of the first established newspapers, black or white, to go online.

Before any meaningful consideration of the black press's online migration and digital metamorphosis can proceed, it seems necessary to address what we mean by the phrase "black press." The digital media environment has radically transformed publishing realities and produced what I call "digitextuality" (a concept that marries digital form to intertextual content). Regarding the differing communicative modes that characterize print and digital texts, George Landow and others have proffered convincing arguments for the existence of significant structural differences separating the communicative modes of print and digital media. For Landow, one key point of departure is that autonomous or stand-alone print texts normally are identified by their unified and centralized natures, whereas the hypertext structure of digital texts, conversely, is defined by a "dispersed, multiply centered network of data organized by a key feature known as electronic linking."[8]

Linking, which is essentially a computerized system enabling instantaneous textual navigation and retrieval that permits readers of digital data to jump from text to text instantaneously with the click of a computer mouse, does not simply structurally define digital information systems against the manual linearity of older print information regimes.

This digital collision with intertextuality (again, "digitextuality") compels Landow to go so far as to assert that hypertexts cause a mode of perceptual and cognitive blurring that "has a marked effect on the conception and experience of boundaries and limits."[9] Specifically this idea of seamless digital boundary crossings of generic, disciplinary, temporal, and spatial lines (that also generate class, national, generational, gender, and the always problematic racial blurring of established norms and hierarchies) vexes any discursive engagement with would-be immutable identity categories in cyberspace. How then to define the particularities of the black press in cyberspace now that the drastically revolutionized nature of "the text," of publication, of authorship, of information dissemination and retrieval, and of the reader all signify so significant a shift in the basic terms and concepts of our topic?

The pertinence of this question becomes evident to anyone confronted with the sheer volume of sites claiming black affiliation. In fact, this problem did not manifest itself to me until I was well into my own research that required consultation with such popular search engines as Yahoo!, Lycos, Infoseek, Alta Vista, and Hotbot, among others. (These searches supplemented my investigation of such black site directories as the Universal Black Pages, Melanet, Everything Black.Com, the Afrocentric Mall, etc.) My specification of the key words and phrases, "black," "black press," African American," "African-American press," "black diaspora," "African diaspora," and so on, yielded a number of "hits" and "site" and "category matches" in the hundreds of thousands. I was, therefore, thrust into a panning-for-gold mentality. What I was prospecting for was the rare black gold of "authentic" black press websites hidden somewhere amid what I soon discovered were inflated numbers for these mainstream search engines' "category matches."[10]

This observation makes clear the fact that new conditions of digital reproducibility have radically altered the nature and status of black publication. The conditions of possibility that engendered the historic print black press (i.e., startup capital, expensive linotype machinery and master printers, a national and global distribution network, sales agents and paper delivery personnel) no longer represent the formidable impediments that once plagued chronically undercapitalized black press ventures. Today almost anyone with access to a computer and a modem can establish a virtual black press operation to plead his or her own cause, as the antebellum black journalists Russwurm and Cornish advocated. Obviously these sea-changes require us to reconsider what constitutes the black press now that the age of cyberspace all but removes brick and mortar obstacles to mass publishing operations. Even more crucial, in my view, is the pressing need to grapple with a new kind and increasing level of epistemological uncertainty when interacting with a putative black press entity in the digital sphere.

One aspect of the rapidly proliferating "black" presses online is the need for researchers and consumers now to confront and acknowledge a newly expansive conceptualization of the "black press," given the increasing difficulty of sorting out actual black press entities from their online simulacra. In an effort to delimit an otherwise endless and unreliable slide of racial signification in this quest for black presses in cyberspace, it seems logical to focus our sampling on a few websites established by legitimate and prominent black press organizations.

Focusing on established black sites and their distinct modes of intertexuality shows us a promising future for the black press. For despite certain risks of identity erasure that can accompany online publication, online journalism might better fulfill some historical ideals of the black press than its traditional print counterparts. Beginning with the *Charlotte Post* (a relatively new online entrant), we can see a black press in cyberspace example that sticks close to its local print roots while using new technologies to globalize "traditional" issues. Moving on to the national forum of Afro-Americ@ (a pioneer in cyberspace), however, reveals a more significant departure from print media—but one that, perhaps, fulfills both "traditional" and contemporary needs of the black press even more extensively by making interactive participation instantaneous. As with other migrations in African-American history, the migration of the black press to the Internet offers promise as well as risk.

The online version of the *Charlotte Post* strongly maintains its ties to the historic black press lineage. The site uses its web-specific "About us" page to foreground its historical successes and credentials: "The *Charlotte Post* has served the African-American community of Charlotte and the metropolitan area for more than 120 years. Each week the *Post* is read by thousands of Charlotte and surrounding area residents interested in the most in-depth coverage of minority issues. For providing this service, the *Post* has continually been awarded national and local awards."[11] The *Post* online includes news stories that make it easy to see that black readers continue to look to their presses, as Roland Wolseley notes, "to find out 'what really went on' when a news story about blacks breaks."[12] What is striking in a Frederick Detweiler observation about several characteristic themes found in black presses during the 1920s, is that they resonate powerfully today with themes such as: "unfair laws, discriminatory acts of whites [and] lynchings, and the positive achievements—new businesses begun, political offices gained, educational honors or progress made by individuals" (quoted in Wolseley).[13] Similarly, in the 1950s, another scholar of the black press "published a system of classifying the contents of black newspapers. . . . First was what he called the characteristic Negro Story . . . the Lynch Story, the Protest Story aimed at Jim Crowism, and the Integration Story . . . the Black Power Story, and Separatism Story, and the Black Revolution Story . . . the Negro Angled Story: news of blacks taking part in white news events . . . The Gossip Story [and finally] the African Story" where African Americans began to identify more personally and politically with the land of their forebears.[14] It is significant that any survey of black presses in cyberspace, including the *Charlotte Post* and the *Afro-Americ@*, manifests the persistence of these themes and stories mainly because the conditions that necessitate these journalistic preoccupations have not abated.

Despite its binding print-based aesthetics, the *Charlotte Post* online seems intent on creating a timely, web-oriented look. Distinguishing this site from the other black press websites is primarily its liberal use of text-related photos, navigational frames, and buttons that provide an important place-keeping function as readers surf the site, and a threaded chat/discussion feature connecting reader responses to specified topics.

Typifying this site's more interactive elements are the *Post*'s provocative e-mail discussions of both traditional and contemporary issues. During the last week of December 1998, "Should the Census Bureau Establish a 'Multiracial' Category to Allow Individuals of 'Mixed Race' to Legally Identify Themselves?" was one hot topic prompting reader response. Of the five reader posts, equivalent to "letters to the editor," all but one reject the idea of legislating a "multiracial" category for mixed race people, citing deleterious political implications.

One reader sees this simply as a divisive tactic threatening black solidarity and what Gayatri Spivak terms "strategic essentialism." The chat respondent posted this concern: "I think that this movement will further divide the black population. I also think that this issue is being used as a buffer between us and white folks. After all, he is not trying to re-classify himself but if he sees any benefit (political), he will sanction it? I want those involved in this issue to think about it!" Another corroborates, adding this perspective: "I think this is and has always been a way to keep America segregated. . . . The government should spend more time and money in finding ways to end segregation because it still exists. We are all Americans!"[15]

The most in-your-face condemnation, however, finds troubling identity politics at the root of this dilemma: "I remember when people were proud to be 'Black' . . . [now they] want to switch. . . . [But] they too will find out, no matter how light you think you are, how dark you are . . . all the man behind the sheet sees is something to swing on the end of his rope."[16] This e-mail respondent reminds *Post* readers that America's one-drop of black blood litmus test for white racial purity still has cultural currency.[17] Even the only dissenting reader posts an ambivalent reply. While answering affirmatively that "mixed race" persons should be legally identified because "it is becoming harder and harder to identify persons by race," this e-mailer confuses her position by asking finally, "What would be the purpose?"

One useful purpose of the black press in cyberspace is the ease and spontaneity of e-mail submission and delivery that encourage a more democratizing ethos in both the consumption and production of journalistic discourse across the board. Whereas the expense of reams of newsprint might have curtailed the available space for publishing most reader feedback, it is conceivable that the virtual spaces of e-publication (electronic publication) are not so restricted and thus are capable of accommodating voluminous instances of logging on and weighing in.

Beyond the hot-button issues that drive most online chat interactions, the black press in cyberspace is most effective when situating contemporary cultural, economic, and technological concerns in their historically important contexts. Such is the case with a *Post* online Christmas week news story entitled "Dolls Reflect, Shape Cultural Identity," by Archie T. Clark II. At issue here is the perennially popular

Christmas gift, the ubiquitous Barbie doll. Clark's article, which revisits the issue of young black children's ongoing preference for white dolls over black ones, makes the case that even today such consumer choices are symptomatic of a persistent "lack of self-esteem and racial identity" in segments of the black community. Raleigh, North Carolina, doll merchant Kamau Kambon offered a provocative response when Clark asked him to consider whether African-American purchases of the traditional Barbie matter.

"You better believe it matters," said Kamau Kambon. Two years ago Kambon, "observed and read about consumers, some of them black, snatching up white Barbies while black Barbies remained on the shelves. He was disappointed. . . . I don't carry too many black dolls because people don't buy them. . . . In 1996 about 96–98 percent of the black dolls manufactured that year were left on the shelves and black people were buying dolls—the white ones."[18] Besides confirming a suspected fiscal disincentive for reluctant white manufacturers to invest in and promote nonwhite dolls, Kambon reveals the near-impossibility of black entrepreneurs to merge sound business practices with the promotion of a "possessive investment" in black racial identity and self-esteem, despite their best efforts.[19] Even blacks, it seems, are affected by what George Lipsitz calls "the possessive investment in whiteness."

Clark's investigation uses historical research into the destructive potential of identity politics in some forms of child's play. Among the historical proofs that Clark revisits are Kenneth Clarke's seminal study and Dr. Darleen Powell Hopson's 1988 replication, which led to and then reconfirmed the *Brown v Board of Education* decision. For Clark, the journalist, it is central for black families to understand that more than "beauty is at stake when a child prefers a doll of a different race."[20] Clark concludes by quoting Baruti Katembo, a math teacher and Raleigh community activist who started a Fourth of July celebration for local black people: "When a child owns a doll, they unknowingly idolize it and want to be like it. . . . As long as we continue to see ourselves as extensions of white people, we will be further and further removed from being able to define ourselves."

Even as Clark's article rests its argument in a historical struggle, it also indirectly supports an important new feature of black websites in an era of ever-increasing e-commerce. The new electronic marketplace affords enterprising black firms unparalleled access to a more level economic playing field despite the emergence of global oligopolies and media monopolies with profit motives to the contrary. The web has become a place where such organizations can market black arts and other Afrocentric commercial goods, and Clark's article may inspire readers to turn to such sites for Barbie alternatives. Even if the mainstream press were to report on black youths and white Barbie dolls, it is extremely doubtful that they would angle this news in terms unfavorable to consumerism, let alone in terms of historically documented mental health issues. By foregrounding its information function in this way, the *Post* online lives up to its own published credo and its historic black press legacy.

Now, for as much as the *Post* upholds the best practices of the historic black press's uplift mission in cyberspace, one of publisher Gerald O. Johnson's planned "new features" returns us to a questionable blast from the print past. In his "What's New" page, Johnson promises to revive the cheesecake photo staples that dotted the pages of even the most venerable of black presses from around the 1920s onward. Apparently Johnson believes that *Post* readers might delight in news about a new feature: "We have added a 'beauty of the month' section. This section will profile some of Carolina's finest. Browsing this section will make you understand why nothing could be finer than being in Carolina."[21] Given the growing popularity of so-called "voyeur sites" featuring unrestricted visual pleasure and access to the presumed everyday life experiences of young, nubile girls and women, perhaps Johnson is only guilty of employing late capitalism's e-business tactics best summed up in Wolseley's terms as, "putting in what sells."[22] Regardless of motive, however, this carryover from the historic black press might be reconsidered.

Clearly the *Charlotte Post* places a premium on digital "data that is both informative and entertaining" for its black cybernauts and net-newbies, yet it still remains tethered to a visual style better suited to its print progenitors.[23] The *Afro-Americ@'s* site, however, deploys contemporary online aesthetics, replete with graphics-rich, quick-loading splash pages, Afrocentric icons, symbols, and imagemaps ("an image that is treated by the browser as a navigational tool").[24] Perhaps this innovative use of technology is not surprising, given that, in 1995 when the

Afro-American newspaper began publishing online, it was the first of the established black or white newspapers to do so.

Primary among the *Afro*'s many distinctions is its design configuration. In contrast to other print newspapers whose online presentations replicate their traditional print-based looks, the *Afro*'s design features are more aligned with and attuned to the new visual aesthetics and functional imperatives of the graphics-driven, digital communicative cues of the World Wide Web. As if becoming a materialization of the ancestral Murphy's injunction to change, the *Afro-Americ@* online is an effective digital text ("digitext") that conforms to the imperatives of today's easy-to-navigate hypertext systems. Moreover, this digitextual format allows it to best administer the multitude of tasks required of a national database for black news by centralizing information, disseminating it to readers, and publishing reader responses.

As seen during the week of 21 December 1998, the front page of the *Afro* site is a visually sophisticated, yet very understated, splash page containing text and image icons that function as the navigational gateway to the rest of the site. Somewhat reminiscent of a print newspaper's masthead, the splash page's title banner contains the text, "AFRO-*america@*" with a three-dimensional drop-shadow effect that is positioned over a cloud-laced sky background or wallpaper graphic. This virtual frontispiece is further organized around four regular topic divisions termed, "culture," "information," "history," and "kid's zone" that are affixed atop a globe-like graphic located at the center of the page. Flanking the right and left sides of this image bearing the regular topic areas are two graphic text boxes linked to the weekly content changes of news, features, information, and special topics. Across the bottom of the page are text and icon combinations entitled, "register," "site map," and "feedback." The fixed subject categories, the graphic text boxes and the icons at the bottom of the page are all hyperlinks that connect visitors to other information destinations within the site by simply clicking on the desired text or image.

During the week of 21 December 1998, a click on the "afro news: news from around the nation of interest to the african-american community" text box connected online readers to the site's national news department. Evocative of a print-based table of contents or index structure with its three-column newspaper style formatting, this page segments both national and regional headlines or capsule descriptions of news and information for the current week. Among the regional stories covered that week were: "Western—Black Community Celebrates Cancellation of Desmond Pfeiffer, Los Angeles, CA"; "South-Eastern—Race Relations Dim According to Study, Nashville, TN"; "National—The Booker File: Services for Boxing legend Archie Moore; Mayor Wellington sought by hitman": "Capitol Hill—CONGRESSIONAL ROUNDUP: Thompson wants reimbursement for Espy; Jackson, Meeks sponsor bills for Supreme Court hiring; Spingarn Medal nominations accepted." Simply "click on" image maps for detailed news.

The *Afro-Americ@* online site represents an effective and audacious amalgam of old and new technology. Put another way, the *Afro* online seems comfortably positioned astride the historical traditions of the venerable newspaper's past and its ambitious future quest for black press endurance in the age of global multimedia behemoths. Notwithstanding the site's forward-looking visual and structural formation, persistent racism results in a discursive trajectory that too often remains hobbled by the need to foreground news, information, and editorial content inflected by the racial problematic that seems little changed since Carl Murphy ran the paper at mid-twentieth century. For example, in his "Congressional Roundup" column, Washington *Afro* staff writer James Wright reports on Congressman Bennie Thompson's (D-Miss) introduction of legislation designed to lessen the financial hardship of black public servants who are victimized by power-hungry, vindictive, and racist independent counsels.[25] He also reports the push by African Americans in Congress to introduce "legislation to pressure Congress" and the Supreme Court to improve their hiring of minority clerks. Other national news for the week celebrates the accomplishments of community members: United Way fundraising records are acknowledged, and Rosa Parks sets the record straight about her civil rights activities at a youth gathering organized by the George Washington University. Having noted the site's all-too-familiar task of having to disabuse white Americans of the belief that African Americans have attained first-class citizenship in a new and improved color-blind society, it becomes necessary not to blame the new high-tech messenger for reporting the continuing practices of low-tech and no-tech racism that still wound the nation.

Where the site's information content parallels its progressive visual form, however, is in its domains of "Culture," "History," and in the variety of interactive opportunities made available online. In that portion of the *Afro*'s site designated as "Culture" are links to a diverse array of content including: "Community Discussions," "Weblinks to Africa," "Art Gallery," "The Polling Place," "Every Wednesday: A Weekly Culture Magazine," "Black Greeks Across the Country," and "Your Cool Links." This "Culture" domain functions to massify, instantaneously, black cultural production via global exhibition and distribution channels systematically disallowed to African Americans by the vested interests of traditional and newly constituted mass media outlets. Moreover, the *Afro*'s appropriation of the Internet's virtual gallery feature for the celebration of black art and artists speaks to the publishers' ability to seize the technology for virtual-space promotional and entrepreneurial activities that counteract African Americans' ongoing race-based exclusions in real space. In terms of interactivity, then, the *Afro-Americ@*'s "Culture" page successfully rearticulates the necessary two-way communication process between ethnic/race presses and their constituent readerships for the changed exigencies of the new digital agora. The print model of reader-to-press interaction rested largely on a press's ability to induce reader responses to published information and then (following established gatekeeping practices) to publish selective feedback therefrom. The website, however, permits uncensored, unmediated, real-time posting to specific areas of the *Afro* site's "virtual" public or cyberspheres.

Also, the prominence of links to other sites endows these black presses with a new and important dimension not possible within the materialist strictures of print publishing. Through the hypertext link or digitextual feature of web publishing, each press offering a "drum list" on its site reinvents the traditional media wire service. Instead of sharing select and limited stories among members or subscribers, those cyberpresses featuring links (or "drum lists" as several Afrocentric sites rechristen them) to all manner of African diasporic sites become virtual global media distribution networks as site readers and lurkers are instantaneously transported to and from other national and international "black presses" in one seamless online flow. This virtual erasure of national borders and statist ideologies has the potential to strengthen the bonds of African diasporic unity in the global struggle for liberation and self-determination in ways that no other tool of communication has yet achieved. We must wait, of course, to see if this phenomenal potential will be actualized.

In terms of the liberation struggles on the homefront, the *Afro-Americ@* site necessarily must detail African Americans' routine victimization by the nation's endemic racism, particularly given the mainstream press displacement of institutionalized racist practices onto so-called "rogue elements" or isolated individuals and events in the culture. Consequently, the black press's journalistic mission rarely escapes the pull of what James Baldwin terms "protest literature." Be that as it may, one key aspect of the *Afro*'s online ability to redirect the terms of the text/reader interface is that reader responses to the news are less marginalized; instead they are welcome, instantaneous, and widely disseminated. The site's web master trusts the site's readers or "end users" to proof their writings and to abide within the code of the honor system where truth and accuracy are concerned. Once you "send" your data to the "Culture" page's domain entitled "Your Cool Links," it is automatically cybercast. This is the equivalent of network television's live broadcasts, without benefit of the three-second delay. This decidedly antigatekeeping feature of the site is in keeping with a neoidealist spirit of the Habermassian public sphere.

Clearly, the *Afro-Americ@* online is a trailblazer caught up in all of cyberspace's semiotic ambiguities and vicissitudes. The site can symbolize the idea of bounding over the obstacles to progress in an eagerly awaited black future vision, or it can symbolize the recuperation of the old in new technological garb. The danger of the latter is a tendency to limit even the desire to explore the outer limits of the new digital media's unique communicative possibilities. The *Afro-Americ@*'s developmental trajectory follows the progressive promise of the former.

This portrait of two select historic black presses' migration to the Internet clearly reveals their commitment to continue the struggle for black political, social, cultural, and economic survival and prosperity well into the digital age.

Notes

1. See for example, Russ Rymer, "Integration's Casualties: Segregation Helped Black Business. Civil Rights Helped Destroy It," *New York Times Magazine*, 1

November 1998, 48–50; Adolph Reed, Jr., , "Dangerous Dreams: Black Boomers Wax Nostalgic for the Days of Jim Crow," *Village Voice*, 16 April 1996, 24–29.

2. Armistead S. Pride and Clint C. Wilson II, *A History of the Black Press*, 261.
3. Ibid., 261.
4. Ibid., 262.
5. Ibid., 263–64.
6. Ibid., 246.
7. Ibid.
8. See George Landow, "What's a Critic to Do?: Critical Theory in the Age of Hypertext," in *Hyper / Text / Theory*, ed. George Landow (Baltimore, Md.: Johns Hopkins University Press, 1994), 23.
9. Ibid.,17.
10. Complicating the search was a plethora of listings for those black press sites that only exist as online publications. This further confirmed my need to re-conceive what I meant by "black press" now that my print signifier has become entangled in the digitextual blurring of a new black press signified in cyberspace.
11. "About Us," *Charlotte Post*, 1998, http://www.thepost.mindspring.com/about%20info/ABHME.html.
12. Roland E. Wolseley, *The Black Press, USA*, 2d. ed. (Ames: Iowa State University Press, 1990), 198.
13. Ibid., 197.
14. Ibid., 198.
15. Ibid.
16. Ibid.
17. In her article "Passing for White, Passing for Black," that discusses a 1980s legal case about a white woman who challenges the racial identity on her birth certificate, Adrian Piper explains the legal ramifications of the nation's longstanding "'one-drop' rule that uniquely characterizes the classification of Blacks in the United States even where no longer in law. . . . According to this longstanding convention of racial classification, a white who acknowledges any African ancestry implicitly acknowledges being Black—a social condition, more than an identity, that no white person would voluntarily assume, even in imagination." See Piper, "Passing for White, Passing for Black," in *Critical White Studies: Looking Behind the Mirror*, ed. Richard Delgado and Jean Stefancic (Philadelphia: Temple University Press, 1997), 427.
18. Archie T. Clark, II, "Dolls Reflect, Shape Cultural Identity," *Charlotte Post*, 1998, http://www.thepost.mindspring.com/news/com/news2%20Page.html.
19. I borrow this concept from George Lipsitz as contained in his book *The Possessive Investment in Whiteness: How White People Profit from Identity Politics* (Philadelphia: Temple University Press, 1998).
20. Clark, "Dolls Reflect," *Charlotte Post*.
21. Ibid.
22. Wolseley, *The Black Press*, 204.
23. John Downey, "Black Weeklies to Merge," *Charlotte Post*, 1997, 14 December 1998.
24. Vincent Flanders and Michael Willis, *Webpages that Suck: Learn Good Design by Looking at Bad Design* (San Francisco: Sybex, 1996), 25.
25. James Wright, "Congressional Roundup," *Afro-America@* National News, Washington, D.C., 21 Dec. 1998, <>.

Contributors

C. K. DORESKI, author of *Elizabeth Bishop: The Restraints of Language* and *Writing America Black: Race Rhetoric in the Public Sphere*, is completing *Citizenship and Its Discontents: Americans at Home in the Second World War* with the assistance of a National Endowment for the Humanities fellowship. Her essays on the cultural and historical contexts of literature have appeared in *Paideuma, Twentieth-Century Literature, Prospects, The Literary Review, African American Review, Contemporary Literature, Prose Studies,* and *CLA Journal.*

ANNA EVERETT is an associate professor in the Department of Film Studies, University of California at Santa Barbara. She is author of *Returning the Gaze: A Genealogy of Black Film Criticism, 1909–1949* (Duke University Press, 2001) and *The Revolution Will Be Digitized: Afrocentricity And The Digital Public Sphere* (University of Utrecht, 2001); in addition, these works are under contract, *Inside the Dark Museum: An Anthology of Black Film Criticism, 1909–1959* (Duke University Press), and *Digital Diasporas: A Race for Cyberspace* (State University of New York Press). She has also written in *Cinema Journal, Film Criticism,* and *Spectator.*

ROBERT FANUZZI is an associate professor of English at St. John's University. He has published widely on Frederick Douglass, William Lloyd Garrison, and the public culture of the New England abolition movement. His forthcoming book, *Abolition's Public Sphere: The Imaginary Institution of Democracy,* investigates the meaning of print, publicity, and republicanism in the antislavery struggle. He is also the editor of an anthology of antislavery literature, forthcoming from Modern Library.

SHELLEY FISHER FISHKIN is a professor of American studies and English at the University of Texas at Austin. She is the author of *From Fact to Fiction: Journalism and Imaginative Writing in America, Was Huck Black? Mark Twain and African-American Voices*, and *Lighting Out for the Territory: Reflections on Mark Twain and American Culture*. She has published numerous articles and reviews on American literary history, American journalism history, and issues of race, ethnicity and gender in American culture.

HANNA GOURGEY received her doctorate in communication studies from the University of Texas at Austin where she studied rhetoric and media. She taught classes in media and politics at the University of Louisville. Her research includes the analysis of African American and Jewish American press as well as the genesis of interpretive communities and cyberspace. Gourgey serves as Director of Strategic Partnerships at Community Options Inc., an organization dedicated to empowering people with disability through work force initiatives and grass roots organizing.

JAMES C. HALL is the author of *Mercy, Mercy Me: African American Culture And The American Sixties* (Oxford) and editor of *Approaches To Teaching Narrative Of The Life Of Frederick Douglass* (MLA). He is currently Associate Professor of African American Studies and English at the University of Illinois at Chicago.

ROBERT S. LEVINE is a professor in the English Department at the University of Maryland, College Park. He is the author of *Conspiracy and Romance* (1989) and *Martin Delany, Frederick Douglass and the Politics of Representative Identity* (1997) and editor of both *The Cambridge Companion to Herman Melville* (1998) and a Bedford Cultural Edition of William Wells Brown's *Clotel* (2000).

ADAM MCKIBLE is an assistant professor of English at the John Jay College of Criminal Justice (CUNY). He is currently working on a collection of essays on little magazines and the development of modernism.

CARLA L. PETERSON is a professor in the Department of English and the Comparative Literature Program at the University of Maryland and affiliate faculty of both the Women's Studies and the American Studies departments. Her major publications include *"Doers of the Word": African-American Women Speakers and Writers in the North (1830–1880)* (1995) and essays in *Feminist Studies*; *American Literary History*; *Challenging Boundaries: Gender and Periodization*, ed. Joyce Warren and Margaret Dickie (2000); *Criticism and the Color Line: Race and Revisionism in American Literary Studies*, ed. Harry Wonham (1996); *Listening to Silences*, ed. Shelley Fisher Fishkin and Elaine Hedges (1994); and *Famous Last Words: Women Against Novelistic Endings*, ed. Alison Booth (1993).

MAREN STANGE is a professor of American studies at the Cooper Union, New York City. She is the author of *Symbols of Ideal Life: Social Documentary Photography in America, 1890–1950* (1989) and many essays on photography and visual culture. Her *Black Chicago in Pictures* is forthcoming from the New Press.

RODGER STREITMATTER is a professor at the School of Communication at American University. His books include histories of African-American women journalists, the gay and lesbian press, and the American dissident press.

MICHAEL THURSTON is an assistant professor of English at Smith College. He has published essays on Langston Hughes, Ernest Hemingway, Muriel Rukeyser, Robert Lowell, and Eavan Boland. His book, *Making Something Happen: American Political Poetry Between the World Wars*, is forthcoming from University of North Carolina Press. *Modernism, Inc.*, a collection of essays edited with Jani Scandura, is forthcoming from New York University Press.

TODD VOGEL is the director of American Studies and visiting assistant professor of English and American studies at Trinity College in Hartford, Connecticut. He is completing a manuscript on marginalized writers and literary whiteness called *Staging Race and Sabotaging Whiteness*. Since 1984, his work as a journalist has appeared in *Business Week*, the *Washington Post*, the *Boston Globe*, and the *Dallas Morning News*.

WENDY WAGNER is visiting assistant professor of English at Bates College. She is currently working on a manuscript entitled *The Reproduction of Race: Motherhood and the Tragic Mulatta in African-American Women's Writing, 1859 to 1933*. Her biographical essay on Amelia Johnson appeared in the *Dictionary of Literary Biography* volume on American Women Prose Writers, 1870–1920.

Index